PARENTAL INCARCERATION

Parental Incarceration: Personal Accounts and Developmental Impact makes available for the first time a collection of personal stories by adults who have had the childhood experience of parental incarceration. These stories help readers better understand the complex circumstances that influence these children's health and development, as well as their high risk for intergenerational crime and incarceration. Denise Johnston examines her own children's experience of her incarceration within the context of what the research and her 30 years of practice with prisoners and their children has taught her, arguing that it is imperative to attempt to understand parental incarceration within a developmental framework. Megan Sullivan, a scholar in the humanities, examines the effects of her father's incarceration on her family and with respect to her own educational and class outcomes, and underscores the importance of the reentry process for families.

The number of arrested, jailed, and imprisoned persons in the United States has increased since 1960, most dramatically between 1985 and 2000. As the majority of these incarcerated persons are parents, the number of minor children with an incarcerated parent has increased alongside this, peaking at an estimated 2.9 million in 2006. The impact of the experience of parental incarceration has garnered attention by researchers, but to date attention has been focused on the period when parents are actually in jail or prison. This work goes beyond that to examine the developmental impact of children's experiences that extend long beyond that timeframe. A valuable resource for students in corrections, human services, social work, counseling, and related courses, as well as practitioners, program/agency administrators, policymakers, advocates, and others involved with families of the incarcerated, this book is testimony that the consequences of mass incarceration reach far beyond just the offender.

Denise Johnston[*] is the director of Families & Criminal Justice, the successor agency to the Center for Children of Incarcerated Parents. A child development specialist, she has developed and directed educational, therapeutic, family support, and advocacy services for more than 25,000 families of justice-involved parents since 1988. Johnston is also author of numerous publications for families and for professionals.

Megan Sullivan is the author of *Women in Northern Ireland: Cultural Studies and Material Conditions* (University Press of Florida, 1999), *Irish Women and Cinema*: 1980–1990 (NOVA Southeastern University, 2001), and many essays and articles. Her essay "My Father's Prison" was awarded the Anthony Prize in Prose from *Between the Lines Literary Journal*. She co-edited "Children of Incarcerated Parents" for *S&F Online*. She is an Associate Dean and Associate Professor of Rhetoric at Boston University.

Parental Incarceration: Personal Accounts and Developmental Impact fills a major gap in the research in that it is the first text of its kind to explore the impact of parental incarceration on children within a developmental framework. It enhances the literature and provides an opportunity for researchers, policymakers, and practitioners to better understand and garner unique insights into the lived experiences of adult women and men whose stories of parental involvement in the criminal justice system have often been ignored in studies of crime, punishment, and mass incarceration. This is a must read for all those looking to improve outcomes for the children of incarcerated parents.

Barbara E. Bloom, *Sonoma State University*

PARENTAL INCARCERATION

Personal Accounts and Developmental Impact

Edited by Denise Johnston and Megan Sullivan

Routledge
Taylor & Francis Group

NEW YORK AND LONDON

First published 2016
by Routledge
711 Third Avenue, New York, NY 10017

and by Routledge
2 Park Square, Milton Park, Abingdon, Oxon OX14 4RN

Routledge is an imprint of the Taylor & Francis Group, an informa business

British Library Cataloguing in Publication Data
A catalogue record for this book is available from the British Library

Library of Congress Cataloging in Publication Data
Names: Johnston, Denise, 1947- author. | Sullivan, Megan, author.
Title: Parental incarceration : personal accounts and developmental impact /
Denise Johnston and Megan Sullivan.
Description: New York : Routledge, 2015. | "2016 | Includes bibliographical references and index.
Identifiers: LCCN 2015035805| ISBN 9781138183216 (hardback : alk. paper) | ISBN 9781138183223 (pbk. : alk. paper) | ISBN 9781315645971 (ebk)
Subjects: LCSH: Prisoners' families. | Children of prisoners. | Children of women prisoners. | Prisoners--Family relationships.
Classification: LCC HV8885 .J64 2015 | DDC 362.82/95--dc23

ISBN: 978-1-138-18321-6 (hbk)
ISBN: 978-1-138-18322-3 (pbk)
ISBN: 978-1-315-64597-1 (ebk)

Typeset in Bembo
by Taylor & Francis Books

Denise Johnston dedicates this book to her children and their father. Megan Sullivan dedicates this book to her husband, Carl Richardson; her mother, Marita G. Sullivan; and her siblings, Maura, Anne, Mary Kate, Kara and Robert.

CONTENTS

Foreword   *ix*
Preface   *xi*
Preface   *xxi*
Notes   *xxviii*
Acknowledgments   *xxxi*
Notes on Contributors   *xxxii*
Contributor Biographies   *xxxiv*

1 Relationships   1
Denise Johnston and Megan Sullivan

Personal stories   20
My Daddy by Betty 20
My Guardian Angel by David Santiago 21
The Unconditional Love by Manuel Reyes Williams 23
Full Circle by Victoria Greene 24
His Children's Conviction by Danielle Chapman 25
My Parents by Aliyah 27
Blue by Larri Calhoun 29
All Grown Up by Hollie Overton 31

2 Safety and Protection   34
Denise Johnston and Megan Sullivan

Personal stories   47
A Life of Crime by Marcus T. Rogers 47
I Think About My Father All the Time by Miranda Longo 48
I Wish Things Had Been Different by Moe-Moe Sullivan 49
Life as an Unhealed Wound by Nate A. Lindell 52

Betty Boop by Percy Levy 57
The Chain by Jasmine 60
Nothing Like My Dad by Aaron Godinez 62
My Parents' Incarceration by Mary 63

3 Care and Guidance   **65**
Megan Sullivan and Denise Johnston

Personal stories   **81**
Man of the Year by Pamela Hayes 81
A Rocky Start by Willard C. Jimerson 82
The Culture of Incarceration by Bruce Bennett 83
My Mother's Incarceration by Natalie Chaidez 88
Life Without by Kris William Benson 91
Everyone in My Family Has Been in Prison by Shadow 94
About My Mother by Abel Hawkins 95
In His Footsteps by Jeremy Mark Read 97
This Indescribable Butterfly by Alisha Murdock 100

4 The Experiences of Parental Arrest, Incarceration and Reentry   **104**
Megan Sullivan and Denise Johnston

Personal stories   **123**
My Name is Tony Shavers by Tony Shavers, III 123
The White Bridge by Carie Spicer 126
That Place by Ifetayo Harvey 128
Visiting Day by Vannette Thomson 129
Dad in Prison by Shari Ostrow Scher 131
My Family by Jessamyn Ramirez 135
We Never Part by Bianca S. Bryant 137
Fathers & Sons by Michael P. Carlin 139
Reentry Story by Daniel Bowes 144

**Conclusions: What We Can Learn From Adults Who
Experienced Parental Incarceration as Children**   **150**
Denise Johnston and Megan Sullivan

Personal stories   **159**
The Most Important Thing by Sharika Lockhart Young 159

References   *162*
Index   *175*

FOREWORD

After much thought and discussion with family during my junior year of high school, I decided to write my college admissions essay on visiting my parents in prison. Despite my initial reluctance to write about such an emotionally fraught topic, I ultimately chose to do so because having incarcerated parents was a defining feature of my childhood. As I wrote in my admissions essay, "Every day I combine two lives: one immersed in the stability of privilege and the other meeting the challenges of degradation." I found the very process of writing about visiting my parents in prison cathartic. I also knew that writing about visiting my parents in prison would make me stand out. Of the relatively few children of incarcerated parents who apply to college, most learn early on that society stigmatizes prisoners and their families; they are too ashamed or confused or uncertain of people's responses to share their stories. And yet, parental incarceration has become, in the last few decades, a quintessential American experience: on any given day 1.7 million American children have a parent behind bars.[1]

Parental Incarceration: Personal Accounts and Developmental Impact is a unique collection of the voices of adults who grew up with incarcerated parents. This timely collection is the first book of its kind. Comprised exclusively of submissions from people who have personally faced the challenges of parental incarceration, it reveals the similarities and differences within a shared experience that, in this country, has become as commonplace as it is heartbreaking. The number of people incarcerated, most of them parents,[2] skyrocketed by more than 500 percent over the last 30 years.[3] The number of children left behind, all too often invisible to policymakers, skyrocketed as well.[4]

I was one of those children. Both of my biological parents were arrested when I was just 14 months old. For their role in a tragically bungled armed robbery of a Brinks truck that left a security guard and two police officers dead, my mother received a 20-years-to-life sentence and my father received a 75-years-to-life sentence. I was lucky to land in a loving, stable family; my new parents already had two sons, my older brothers. A White male in an upper middle class family, I benefited from the best private school education Chicago had to offer. The support of academic tutors and therapists enabled me to overcome significant behavioral and learning challenges stemming from my parents' incarceration: I didn't learn to read until the third grade, I skipped classes, and, when I did go to class, my teachers often sent me to the principal for misbehaving. I was earning poor grades and generally creating problems for everyone around me. Over the years I learned to channel my energy into productive outlets like school work and sports; throughout, I visited my biological parents frequently. We maintained our relationships between visits with letters and phone calls. By the time I was finishing high school, earning straight As, I began to publicly share my experience through lectures, conferences, and writing. My college essay served me well but I realized that my experience would never have a broader impact if it was buried in an admissions' office folder. I eventually published my college essay[5] and shared my story with virtually everyone I encountered in college and beyond.

My hope, then as now, was twofold: break through the shame that silence perpetuates, and highlight how even the most troubled children with incarcerated parents can find their strength with the requisite resources. Rather than providing extra support for children who lose their parents to prison, society's response is to allow children to be punished, de facto, for their parents' transgressions.

As the stories that follow reveal, children with incarcerated parents, on average, grow up in urban poverty, are black or brown, and are largely cut off from the privileges of quality schools and higher education.[6] Yet these voices are so much more than average. For example, Michael P. Carlin (Chapter 4) vividly portrays his relationship with his often imprisoned father, and explains how Carlin himself ended up spending time in prison, a multi-generational cycle of incarceration. Another contributor, Jessamyn Ramirez (Chapter 4), describes growing up in a downward spiral of poverty, drug abuse, and criminality. One day when Ramirez was just 6 years old, while standing in line at a supermarket with her mom, Ramirez shouted out how happy she was to have her mom home from prison. The awkward silence and dirty looks from the other people in line were her first early lesson in the stigma that leads most children with incarcerated parents to hide their circumstances from the world.

Parental Incarceration: Personal Accounts and Developmental Impact empowers and gives voice to people whose stories of parental incarceration are largely left out of mainstream media coverage of crime, punishment and mass incarceration. The publication of these essays, and each contributor's decision to share an intensely personal story, were acts of courage that will help break through the stigma and shame that leads most children with incarcerated parents to bury their truths. Committing these stories to writing is a particularly significant step in ensuring that researchers, academics, and policymakers examining the criminal justice system never again have an excuse for ignoring the voices of the children left behind.

Chesa Boudin[7]

PREFACE

Early in the 1990s, I was asked to appear on the *Jenny Jones Show*. It was a typical television talk show and, as founding director of the Center for Children of Incarcerated Parents, I was invited to provide context for an episode on incarcerated mothers and their children. The producers also consulted me about how to question kids regarding their mothers in prison. My advice was simple: "Don't expect to get much information from them about their experience." At show time, the children cried a little, kept their faces down and mumbled when asked how they felt about their moms' incarceration.

As I watched this painful process, it occurred to me that someone ought to be talking to adults who experienced parental incarceration as children. Instead of the noncommittal, monosyllabic but developmentally appropriate answers we get from children, adults would have a long-term perspective and could give us a mature analysis of their experience.

I knew this in part because of my training as a pediatrician and child development specialist, in part because of my years of work with incarcerated parents and their children, and in part because I had two daughters who had lived through my incarceration when they were young and had only been able to process the experience as they got older. It seemed like an important idea at the time and I planned to pursue it with programs and publications but things got so busy and there were so many other ideas …

Almost two decades passed. During this period, the Center served more than 25,000 families, delivering a wide variety of programs for pregnant prisoners, infants and children of prisoners, incarcerated parents, caregivers of prisoners' children and professionals who work with families involved in the criminal justice system. In 2010, I was asked to write an article[8] about the Center's work for an online journal. One of the journal's co-editors, Megan Sullivan, also had an interest in the adult children of incarcerated parents. We began to discuss the possibility of collecting stories about parental incarceration from adults who'd had the experience as children. This book is the result of that collaboration and the first of its kind, presenting a collection of stories that have not yet been heard.

What Is the Child of an Incarcerated Parent?

The most inclusive definition of "children of incarcerated parents" encompasses children who have ever had a parent or primary caregiver detained or incarcerated in a jail or prison. That is the definition used to select contributors to this book. Narrower definitions exclude children whose parents are not currently incarcerated as well as children of incarcerated primary caregivers, parents detained but not sentenced, and/or parents incarcerated in jails.

Beyond this book, the definition used is important in determining the numbers of children of incarcerated parents and the issues that need to be addressed in their interest. For example, limiting the designation to children of current prisoners reduces the size of the population by about 80 percent and precludes a useful discussion of the many developmental issues that are related to parental involvement in the criminal justice system.

How Many Children of Incarcerated Parents Are There?

In 2014, an estimated 1.4 million U.S. children had a parent in jail or prison.[9] However, the focus on parental incarceration as the time period when parents are incarcerated is an adult-oriented perspective. This book takes a child-oriented, developmental perspective that recognizes children's significant experiences have effects beyond the actual time period in which those events occur.

In 2010, the Center for Children of Incarcerated Parents estimated that there were more than 10 million U.S. minors who had experienced parental incarceration.[10] This is several times the current number of prisoners' children and a very large group of people, yet little is known about them outside of the times that their parents are behind bars.

There have been no published estimates of the number of U.S. adults who experienced parental incarceration as children.

Who Are the Children of Incarcerated Parents?

Children of prisoners differ in some significant ways from the larger population of U.S. children.

Age

The majority (51 percent) of prisoners' children are under 10 years of age.[11] This proportion is slightly less than the proportion of all U.S. children under the age of 10.[12] It's important to note that the average age of prisoners' children changes with the mean length of parental sentences; when prisoners serve longer sentences, the proportion of their children who are under 10 years of age declines.

Race/Ethnicity

Incarcerated parents are mostly people of color and this is also true of their children. But the current distribution of race/ethnicity among these parents and their children does not apply to adults who experienced parental incarceration in childhood, since racial disproportion in the criminal justice system was less marked in earlier eras.[13]

The majority of families served by the Center for Children of Incarcerated Parents were comprised of people of color. However, over the years, the profile of the families served by the Center began to change, with an increasing percentage of bi- or multiracial children. For example, more than a third of child participants in a mother–child prison visitation program conducted by the Center from 2006 to 2010 fell into this category.[14] Similarly, about a third of the children in families served by my current agency, Families & Criminal Justice, are bi- or multiracial.

Development of Prisoners' Children

The most important information about any child is the status of his/her development. Children's development is shaped by their experiences[15] and information about those experiences is critical in understanding their potential outcomes. Unfortunately, we know very little about the development of prisoners' children.

Children's developmental outcomes are the result of the effects of the developmental resources/supports they receive and the effects of the developmental insults they experience.[16] Apart from their experiences related to parental incarceration, we don't have enough information about either type of experience in the lives of prisoners' children to have a clear understanding of their development as a group. For many years, this information has remained beyond the reach of a field focused on the prison.

The research[17] that has provided the most information on this important topic was done in the community, away from the jail and prison. Essentially, these investigations examined children of incarcerated parents as children, applying the same framework used to examine the lives of other children. But there are far too few of these studies.

It is my personal and professional experience that parental incarceration, in itself, has limited effects on the development of children. My work with children of families involved in the criminal justice system, like my experience with the development of my own kids, makes it clear that the constellation of life events associated with parental incarceration – including those related to parental absence, lack of education, substance dependency, mental illness and unemployment – are responsible for the developmental outcomes seen among prisoners' children. It would be good to be able to test this conviction against empirical data on adult children of incarcerated parents, but virtually none has been available.

Within this context, one of the most valuable contributions of *Parental Incarceration: Personal Accounts and Developmental Impact* is the delicate light it shines on the long-term development of prisoners' children.

The Influence of Parent Gender

The gender of children's incarcerated parent is a critical factor in their outcomes for at least four reasons.

First, life experiences related to parent gender affect children of incarcerated parents in the same way they affect children in the larger society. So, for example, just as in the larger society, incarcerated mothers are more likely than incarcerated fathers to have been the primary caregivers of their children and to have more involvement in daily parenting.[18] In my practice, I've seen that about one in three mothers in jail and prison provided regular, daily care for their kids prior to incarceration, compared to a very small number of jailed or imprisoned fathers.

Second, women prisoners have significantly more contact with their children than male prisoners. This might be expected since they are more likely than incarcerated fathers to have lived with any or all of their children prior to incarceration[19] and to reunite with their children following incarceration.[20]

Third, incarcerated mothers are more likely than incarcerated fathers to have histories of conditions and experiences that can adversely affect parenting, including mental health problems, substance dependency and homelessness.[21] In addition, unlike incarcerated fathers, the majority have romantic/reproductive partners who are also involved in the criminal justice system.[22]

Fourth, some behaviors of incarcerated fathers insure that they will be separated from their children permanently or for longer periods than incarcerated mothers. For example, they are more likely to have histories as perpetrators of domestic violence.[23] They are also more likely to be incarcerated for other serious and/or violent offenses.[24] As a result, they serve longer sentences of incarceration at higher custody levels than incarcerated mothers and have less access to their children.

How Do Children Experience Parental Incarceration?

The experience of parental incarceration encompasses the parent's pre-arrest criminal activity, parental arrest, parental detention and adjudication, parental incarceration and parental reentry.

Parental Criminal Activity

It is common sense that witnessing parental criminal activity would adversely affect children and this is supported by empirical research.[25] Indeed, as reflected in the collected stories in this book, children's experiences of criminal and other inappropriate parental behavior appear to create more lasting emotional pain and negative effects on development than parental arrest and incarceration. This was true for my children and for the other children of prisoners I have known personally and professionally.

Presence at Parental Arrest

In 1991, while conducting a study of jailed mothers, I found that about 20 percent of their children had witnessed maternal arrest.[26] Findings of later research were remarkably consistent with this proportion.[27]

In my personal and professional experience, witnessing the arrest of a caregiving parent is often traumatic for children. My own children both witnessed several paternal arrests; my youngest child also witnessed two of my arrests and still gets distressed when she remembers those experiences.

Knowledge of Parental Incarceration

We don't know what proportion of prisoners' children are told about parental incarceration or what they are told about it. Many children of prisoners have never lived with their incarcerated parents or have lived apart from them for an extended time, and this undoubtedly influences whether or how they are told.

Several contributors to this book report being hurt or angry that they were not told about their parents' circumstances. In my professional experience, this is common. Whenever I teach a child development class for incarcerated parents, a substantial number of second-generation prisoners recall how – even as small children – they felt excluded and insignificant when such important information was withheld from them.

From my experience, I can say that it's hard for parents to tell their children they've committed a crime serious enough to put them in jail or prison. Most arrested and incarcerated parents hope to protect their children from this kind of pain and embarrassment. In addition, there are layers of shame associated with committing and getting caught for criminal behavior, and parents' own feelings may keep them from telling children what they have done.

My children were told each time I was arrested and incarcerated but sometimes not immediately after those events happened. I didn't explain or ask anyone else to explain my charges to them or describe the events that led to my arrest. While they later got this information, they were unhappy that it was not provided at the time.

Almost all experts who have weighed in on the subject recommend that children be told when their parent is in jail or prison.[28]

Children's Understanding of Parental Arrest and Incarceration

Kids who are old enough to watch children's media usually know the meaning of the words "police," "arrest" and "jail." But children's understanding of the personal meaning of parental arrest and incarceration varies with their age and developmental stage, as well as with their familiarity with the justice system and incarceration, in general.

Almost half of the contributors to this book had parents who were incarcerated at the time they were born or in their infancy. Children in this age group have no direct memories or understanding of parental incarceration but may have "constructed" memories consisting of information given to them by others; for these very young children, parental arrests are almost never traumatic. Conversely, slightly older children – toddlers and preschoolers – are the most developmentally vulnerable to bad experiences, including traumatic parental arrests. For example, my youngest daughter not only witnessed two of my arrests in her early childhood, but my second incarceration was the first extended parental absence she had experienced. These episodes were devastating for her.

Older children of prisoners usually understand what arrest and incarceration mean, making the experiences less frightening. My oldest child had a good understanding of these topics because her father had been in prison when she was young and many of our relatives and friends had been incarcerated. By the time of my arrests – none of which she witnessed – she was an adolescent and had been separated from me several times. For her, my arrests and incarcerations were embarrassing but not unknown experiences.

An important part of a child's understanding of parental incarceration involves considera-tion of its future implications for his/her own life. None of this book's contributors who had incarcerated mothers addressed this issue; neither did the female contributors who had incarcerated fathers. But it was the focus of his entire story for one son of an incarcerated father and an important issue for several other male contributors who experienced paternal incarceration.

I would say that both of my children were badly affected by my arrests and incarcerations but less so by their father's. Because they were different ages, they were affected in different ways and for different reasons by their experiences. Surprisingly, although both had norma-tive brushes with law enforcement as teenagers, neither of my kids seemed to see long-term implications of their parents' criminal justice involvement for their future lives.

Parent–Child Contact during Incarceration

In most early studies of incarcerated mothers, the pain of parent–child separation was iden-tified as one of the most negative consequences of maternal incarceration.[29] These reports led both corrections and advocates to the focus on parent–child visitation as the way to benefit and improve the outcomes of prisoners' children. Where, prior to 1970, there had been only a handful of parent–child visitation programs in U.S. jails and prisons, by the mid-1980's there were hundreds, some offered in special, child-friendly settings.[30]

One of the correctional facilities where I was incarcerated had such a program. Like most extended-contact visitation programs, it served only custodial, caregiving mothers and limited participation to children under 10. As a result, only my youngest daughter could participate. It was an incredibly valuable experience for both of us. It helped my daughter adjust to my absence for what was a very significant portion of her young life. In addition, seeing her regularly in a relatively relaxed setting helped me figure out a lot about the meaning of my incarceration for my child. In fact, she painted it for me at one visit: a beautiful green and blue crying heart.

At other times my children and I visited through glass barriers. Again, their age was a factor in how this worked. It was not a problem for my older daughter but my youngest hated it and would sometimes bang the window with the telephone handset. Later, while working at the Center, I encountered several toddlers and young kids who had real problems with bar-rier visits, including one child who said such a visit was like seeing her mother on television and that she was not sure the experience had been real.

Whether through barriers, in the regular prison visiting room or in special parent–child programs, only a minority of incarcerated parents and their minor children actually have visits.[31] This is despite decades of child welfare research that has established that physical parent–child contact during separations is beneficial to the child, to the parent and to the parent–child relationship.

My professional experience is consistent with the research; most of the incarcerated parents I've worked with haven't received jail or prison visits from their children. Although there are many logistical barriers to parent–child visitation – for example, children of prisoners must have written permission from their custodial parent to visit the prison or their caregivers must have the parent's Power of Attorney for the purpose of visitation, prisons are typically located far from children's homes, and travel to visits costs a lot – the barriers I have most often observed were relational. For example, one of the most common reasons children don't visit their incarcerated fathers is that they don't have active relationships with their dads. Another common reason is lack of caregiver support for parent–child visitation, often due to parent–caregiver conflicts.[32]

However, a small number of prisoners' children visit their incarcerated parents regularly. This type of visitation provides the strongest support for parent–child relationships but can also present logistical and financial challenges to families. In my personal and professional experience, parent–child correctional visitation occurs most often among families in which: 1) parents and children lived together prior to the incarceration; 2) there is a strong emotional and/or co-parenting bond between the incarcerated parent and his/her children's caregiver; and 3) the family has the human and material resources to support visitation.

Parental Reentry

There is very limited information about how children experience the reentry of their incarcerated parents. In my professional experience, several factors contribute to the low rates[33] at which formerly incarcerated parents and their children live together after parental incarceration:

- Many of the children have never lived with their incarcerated parent.[34]
- The dissolution of relationships between incarcerated fathers and the mothers of their children during paternal incarceration is the norm,[35] reducing the likelihood that fathers will be able to return to their children's homes after release.
- A significant minority (at least 15 percent) of incarcerated parents have lost their parental rights to one or more children.[36]

My own research suggests that most children who have experienced parental incarceration do not live with their parents who have been incarcerated.[37] This is consistent with my practice experience; except for the families of women participating in residential, mother–child correctional programs, most parents and children served by the Center for Children of Incarcerated Parents did not reside together after the parents were released from jail or prison.

My personal reentry experiences were different from the norm, at least in part because I was married. My husband and I remained in our relationship during our incarcerations and returned to our children's home afterwards. While we struggled with many of the typical obstacles to successful reentry – including unemployment, lack of transportation and housing insecurity – we were not alone in the struggle. And, while we faced many of the typical obstacles to parent–child reunification, our extended family and the parent who had been home with the kids always helped the one who had been gone. Based on my own experience, it appears that a "good enough" marriage and other strong family relationships are the core support for successful reentry. My professional experience and the research literature[38] also support this conclusion.

Outcomes of Children of Incarcerated Parents

There is very little known about the child or adult outcomes of prisoners' children. Existing research has most often focused on the outcome of intergenerational criminality/incarceration[39] and the child behaviors that typically precede it, including aggression.[40] There have been few or no studies of children's relationships, their educational experience (as opposed to school behavior and performance), their interests or their achievements. Anecdotally, we know a lot about how some of them feel but, empirically, we know almost nothing about what most of them do.

There is virtually no information available about what happens to prisoners' children as adults. Research provides some sense of the proportion that become incarcerated as adults – in one small study, about one in twelve sons of incarcerated fathers and about one in five sons of imprisoned mothers[41] – and this suggests a larger number have criminal justice system involvement short of incarceration. But we don't know what percentage complete high school, go on to college, develop serious physical or mental illness, become employed, suffer homelessness, get married, have children, or achieve success in their careers.

In this respect, the contributions to this book are extremely valuable, providing the first glimpse into the adult lives of a large and little-known population. Among contributors to *Parental Incarceration: Personal Accounts and Developmental Impact*:

- 26 percent have attended college (compared to 46.3 percent of the U.S. population in 2012[42]).
- 17 percent are married (compared to 51 percent of the U.S. adult population[43]).
- 51 percent have children.
- 14 percent report outcomes that are significantly worse than those of their incarcerated parents – in terms of more serious crimes, longer incarcerations and more human losses.
- 60 percent are experiencing lives that are significantly healthier, more stable and more productive than those of their incarcerated parents.

Fortuitously, my own children survived parental crime, arrest and incarceration with relatively minimal consequences. Like most other children of parents involved in the criminal justice system, they experienced developmental insults like household economic strain and instability, parental addiction, parent–child separations and exposure to violence. However, they also experienced developmental resources like a stable and lasting relationship between their parents, continuity of parental caregiving, a good education and parental recovery. Unlike many children of incarcerated parents, the developmental resources and supports in their lives outweighed the developmental insults they suffered. They and their families are doing well. I am so proud of them for surviving and overcoming the pain and trials their father and I put them through. Like the saying goes, they are "stronger than yesterday."

Things We Don't Know

There are many things we don't know about the children of incarcerated parents. This is largely because, historically, these kids have come into view at the moment of parental arrest and remained of interest only until their parents were released from incarceration.

The things we don't know can be as important as the things we know in achieving an accurate understanding of the lives and outcomes of these children:

- We don't know their life course or significant experiences from birth to adulthood.
- We don't know how they were parented on a day-to-day basis.
- We don't know much about how they develop. We do not yet have information about their development that has been collected intentionally and as the focus of research, prospectively and longitudinally. In particular:

  a   We know very little about the individual, family and neighborhood resources and supports that are available to children of incarcerated parents.

  b   Other than studies of programs like infant nurseries, we have little information about children of incarcerated parents as infants and toddlers, the period that serves as the platform for later development.

  c   We have virtually no information about any shared competencies and strengths of this large population of children.

- We also don't know about the lives of all groups of prisoners' children:

  a   We do know that many current prisoners had incarcerated parents and there is a wealth of literature in multiple fields related to intergenerational crime and incarceration. So early problem behaviors, delinquency, and adult criminality, arrest and incarceration form the one developmental pathway of these children that is clear to us.

  b   We also know that another group takes a pathway to obscurity *as children of incarcerated parents*. For example, in spite of vigorous efforts to recruit writers who are not themselves involved in the criminal justice system, less than 20 percent of the manuscripts received for this book came from adults in that category. This suggests that many children of prisoners who are doing well as adults may not be interested in revisiting and/or disclosing their histories.

  c   In particular, we know very little about other groups of children of incarcerated parents – the boys who were raised by single moms and went on to become working family men; the girls who grew up alone and afraid but achieved academic and professional success; the kids who resolved the pain and loss of a permanently absent mom or dad and/or conflicted families, going on to establish and sustain healthy relationships. Understanding these developmental trajectories and their outcomes in such a large population will undoubtedly benefit not only families of prisoners but also add to our knowledge of children and families.

It's also critically important to keep in mind that there are things that we don't know we don't know. For example, prior to the 1990s, it was not generally recognized that children of incarcerated parents experienced significant trauma beyond the adverse effects of parental arrest/incarceration. How wrong this was can be seen from the stories in this book describing childhoods lived in that period and characterized by cascades of traumatic experiences unrelated to their parent's involvement in the criminal justice system. So, in examining the poorly documented lives of prisoners' children, it is imperative that we always consider the possibility that *what* we are seeing in the children is not related to *why* we are looking at them.

Parental Incarceration: Personal Accounts and Developmental Impact

This book is intended to provide a first glimpse of the lives of prisoners' children beyond their survival of parental crime, arrest and incarceration. The stories it presents show that there are a range of possible adult outcomes and futures for children of incarcerated parents.

The editors' personal experiences with parental incarceration have provided one context for this task. In addition, my 30 years of work with justice-involved families has allowed me to place our contributors' stories within the context of the scholarly works in my field as well as my practice with a very large number of children of incarcerated parents.

It is a tremendous honor to be able to share these stories with other researchers and practitioners, with other incarcerated parents and children of prisoners, and with our readers.

Denise Johnston

PREFACE

Much of my life has been bracketed by hard work. As a child I worked hard to be good; as an adolescent and teenager I worked hard to do the right thing; and as an adult I worked hard in school and toward my career. Around the year 2002 I came up for air. I received tenure at a private research university on the east coast of the U.S., and so I had the time, in the form of a one-year sabbatical, to parse out the conundrum I had previously backed up against, pushed aside, tried to ignore: my father's incarceration and its effects on me.

I knew my father's arrest and incarceration had affected me, but it was difficult to articulate exactly how or what these particular effects were. In large part because of the stigma associated with incarceration, I rarely spoke about my father. The few times I did, however, people assumed I must have been emotionally impacted by my father's imprisonment. I *had* missed my father while he was incarcerated, and I *did* acknowledge the psychological implications of such a loss. Yet I also believed the effects of my father's incarceration on me were not primarily rooted in the psyche. It felt to me that the most troublesome effects had to do with the changed economic circumstances that accompanied, and lingered long after, my father's incarceration.

No doubt because of my academic training, but also because my father had died in 1986, when I determined to unravel the conundrum of my father's incarceration and its impact on me I began the only way I knew how: I conducted research. I went to the library and found decades old newspaper articles detailing my father's arrest; I reread the few letters I had saved from the several he had written from prison; and I requested information from the State of Connecticut Department of Correction.

Most of the newspaper articles merely confirmed what I already knew: in March of 1975 Robert J. Sullivan received a two-to-five-year sentence for larceny, first degree, and was sent to what was then Connecticut's maximum security prison. A series my hometown newspaper published about corrupt lawyers – a series that featured my father and for which the newspaper received a Pulitzer Prize – rounded out the details: the money my father had embezzled, the period of time he had been under surveillance, his addiction to gambling, and that he had been disbarred. All the reports mentioned Robert J. Sullivan was a married father of six children.

The letters I reread supported my recollections: my father had been an avid reader, and he had thought about his children while he was incarcerated. The only revelatory information I discovered came perhaps unintentionally from the Department of Correction. A Department of Correction form I received under the *Freedom of Information Act* described my father:

> Inmate # 63436
> Race: white
> Height: 5 ft. 11 in.
> Sex: male
> Hair color: brown
> Eyes: hazel
> Marital Status:
> Dependents: 0

My father had been a handsome man, and his *black* hair and *blue* eyes had often been remarked upon by others. He had married my mother in 1959 in a church ceremony presided over by her uncle, a priest, and in the ensuing years my parents had six children together. It's possible that the person who typed the answers on this form had questioned my father about his marital status and whether or not he had children; it's possible my father had lied or declined to discuss these facts. But I don't think so; by all accounts the day my father was sentenced had been a day of truth-telling. I suspect a Correction Officer had hurriedly completed the form and hadn't bothered with what he had considered extraneous information: Robert J. Sullivan's exact hair and eye color, inmate # 63436's status as a husband and as the father of six children who were then between the ages of three and 13.

The Department of Correction form confirmed what I had intuited: despite the fact that my siblings and I were affected by our father's incarceration, our status as his children had been ignored. I'm confident now that this literal and figurative erasure contributed to the difficulty I later had articulating exactly how my father's incarceration affected me. Although the form was completed in 1975, it remains a fairly apt metaphor for the status of children whose parents are incarcerated in 2015. And it prompted me further to tease out the somewhat tangled connections between a parent's incarceration and a child's experiences. What I discovered informs the themes of this book.

Children's Relationships and Development

Parental Incarceration: Personal Accounts and Developmental Impact begins with a discussion of the relationships between children and their parents, caregivers, and siblings, because research shows these early relationships are predictive. Evidence indicates that how a child is cared for directly or indirectly determines his/her outcomes. My family's circumstances would be altered by my father's arrest, but my siblings and I had been well loved and cared for beforehand, and we would continue to be well loved and cared for afterward. In this way, we suffered far less than many other children. I also believe it is primarily this love and care, mostly provided to us by our mother, that enabled my siblings and me to develop appropriately into the five women and one man we are today.

Not unlike many women of her generation, my mother never finished college, and she helped support my father's education and career. She also had always been our primary caregiver. My siblings and I often only saw our father for breakfast, just before we went to bed at night, and on the weekends. For this reason, the fact that he was physically absent from our home when he went to prison was not as traumatic as it might have been. Also, like many children of incarcerated fathers, because we remained in the care of our mother/primary caregiver, my siblings and I experienced far less disruption than we might have.[44] Because our mother modeled good relationships with her sibling, friends and neighbors, my siblings and I learned how to be good siblings, friends and neighbors. All this is to say that while we mourned the loss of our father, his incarceration did not necessarily harm our relationships with others. Much more difficult were the changed circumstances that befell us.

The Impact of Economic Class

Prior to my father's criminal activity and arrest, my family enjoyed many privileges: we were White and middle class in a society that rewarded both; we lived in a lovely home in a safe neighborhood; my siblings and I attended private (parochial) school; and my family existed within a community of relatives and friends. Yet on the day my father was incarcerated we became poor, and we lost our family's only source of income. Actually, we had become poor beforehand: my father had gambled away all of our family's money as well as his clients'. (The only thing he could not touch was our house, which was in my mother's name.)

The first year my father was in prison, a family friend paid our mortgage, and then somehow my mother cobbled together enough money from her earnings at various low-wage jobs. Later, she would work one of these jobs at night, and my siblings and I – then between five and 15 years old – would care for each other. My mother was able to pay the mortgage and keep our home, and my family was eligible for food stamps. We usually had enough food to eat, but there were times when we did not have oil to heat our home. At school we were given free tuition and free milk. In short, we were not unlike what statistics tell us about the many women and children who face housing and food insecurity after a father/partner/wage earner is imprisoned.[45]

During this period we were eligible for welfare benefits, but my mother declined them. I assume if we had received welfare benefits, then we would have had access to subsidized health care as well. As it was, we did not have health insurance while my father was incarcerated and for some time afterwards. My siblings, mother and I utilized free medical and dental clinics. I do not believe our health suffered as a result. However, I do think the combination of our lack of health insurance and our family's emotional and financial turmoil meant that my siblings and I did not have the consistent health or nutritional care we might otherwise have received. I also believe that for years, even decades afterward, our health care needs were sometimes a necessary afterthought in the journey of trying to get by, in the long climb toward financial security.

Care and Guidance: Health, Community and Education

Researchers know too little about the physical and emotional health of prisoners' children.[46] For example, there is no research to tell us what happens when a child's health care needs coincide with a parent's incarceration. Just prior to my tenth birthday, and six months before my father was incarcerated, I had open heart surgery. I was in the hospital for two weeks, and I was put on a heart–lung machine while doctors sewed up a hole in my left ventricle. Afterward, in an intensive care unit, I received doses of morphine; many days later, I helped nurses check the 50 stitches that scampered across my chest. I know now that my father was being investigated when I was in the hospital; I can only imagine the stress these two events – my hospitalization and my father's potential arrest – must have caused my parents and, in turn, their children. I continued to visit my heart surgeon for months after my surgery; I know I saw him when my father was in prison. I also know he did not charge my mother for these post-operative visits.

In many ways my siblings and I were fortunate to remain in our community after my father's arrest and incarceration. We had a network of people in this community who knew and cared for us; we had family members who could lend us emotional support; and we did not have to be uprooted. Yet there were trade-offs: my siblings and I also felt stigmatized in this community. There is some suggestion that families who have never been exposed to criminal activity prior to a parent's arrest and incarceration may feel more stigmatized than other families.[47] I know there was an odd disconnect between the fact that there had been media attention about my father's arrest but that so few people in our community spoke about him to us. In public, my siblings and I almost never spoke about what had happened; we were embarrassed, and we did not know how to articulate our feelings. I understand my family's and our community's reluctance to speak openly about my father in the context of the culture I was raised in: an Irish-American Catholic culture that did not easily discuss certain topics. Yet I also recognize how our larger, U.S. culture sidesteps discussions about incarceration. Other than advocates and those who work directly with prisoners, most people do not talk about or even fully consider incarceration. Children internalize this taboo and learn little about prisoners and their families. As a result, children often lack the vocabulary to discuss any concerns or thoughts they may have when incarceration affects them.

Today, because I am an educator, I wonder whether and how teachers and school administrators might have addressed what was happening to my family. When my father was incarcerated, four of my siblings and I attended the same school. We received free tuition from this school, so in many ways the school helped us tremendously. Yet I wonder what might have happened if my siblings and I had happened upon a book in the school library written about children like us. I wonder what would happen today if schools could provide an opportunity for students to learn more about a large segment of their country's population, those behind bars.

In 2015, we have some evidence of how children of prisoners feel in school and how teachers react to parental incarceration,[48] but I believe my education was affected by my father's criminal activity and incarceration and my family's ensuing financial precariousness in specific ways. First, those early weeks and months of my father's incarceration were difficult; when I think back now I believe my siblings and I were confused and traumatized. Our father's absence, our lack of resources, our mother's brave front, and the media attention was anxiety producing. I can only guess that my siblings and I did not perform optimally in school during this period. Second, for many years after my father's incarceration and release, my family operated in a kind of survival mode. My mother worked hard to keep us clothed and fed; my siblings and I worked hard to take care of one another and our house and to find odd jobs to help out. As a result, and at least for the four eldest of us, my mother could not adequately attend to our academic needs. In later years, when my mother was less worried about our financial survival, she was able to attend to the academic needs of my youngest siblings. I see the difference this made.

I think people either assume there is little or no impact on a child's education when a parent is incarcerated, or they assume the opposite: that a child of incarcerated parents probably will not fare well academically. As it happens, the truth is far more complicated; my hope is that as a culture we can begin to look more carefully at the relationship between a parent's incarceration, financial insecurity, and a child's academic access and success.

Addiction, Arrest and Incarceration

Many incarcerated parents have substance abuse problems.[49] I would later learn my father's addiction to gambling was related to his alcohol abuse, but in those early years this alcohol abuse did not obviously affect my siblings and me. When he was released from prison, my father came home to live with my family, but he was still drinking, so my mother asked him to leave. For this reason, my siblings and I were less affected by our parent's alcohol abuse than are many children. Yet the constellation of factors related to my father's incarceration – his addictions, our financial precariousness, and our culture's inability to address the issue – clearly impacted my siblings and me. The same is true for many children whose parents have been or are incarcerated. Often incarceration does not appear in a vacuum; often it sits tellingly alongside of addiction.

My siblings and I did not witness our father's arrest; as far as I know we were never exposed to his criminal activity either. Firsthand reports from contributors to this book indicate witnessing a parent's arrest is traumatic, as is witnessing criminal activity. I'm glad my siblings and I did not see our father arrested. Yet there is a kind of trauma associated with kissing your father goodbye at the breakfast table one morning and then coming home from school to discover he has been sent to prison. I believe my parents tried to warn my siblings and me about our father's potential incarceration. I recall they gathered us together one morning and told us our father had made mistakes and was going to talk to a judge. I recall my mother watching me closely; I think now she was concerned about my health. Yet my siblings and I did not deduce from this conversation that soon we would not see our father again for nearly two years.

Once he was sentenced, my siblings and I were told the truth about our father's incarceration, and I'm grateful for that. Although some children are not told where a parent is when he/she goes to prison or jail, my mother could not have kept this information from us; nor did my parents want to keep this information from us. My eldest sister visited my father once, but she never talked about it. My other siblings and I never visited; my parents did not want us to. The majority of children do not visit their incarcerated parents in prison.[50]

I believe my parents made the best decision they could have at the time. However, I also know my father's brief reentry back into our family after his release was difficult in part because my siblings and I did not know how to talk to him. We did not talk to my father on the phone when he was incarcerated because we could not afford collect calls from him. My mother visited him often, but she said very little to my siblings and me about these visits. My father wrote to us, and there is some evidence of the benefits of parental correspondence from jail or prison.[51] I know I cherished my father's letters. However, there is a difference between corresponding with and talking to a parent. I do not believe these letters helped me remember how to communicate with my father upon his release.

Reentry

As my co-editor states in her preface, there is limited information about how children experience the reentry of their parents. Research confirms the majority of children of incarcerated fathers do not live with their fathers after these men are released from prison or jail.[52] My family's reentry story supports these findings. I recall the year my father was released and moved back into our family's home as one of the more stressful periods of my childhood. Initially, we were thrilled to have our father home. My siblings and I made cards and a cake the day he returned; later we squished together on the couch with our father and ate buttered popcorn and watched television. More than once during this period, we had the unusual and fun experience of going grocery shopping with him. Unlike our mother, our father let us stand on the grocery cart and choose sugar cereals to buy. Quickly, however, this mini-vacation ended.

My parents argued – about money, about my father's drinking – and my father always seemed to be frustrated, on edge, in a bad mood. My siblings and I were confused; we found it difficult and unusual to be chastised by our father, as our mother had always been our disciplinarian. My father was unemployed, disbarred, and living in the same community that had seen him arrested. Before the year was up my father moved out of the home. For a few years afterward my siblings and I saw him sporadically; he would visit us for two Sundays in a row, and then we would not see or hear from him for months. He never paid child support; I don't believe he ever had secure employment again; we did not know where he lived. After several years of sporadic visits, we lost all contact with our father. He resurfaced in the months just before his death from cancer. My family's reentry story is remarkably similar to what other families experience.

Outcomes

One of the reasons my co-editor and I wanted to compile this book is because there is so little information available about adults whose parents are or were incarcerated. As my co-editor indicates in her preface, we have some information about the percentage who become incarcerated, but we do not know how the vast majority of adults live in the years and decades before and after a parent's incarceration. The stories by our contributors help fill in this gap. I hope that by writing about this topic, my co-editor, these contributors and I will encourage others to tell their stories.

My siblings and I fared well in spite of our father's incarceration. Our childhood, adolescent and teenage lives were difficult, and there are long-term if still difficult to articulate repercussions of my father's actions. Yet, overall, we fared well, and this is chiefly because of the excellent support, love and guidance we received from our mother. We also fared well because of the racial and community advantages we had. Neither my siblings nor I have been involved in the criminal justice system; among us there are four educators and one health care worker, four solid and committed marriages, and nine healthy grandchildren (my nieces and nephews). We are all devoted to our mother, and, for the most part, we all have good relationships with one another, extended family, friends and colleagues. My siblings have been very supportive of my writing, and they are proud that I am helping others learn more about children of incarcerated parents. However, they did not wish to contribute to this book. They lived the story; that was enough.

Megan Sullivan

NOTES

* Author names for this book are alphabetical and do not reflect first or second author status.

1 Glaze LD, Marushak LM. (2008). *Parents in Prison and Their Minor Children*. NCJ Publication 222984. Washington, D.C.: US Department of Justice, Bureau of Justice Statistics. Available at: http://bjs.ojp.usdoj.gov/content/pub/pdf/pptmc.pdf.
2 *Ibid.*
3 The Sentencing Project. (2014) *The Sentencing Project News – Incarceration*. Available at: www .sentencingproject.org/template/page.cfm?id=107.
4 In the last 20 years alone, the number of children with a parent in prison – not jails or other detention centers – has increased by 82 percent. See: Schirmer S, Nellis A, Mauer M. (2009). *Incarcerated Parents and Their Children: Trends 1991–2007*. Washington, D.C.: The Sentencing Project. Available at: www.sentencingproject.org/doc/publications/publications/inc_incarceratedparents.pdf.
5 Boudin C. (2001). In prison again. *Salon.com*. Available at www.salon.com/2001/01/18/visiting.
6 Schirmer et al. *Ibid.*
7 A Yale College and Yale Law School graduate, Chesa Boudin studied at Oxford on a Rhodes Scholarship. The author of several scholarly articles and books on topics ranging from Latin American politics to the rights of children with incarcerated parents, Chesa currently works as a public defender in San Francisco.
8 Johnston D. (2010a). A developmental approach to work with children of prisoners. *S&F Online*, 8(2). Available at: http://sfonline.barnard.edu/children/johnston_01.htm.
9 Families & Criminal Justice. (2014). *How Many Are There? Estimated Counts of the Children of Incarcerated Parents in the United States*. Available at: http://familiesandcriminaljustice.org.
10 Center for Children of Incarcerated Parents. (2010a). *How Many Are There? Estimated Counts of the Children of Incarcerated Parents in the United States*. Eagle Rock, CA: Authors.
11 Glaze LD, Marushak LM. (2008). *Parents in Prison and Their Minor Children*. NCJ Publication 222984. Washington, D.C.: US Department of Justice, Bureau of Justice Statistics.
12 US Census. (2012). *The 2012 Statistical Abstract of the Census: Population*. Available at: www.census.gov/compendia/statab/cats/population.html.
13 Langan PA. (1991). *Race of Prisoners Admitted to State and Federal Institutions, 1926–86*. NCJ Publication 125618. Washington, D.C.: US Department of Justice, Bureau of Justice Statistics; Lynch JP. (2012). *Corrections in the United States*. Washington, D.C.: US Department of Justice, Bureau of Justice Statistics.

14 Johnston (2010a). *Ibid.*

15 Sroufe LA, Egeland B, Carlson EA, Collins WA. (2005). *Development of the Person.* New York: Guilford Press.

16 *Ibid.*

17 See Fragile Families Study publications at www.fragilefamilies.princeton.edu/index.asp. Also see Johnston D. (1992). *Children of Criminal Offenders: Report to the California Assembly Office of Research.* Pasadena, CA: Center for Children of Incarcerated Parents; Johnston D. (2002). What works: Children of prisoners. In Gadsden V. (Ed.), *Heading Home: Offender Reintegration in the Family – What Works.* Lanham, MD: American Correctional Association; Stanton A. (1980). *When Mothers Go to Jail.* New York: Lexington Books.

18 Glaze, Marushak. *Ibid.*

19 Glaze, Marushak. *Ibid.*

20 Johnston (2002). *Ibid.*

21 Glaze, Marushak. *Ibid.*

22 Johnston (2002). *Ibid.*; Phillips S, Erklani A, Keeler GP, Costello EJ, Angold A. (2006). Disentangling the risks: Parent criminal justice involvement and children's exposure to family risks. *Criminology and Public Policy,* 5(4): 688–702.

23 Dutton DG, Hart SD. (1992b). Risk markers for family violence in a federally incarcerated population. *International Journal of Law and Psychiatry,* 15: 101–112; Fishman LT. (1990). *Women at the Wall: A Study of Prisoners' Wives Doing Time on the Outside.* Albany, NY: State University of New York Press; Nurse AM. (2002). *Fatherhood Arrested: Parenting from within the Juvenile Justice System.* Nashville, TN: Vanderbilt University Press; Tripp B. (2003). Incarcerated African American fathers: Exploring changes in family relationships. In Harris O, Miller R. (Eds.), *Impacts of Incarceration on the African American Family.* New Brunswick, NJ: Transaction Publishers.

24 Glaze, Marushak. *Ibid.*

25 Dallaire D, Wilson L. (2010). The relation of exposure to parental criminal activity, arrest and sentencing to children's maladjustment. *Journal of Child and Family Studies,* 19: 404–418; Dallaire D, Zeman JL, Thrash TM. (2015). Children's experiences of maternal incarceration – specific risks: Predictions to psychological maladaptation. *Journal of Clinical Child and Adolescent Psychology,* 44(1): 109–122.

26 Johnston D. (1995d). Jailed mothers. In Gabel K, Johnston D. (Eds.), *Children of Incarcerated Parents.* New York: Lexington Books.

27 Dallaire, Wilson. *Ibid.*; Johnston (1995d). *Ibid.*; New York State Division of Criminal Justice Services. (2013). *Children of Incarcerated Parents in New York State: A Data Analysis.* Albany, NY: Authors; Silbaugh, cited in Nolan C. (2003). *Children of Arrested Parents.* Sacramento, CA: California Research Bureau.

28 Families & Criminal Justice. (2012). *Where's Daddy? Telling a Child about Paternal Incarceration.* Los Angeles: Authors; New Jersey Department of Corrections. (2007). *What about Me? When a Parent Goes to Prison: A Guide to Discussing Your Incarceration with Your Children.* Trenton, NJ: Authors; Sesame Street (2013). *Little Children, Big Challenges: Incarceration.* Available at: www.sesamestreet. org/cms_services/services?action=download&uid=24467219-1a98-4240-9fc3-cc738714e819.

29 Baunach, PJ. (1979, November). *Mothering from Behind Prison Walls.* Paper presented at the annual meeting of the American Society of Criminology, Philadelphia; Bertram J, Lowenberg C, McCall C, Rosenkrantz L. (1982). *My Real Prison Is … Being Separated from MY CHILD.* San Francisco: Prison MATCH; Glasser, I. (1990). *Maintaining the Bond: The Niantic Parenting Programs.* Niantic, CT: Families in Crisis; Henriques, Z. (1982). *Imprisoned Mothers and Their Children.* Washington, D.C.: University Press of America.

30 Cannings, K. (1990). *Bridging the gap: Programs and services to facilitate contact between inmate parents and their children.* Ottawa: Ministry of the Solicitor General of Canada.

31 Glaze, Marushak. *Ibid.*; Mumola C. (2000). *Incarcerated Parents and Their Children.* NCJ Publication 182335. Washington, D.C.: Bureau of Justice Statistics.

32 Carlin, M. (2000). Asserting parental rights from prison. *Family and Corrections Network Report,* 22: 1–3; Johnston (2010a). *Ibid.*

33 Johnston (2002). *Ibid.*

34 Johnston (2002). *Ibid.*

35 Carlson M, Furstenberg F. (2006). The prevalence and correlates of multipartnered fertility among urban U.S. parents. *Journal of Marriage and Family*, 68(3): 718–732; Hairston C. (1991). Family ties during imprisonment: Important to whom and for what? *Journal of Sociology and Social Welfare*, 18: 87.

36 Applied Behavioral Health Policy. (2005). *An Epidemiological Study of the Prevalence and Needs of Children of Incarcerated Parents*. Phoenix, AZ: University of Arizona; Walker C. (2003), *Parents Behind Bars Talk about Their Children: A Survey of Allegheny County Jail Inmates*. Pittsburgh, PA: Pittsburgh Child Guidance Foundation.

37 Johnston (2002). *Ibid.*

38 For a review of the literature, see Warland C. (2014). *Healthy Relationships, Employment and Reentry*. Washington, D.C.: National Resource Center for Healthy Marriage and Families. Available at: https://library.healthymarriageandfamilies.org/cwig/ws/library/docs/MARRIAGE/Blob/88902. pdf?w=NATIVE%28%27TITLE+ph+is+%27%27healthy+relationships+employment+and+reentry %27%27%27%29&upp=0&rpp=25&order=native%28%27year%2FDescend%27%29&r=1&m=1

39 For a review of the literature, see Center for Children of Incarcerated Parents. (2010b). *Research Monograph No. 3 (Revised): Intergenerational Incarceration*. Eagle Rock, CA: Authors.

40 Craigie T. (2011). Effect of paternal incarceration on early child behavior problems. *Journal of Ethnicity in Criminal Justice*, 9(3): 179–199; Murray J, Farrington DP, Sekol I. (2012). Children's antisocial behavior, mental health, drug use and educational performance after parental incarceration. *Psychological Bulletin*, 138(2): 175–210; Wildeman C. (2010). Paternal incarceration and children's physically aggressive behaviors. *Social Forces*, 89(1): 285–309.

41 Dallaire DH. (2007). Incarcerated mothers and fathers: A comparison of risks for children and families. *Family Relations*, 56(5): 440–453.

42 US Census. (2012). Available at: http://factfinder.census.gov/faces/tableservices/jsf/pages/productview. xhtml?pid=ACS_14_1YR_S1501&prodType=table.

43 Cohn D, Passel JS, Wang W, Livinston G. (2014). Barely half of U.S. adults are married. *Pew Research – Social and Demographic Trends*. Available at: www.pewsocialtrends.org/2011/12/14/ barely-half-of-u-s-adults-are-married-a-record-low.

44 Glaze LD, Marushak LM. (2008). *Parents in Prison and Their Minor Children*. Publication No. 222984. Washington, D.C.: US Department of Justice, Bureau of Justice Statistics.

45 Geller A, Franklin AW. (2014). Paternal incarceration and the housing security of urban mothers. *Journal of Marriage and Family*, 76: 411–427.

46 New York Initiative for Children of Incarcerated Parents. (2012). *Fact Sheet: Parental Incarceration's Impact on Children's Health*. New York: Authors.

47 Gabel S. (1992). Children of incarcerated and criminal parents: Adjustment, behavior and prognosis. *Bulletin American Academy of Psychiatry Law*, 20(1): 33–45.

48 Dallaire D, Ciccone A, Wilson LC. (2010). Teachers' experiences with and expectations of children with incarcerated parents. *Journal of Applied Developmental Psychology*, 31: 281–291.

49 Glaze, Marushak. *Ibid.*

50 Glaze, Marushak. *Ibid.*

51 Poehlmann J, Dallaire D, Loper AB, Shear LD. (2010). Children's contact with their incarcerated parents: Research findings and recommendations. *American Psychologist*, 65(6): 575–598.

52 *Ibid.*

ACKNOWLEDGMENTS

Denise Johnston and Megan Sullivan would like to thank Ellen Boyne and the editorial staff at Routledge for their time and expertise.

Denise Johnston would like to acknowledge the thousands of justice-involved families who shared their experiences and their lives with her and the agencies she directed – Phase Reentry Programs, the Center for Children of Incarcerated Parents, and Families & Criminal Justice – over the last three decades. She is particularly grateful to have known and worked with a number of remarkable individuals including Michael Carlin, Juanita Massie and Launi Perry, who went from prisoner to participant to peer support provider and/or practitioner under the auspices of those agencies. And she says a very special thank you to the dedicated practitioners who have taught and learned alongside her for so many years: Lorena Delgado, Adam Ramirez, Tamara Satterwhite and Dolores Thomas. Finally, she would like to thank her children who helped her with this book in many, many ways.

Megan Sullivan would like to thank the contributors to this book. She would also like to thank Boston University and Linda Wells for two sabbaticals. Finally, Megan would like to thank Dean Natalie McKnight, whose support, mentorship and friendship has meant all the difference for Megan's research and career.

NOTES ON CONTRIBUTORS

The men and women who contributed their stories to this book come from all regions of the U.S. but especially those states – like California, Ohio, Pennsylvania, Texas and Washington – with the highest incarceration rates in the last decades of the twentieth century. They were from 18 to 59 years of age at the time they wrote their stories.

Among the contributors, 60 percent are female and 40 percent are male. African Americans and European Americans each make up 37 percent of the contributor group; another 15 percent are Latino/a and 6 percent are American Indian. Six percent are bi- or multiracial.

The majority (66 percent) of contributors were raised in very-low-income families.

All of the stories in this book are about the experience of parental incarceration in childhood. The 35 writers who contributed stories had a total of 45 incarcerated parents. Sixty percent had just a father incarcerated and 11 percent had just a mother incarcerated but 29 percent experienced the incarceration of both parents. Altogether, 89 percent of contributors had an incarcerated father, a proportion similar to that of minor children of U.S. prisoners in the last decade.

The family context for the experience of parental incarceration varied widely among the writers. A total of 39 percent lived with their parents who were incarcerated for sustained periods prior to and/or after parental incarceration. Some 34 percent lived irregularly or for a limited time with their parents who were incarcerated, but 26 percent never lived with their parent who was in jail or prison.

Less than half of the contributors consistently received primary caregiving from their parents who were incarcerated. Among the writers, almost all of those who had an incarcerated mother described their mothers as their primary caregivers for some period of their childhoods but only two writers who had an incarcerated father described him in those terms.

During parental incarceration, about two-thirds of contributors lived at least some of the time with their other birth parent, including 95 percent of the children of incarcerated fathers and 12 percent of the children of incarcerated mothers. About 17 percent describe spending some time in foster care as a child, including about 20 percent of those with just a mother incarcerated and 36 percent of those with two incarcerated parents. None of those with only an father incarcerated were placed in foster care.

In the U.S. criminal justice process, all arrested individuals are detained – at least temporarily – in a local jail, so all of our contributors had the experience of having a parent in jail. All but two also experienced incarceration of their parents in state or federal prisons.

The parents of a significant number of contributors are deceased. More than a third have experienced the death of a formerly incarcerated parent, including 12 percent whose parent died by violence. In contrast, only one contributor has experienced the death of a never-incarcerated parent.

The contributors are engaged in a range of occupations, including student, waitress, nursing assistant, real estate salesperson, retail salesperson, school teacher, television producer, university professor and attorney. However, 12 percent were unemployed, 9 percent were in residential treatment and 6 percent were homeless at the time they wrote their stories.

Intergenerational criminal justice system involvement is common among the contributors. Overall, half have had criminal justice contact, including 79 percent of male contributors and 19 percent of female contributors. Intergenerational incarceration occurred in 33 percent of those who had experienced only paternal incarceration, 50 percent of those who had experienced only maternal incarceration and 70 percent of those who had experienced incarceration of both parents. Thirty percent of contributors were incarcerated at the time they wrote their stories.

Finally, gender had a marked effect on all experiences related to parental incarceration. For example, female children of incarcerated parents had better health, education, employment and criminal justice outcomes than male children, while the children of incarcerated mothers fared worse than those with incarcerated fathers.

CONTRIBUTOR BIOGRAPHIES

Aliyah was born in Puerto Rico and raised in Southern California. Her father went to jail many times, beginning when she was 5 years of age; he is now deceased due to the consequences of his lifestyle. Aliyah is a single, 26-year-old mother of two children. She is currently serving her third sentence at a California State prison. Last year, she received her GED, and she is currently in training for the prison Fire Camp program that will allow her to become a firefighter while still incarcerated.

Bruce Bennett grew up in Vancouver, Washington, frequently moving and changing schools in response to his family's lawlessness. His mother and stepfather were both arrested and incarcerated during his childhood. At 23, he was imprisoned for killing his aunt's abusive husband. After a rough start that involved drug use, fighting and attempts to escape, Bruce read his first book in prison and began to educate himself, eventually earning a college degree. He is an author of essays, short stories, a screenplay and three books. He has two children and one grandchild with whom he shares loving, supportive relationships. Bruce expects to be released by 2021.

Kris William Benson was born in Sacramento, California. He moved to Florida when he was 3 years of age and spent most of his childhood in the Volusia County area. When he was in his mid-teens, his mother was arrested and jailed for a year. Kris is currently serving a life sentence in the Florida Department of Corrections. Recently, he has fully given his life to Christ and is in a position of leadership in a faith-based reentry program, helping other prisoners prepare themselves to transition back into society and become productive citizens.

Betty M. is a native of Mississippi who has lived in 11 states. Betty did not know her father who was incarcerated. She had never spoken or written about her father's incarceration when she saw the flyer asking for stories from adult children of incarcerated parents. Betty has had seven children. Her youngest daughter has lived with a legal guardian since she was a baby and Betty is still trying to get her back. Betty is currently homeless and living in a shelter.

Daniel Bowes is the supervising attorney of Legal Aid of North Carolina's Second Chance Employment Project which provides free legal services to low-income North Carolinians with criminal records. He is also a staff attorney at the North Carolina Justice Center where he coordinates the advocacy efforts of the NC Second Chance Alliance. He lives in Durham, North Carolina, with his partner, Linda.

Bianca S. Bryant is a native of Memphis, Tennessee. She was first prompted to talk about her experience as a child of an incarcerated parent by a beloved professor at Smith College, where she earned her undergraduate degree. Since then, Bianca has been dedicated to understanding the criminal justice system and how she can help heal young hearts impacted by incarceration and the war on drugs.

Larri Calhoun is the adult daughter of an incarcerated father. She would not have written or published "Blue" without the support of Mailee and Zoe from Project WHAT! Project WHAT! raises awareness about children with incarcerated parents. *WHAT!* stands for We're Here And Talking. Although she is no longer in Project WHAT!, Larri continues to think often about Mailee, Zoe and the others from her group.

Michael P. Carlin was born and raised in a mining community of Eastern Pennsylvania. An only child, he lived with his mother and maternal grandfather when he was a child. During his childhood, his father was in prison for more than eight years. As a juvenile and adult, Michael himself was incarcerated. After serving 16 years in state and federal prisons, he was released in 2001, reunited with his son and went to work for the Center for Children of Incarcerated Parents. He has authored several articles on paternal incarceration, as well as several autobiographical stories.

Natalie Chaidez was born and raised in Southern California. She was an honor student and award-winning athlete as a child. When she was 17, her mother was arrested and incarcerated. During her first year at university, while their mother was in jail, Natalie became the primary caregiver for her younger sister. She has worked in the entertainment industry as a screenwriter and producer for more than 20 years. She currently produces a successful television series, has two adult children, and lives in Glendale, California.

Danielle Chapman is married, with two sons and a granddaughter. She lives in Fontana, California, and works in emergency road services. Her father, incarcerated since she was 13, remains in prison.

Aaron Godinez is a native of New Mexico. He grew up with his mother and his brothers in the South Valley area of Albuquerque and attended local public schools. He was 18 years old when he wrote his essay on his father's multiple incarcerations. Writing his essay helped him to think about his future, moving away from his father's influences and expanding his horizons. In 2014, Aaron took his mother's last name and moved to the East Coast to study acting.

Victoria Greene was born and raised in Georgia. She is the daughter of an incarcerated mother and works in a county jail, providing faith-based services to incarcerated women.

Ifetayo Harvey is from Charleston, South Carolina. She spoke at the International Drug Policy Reform Conference in 2013 and to NPR in 2014 about her experience growing up with a parent in prison. Ifetayo's work has been featured in the *Huffington Post*, on *Alternet .com*, and in *The Atlantic*.

Abel Hawkins was a 31-year-old African-American, Cuban and Belizean man when he wrote his essay on his parents' incarceration. Incarcerated as a juvenile, Abel was emancipated at 17, and began searching for his parents. Although he was unable to locate his father, he discovered that his mother was deceased. He resided with extended family members in Northern California during the last eight years of his life. He died in 2015 from injuries sustained in an automobile accident.

Pamela Hayes is a retired community college administrator. Her father was imprisoned during her childhood. In 2012, she founded a reader's group at the North Carolina Correctional Institution for Women; she currently facilitates this group. Pamela lives in Cary, North Carolina, with her husband, Geoff.

Jasmine is a homemaker and part-time interior decorator. She is 30 years of age, White and married; her husband owns a data management business. Her father was imprisoned during her early childhood. Jasmine married immediately after high school and had two daughters. A drinking problem led to her arrests for driving under the influence. As a young adult, she was incarcerated for vehicular manslaughter and served six years in prison before her release in 2014. Jasmine remarried and recently had her third child, a son. She lives with her husband and children in Central California.

Willard C. Jimerson is the son of two incarcerated parents. He is currently incarcerated in the state of Washington.

Percy Levy is an Urban Fiction author currently serving time in a correctional institution in Connell, Washington. His mother was incarcerated multiple times during his childhood. He has been locked up for more than 13 years and has had little to no contact with his children during this period. He has acquired an associate degree while being incarcerated and is continuing to live his dream through his writings, which are all available on Amazon.com.

Nate A. Lindell was born in Wisconsin but moved from state to state in the Midwest during an isolated, traumatic childhood. His mother was arrested and jailed when he was 9 years of age. After a period in foster care and a stint in a boys' ranch program, he began a short criminal career that ended with his arrest for murder as a young adult. Now 33, Nate has spent the last 13 years in solitary confinement and/or disciplinary housing in several maximum security prisons.

Mary is a member of the Cahuilla tribe. Both of her parents were incarcerated during her childhood. She has struggled with substance abuse since she was 11, which caused her the loss of her oldest and youngest children to adoption. Mary recently completed an intensive treatment program and began working. She currently lives with her mother and two of her children in the Hemet area of the Inland Empire, in Southern California.

Miranda Longo was born in Mexico and raised in Arizona and Southern California from infancy. Her father was incarcerated several times during her childhood. From her teenage years, she worked to support her mother and children. Her two school-age daughters have lived with their father since her incarceration. After completing a prison sentence of 48 months in 2014, Miranda was deported.

Alisha Murdock is 23 years of age. She experienced maternal incarceration off and on for most of her life but after her last release, Alisha's mother began working hard to rebuild their relationship. Alisha is proud of herself for making the right decisions that would be good for her and good for her mother to see, as well; she believes that a lot of the time, children end up showing their incarcerated parents new paths. In August of 2015, Alisha's mother passed away. Alisha was happy that she had the chance to be with her mother and to see her mother happy for those last 23 months of her life.

Hollie Overton was born in Chicago and raised in Texas. Her father was incarcerated during her childhood. She is a television writer, currently working on ABC Family's upcoming drama Shadowhunters, based on the best-selling book series "Mortal Instruments." Her debut thriller "Baby Doll" will be published by Hatchette USA and Random House UK in July 2016.

Jessamyn Ramirez grew up with two parents who were frequently incarcerated throughout her childhood. She lives with her husband in the Highland Park district of Los Angeles, California, where she works in nursing. Previously an employee of the Center for Children of Incarcerated Parents, Jessamyn now volunteers in a program that provides services for pregnant prisoners.

Jeremy Mark Read was born and raised in the state of Washington; he is a 33-year-old husband and father of three. His father was incarcerated for most of his childhood. Jeremy has been incarcerated since he was 16 years old. During his incarceration, he has completed high school and earned a certificate for victim advocacy from Adams State University. He plans to continue his education after release and to start a ministry helping families and their incarcerated loved ones find healing, restoration and reconciliation. Jeremy will be paroled in 2018.

Marcus T. Rogers is the adult child of two incarcerated parents who was incarcerated himself at the time he wrote his story.

David Santiago was born in Lawrence, Massachusetts, and raised in the Beacon projects. His father was convicted of murder when he was one year old. He moved in and out of the foster care and youth detention system until he was 17. He is now serving a seven-year sentence in an Ohio prison and is due to be released in 2016. David is the father of two young children. He writes, "Life can only be wasted if there is no love. Love endures all pain…"

Shari Ostrow Scher has spent her 50-year career in Family Involvement and Early Childhood Education. She currently teaches at Hood College in Frederick, Maryland. She is founder and president of two non-profit organizations: Children of Incarcerated Parents Partnership, and Children of Promise, Children of Hope, a library project in the Dominican Republic. Her family includes her husband, three grown children, her daughter-in-law and her granddaughter.

Shadow is an American Indian woman, a member of the Jicarilla Apache Nation on her mother's side and the Standing Rock Sioux and the Cheyenne River Sioux Nations on her father's side. Both of her parents were incarcerated when she was a child. Shadow has been incarcerated three times. She is currently participating in a mother–child residential treatment program with two of her three children.

Tony Shavers, III was born and raised in Oakland, California. He discovered his passion for creative writing in the fourth grade. Through Project WHAT!, Tony was able to effectively communicate his feelings about being the child of an incarcerated parent; the program also helped to shape the positive relationship he now shares with his father, who was recently released from prison. Tony is a young man with a vision for his life, a desire to create a scholarship fund for youth, and a commitment to improve policies that affect children of incarcerated parents. Tony currently trains entrepreneurs and helps people go after their health and financial desires.

Carie Spicer has a master's degree in Business Administration. She enjoys traveling and spending time with her family and friends and has a passion for helping others.

Moe-Moe Sullivan is a 22-year-old African American woman who believes in social justice and hopes *Parental Incarceration* sheds light on the disproportionate number of Black people being sent to jail. Moshina is a student at City College of San Francisco, a member of the Youth Advisory Board of San Francisco's Independent Living Skills Program, and an advocate for people in prison and at-risk teens. She is featured in the book *How Children Succeed* by Paul Tough and in his essay "The Poverty Clinic."

Vannette Thomson is a proud graduate of Sam Houston State University. She is a published author, a victim advocate, and a person who has overcome adversity. Vannette is currently writing a children's book based on "Visiting Day" and her memoir. She is inspired by her faith, her husband, and the gift of motherhood.

Manuel Reyes Williams was born and raised in Milwaukee, Wisconsin. Both of his parents were incarcerated during his childhood. He was imprisoned for four years, and during that time wrote the story he contributed to this book. Manuel was released from prison in 2014.

Sharika Lockhart Young is the mother of four beautiful children. She is inspired by her father, who is still incarcerated. Her passion to create change has led her to begin writing a book about the impact of an incarcerated parent on a child.

1

RELATIONSHIPS

Denise Johnston and Megan Sullivan

Child development occurs within a nest of human relationships, so it is fitting to begin this very first exploration of the lives of adults who experienced parental incarceration in childhood by considering their early relationships. While they form a large and diverse group, these individuals share the important characteristic of disrupted family relationships. In this chapter we offer contributors' stories about parent–child and other critical relationships among prisoners' children.

A Developmental Perspective on Relationships

The Minnesota Study of Risk and Adaptation from Birth to Adulthood[1] began in 1976 as an effort to provide a coherent picture of the complexity of child development within contexts of social and relational adversity. The researchers defined development as changes in the organization of behavior in response to experience. They identified early primary relationships and care as the central influences on the way children organize their behavior. For example, healthy relationships with siblings are based upon secure, healthy relationships between infants and their parents/primary caregivers. Later in childhood, healthy relationships with both parents/primary caregivers and siblings are the foundation for children's success in peer relationships.

All of these findings inform our understanding of relationships among children of incarcerated parents.

Relationships with Birth Parents

The 25-year report of the Minnesota Study concluded that

> Nothing is more important in children's development than how they are treated by their parents, beginning in the early years of life.

At every stage of child development, a history of supportive care directly or indirectly determines child outcomes. Supportive caregivers have a high level of interest in and responsiveness to children. Their care produces important child outcomes, including self-regulation, positive expectations of the self and positive expectations of others.

Supportive care is provided within a context of family and community resources and challenges.[2] If caregivers receive adequate material and emotional resources from their families and communities, they are able to provide supportive care for children. If caregivers' needs are not met, they will be unable to meet the needs of the children in their care.

For example, the parenting they received and their adverse childhood experiences can be expected to reduce the ability of many incarcerated mothers and fathers to provide supportive care to their children. As poorly educated, unemployed, low-income parents living in disadvantaged neighborhoods, the resources they obtain are typically outweighed by the challenges – like substance abuse/addiction, domestic violence and mental illness – they face.[3]

Clearly, we should expect that some incarcerated parents will have difficulty providing appropriate relationships for their children. Yet we have almost no information about exactly how prisoners care for and relate to their children in the community.

Influences on Parenting among Incarcerated Parents

To better understand these parent–child relationships before and after incarceration, we can explore several significant influences on parenting known to be present in the lives of justice-involved parents.

Multi-partnered Fertility

One influence on parent–child relationships is established before the time of conception, as some women and men enter into serial or concurrent reproductive partnerships. Multi-partnered fertility – having babies by more than one reproductive partner – produces significant disadvantages for children.[4] Children born to fathers who have children by other mothers have less contact with their fathers and receive fewer supports for their development than other children.[5]

> My younger brother had a different father than me and my sister. I was very jealous of my little brother because he got a lot of attention and he had a father in his life who would come around on his motorcycle and they would go out together. I was confused and hurt to have never been able to have a father to do things I pictured my brother and his father doing, like fishing and camping. Or just having someone to look up to.
>
> *David S., adult child of an incarcerated father*

Multi-partnered fertility is a norm among incarcerated parents.[6] As a result, a significant proportion of prisoners' children will not live with their birth parents who have been incarcerated.[7]

> When she was 23, [my mom] moved in with a man who became the father of my oldest two brothers ... Then he started using hard drugs and they broke up ... A few years

later she met my father, an older man. ... They lived together for two years and had my brother. Then, just after my mom got pregnant with me, my father was arrested and sent to state prison.

Abel H., adult child of an incarcerated father

[My brothers and I] mostly had different fathers. I never knew my father but my two brothers just older than me called him Daddy.

Betty M., adult child of an incarcerated father

Multi-partnered fertility is a common reason for disruptions in relationships between incarcerated parents and their children. In addition, it decreases the supports available to caregiving mothers,[8] including mothers who will be or have been incarcerated.

Trauma

Lack of safety and protection, and resulting traumatic experiences, have occurred across the lifespan for most incarcerated persons.[9]

My mom was good in school until she got molested by family "friends." It was a regular thing that started when she was 8. She took it 'til she was 11 and then ran away.

Abel H., adult child of two incarcerated parents

[My mom] once told me that [my birth] was the result of a rape.

Nate L., adult child of an incarcerated mother

After I had been incarcerated for a couple of years, my formerly incarcerated father wrote to me. In his letter, he told me about his molestation as a child.

Jasmine, adult child of an incarcerated father

Traumatic experiences have long been recognized to have important consequences for all intimate relationships,[10] including the parent–child relationship. A recent review of research on this topic found that traumatization can cause parenting limitations, and these limitations can disrupt the development of young children.[11] This happens when traumatized parents are emotionally less available and when they perceive their children more negatively than parents without trauma symptoms. Young children of parents who have been traumatized may be easily deregulated or distressed and older children face more difficulties in their psychosocial development than children of parents without symptoms of trauma.

Mothers with a history of early life trauma may be more intrusive with infants.[12] Mothers with a history of sexual abuse are more likely to engage in aversive parenting practices including physical punishment;[13] they are also more likely to display flatness of affect and disengagement with their children[14] and this behavior appears to have a trauma-related biological basis.[15]

Even without any additional influences, the relationships that many incarcerated mothers and fathers have with their children are strongly and adversely affected by their extensive histories of trauma.

Parental Drug Use and/or Mental Illness

Many incarcerated parents have substance abuse and/or mental health disorders.[16] Substance abuse and addiction have been found to have negative effects on parenting.[17] For example, a strong association has been found between parental substance abuse and child neglect or maltreatment.[18] Similar adverse effects on parenting have been associated with parental mental illness and especially with co-occurring disorders.[19]

These problems may strongly affect the relationship between incarcerated parents and their children, and influence the children's life course.

> I spent … years running away from every foster home to catch up to my drug-addicted parents, believing I could make them get clean.
>
> *Aliyah, adult child of two incarcerated parents*

> Needless to say, my relationship with my mom was horrible. She was completely consumed by her addiction and legal troubles … I lost all respect for her, and saw her as a dangerous, selfish, manipulative and dishonest person who would use anyone and anything to serve her own needs, while being completely unconcerned with her children's.
>
> *Natalie C., adult child of an incarcerated mother*

> I began using drugs to spend time with my parents … I began to learn the criminal side of life through my father and at the age of 14, I began to sell drugs. It was a lucrative endeavor and I was hooked. During that year, I began using heroin and this would prove to be the root cause of my criminal record to this day.
>
> *James C., adult child of two incarcerated parents*

For many years, the association between parents' involvement in the criminal justice system and parental addiction/mental illness has made it difficult to identify the actual effects of parental incarceration. More recently, careful study of families involved in the criminal justice system has found that both children's developmental outcomes and parental incarceration are related to the same risk factors, including parental addiction and mental illness.[20]

Other Influences

Addressing adverse childhood experiences (ACEs), the American Academy of Pediatrics has written:

> Adults who have experienced ACEs in their early years can exhibit reduced parenting capacity or maladaptive responses to their children. The physiological changes that have

occurred in the adult's stress-response system as a result of earlier trauma can result in diminished capacity to respond to additional stressors in a healthy way.[21]

As well as trauma, parental substance abuse and parental mental illness, adverse early experiences that are common among incarcerated parents include parental separation/divorce, the witnessing of domestic violence and crime/arrest/incarceration in an immediate family member.

Parent–Child Separations

Almost all children of prisoners experience multiple parent–child separations. Most of these are not due to parental incarceration, but rather to parental drug use, criminal activity and changes in the relationship between birth parents.[22] For incarcerated mothers, placement of children in foster care is another common reason for separations.[23]

Parent–child separation may cause a range of emotional reactions in both children and parents.[24] Children may also develop fear of emotional closeness, increased sensitivity to later separations and increased vulnerability to both emotional and cognitive problems.

Separations are known to have adverse effects on the parent–child relationship, as well as on long-term child development.[25]

> I was a whimpering cub lost for thoughts to protest my mother's absences.
>
> *Manuel R.W., adult child of two incarcerated parents*

> My father's incarceration … set in stone the loneliness and pain that characterized our relationship.
>
> *Michael C., adult child of an incarcerated father*

The effects of separation can be mitigated by visitation and other forms of parent–child contact.[26] However, most children of prisoners do not visit their parents in jail or prison.[27] As a result, separations due to parental incarceration may have a powerful effect on parent–child relationships.

Relationships with Incarcerated Mothers

Among contributors to this book, 40 percent had an incarcerated mother. This number includes 11 percent who report only maternal incarceration and 29 percent who report the incarceration of both birth parents.

> When my mom was 17, she had my sister, then a couple of years later she had me … When I was small my parents split up. My mom had always been a drinker and pretty violent, but she got worse after my dad left … I always tried to stay close to my mom and I would even follow her to the neighborhood bars. I stayed so close to her they called me Shadow Girl.
>
> *Shadow, adult child of two incarcerated parents*

Excluding self-reports of mother and child reactions to maternal incarceration, more than 40 years of research has produced some important information about the content and quality of relationships between incarcerated mothers and their children. Studies have found that many of these mothers – even those incarcerated in jails for short periods – have a limited fund of basic knowledge about their children,[28] suggesting limited involvement in children's daily lives and a limited parent–child relationship.

> [My mother] was incarcerated on and off from [my birth] until I graduated college at 22 years of age. Most of her arrests were for charges such as theft, forgery, fraud, probation violation and other petty crimes she committed to support her crack cocaine and heroin habits, both of which she used along with alcohol and other drugs ... While my aunts raised me, [my mother] would show up occasionally, but her visits were always short and ended in disaster and sometimes emotional trauma.
>
> *Victoria G., adult child of an incarcerated mother*

The biggest study of incarcerated mothers ever conducted – in which approximately half of all imprisoned mothers in the U.S. were surveyed – found that one of the clearest direct effects of maternal incarceration is the weakening of mother–child relationships in proportion to the number of times mothers are incarcerated.[29] With each episode of maternal incarceration, the likelihood of mother–child reunification is decreased.

> When I was one year old, my mom was arrested. [M]y brother Sammy and I went into foster care ... When I was two, my mom [got into a prison program] ... [After that] we all lived together for about two years but she got arrested again ... Sammy and I went back into foster care. ... We stayed in that foster home until I was 14 ... she never came to get us.
>
> *Abel H., adult child of two incarcerated parents*

Research on attachment between incarcerated mothers and their children has found that more than a third of children studied had optimal or "secure" representations of their attachments to their mothers.[30] Attachment security is produced by warm, nurturing and responsive parenting, suggesting that a significant proportion of incarcerated mothers have healthy, appropriate relationships with their children prior to arrest.

In an early draft of her essay, one contributor wrote this:

> In spite of her drug use and incarcerations, my mother stayed close and took me with her everywhere. She was in our home every day that she was not in jail and once she stopped using drugs, she became a really good mom. Everyone says I am a lot like her, and this makes me happy.
>
> *Jessamyn R., adult child of two incarcerated parents*

Relationships with Incarcerated Fathers

Among contributors to this book, 89 percent had an incarcerated father. This number includes 60 percent who report only paternal incarceration and 29 percent who report the incarceration of both birth parents.

We know much less about the content and quality of relationships between incarcerated fathers and their children than we do about relationships between incarcerated mothers and their children. Most incarcerated fathers were not living with their children prior to incarceration[31] but there is evidence that a large minority of these non-resident fathers had frequent contact with their children.[32] However, no studies have provided a substantive description of the characteristics of father–child relationships in these families. *Parental Incarceration: Personal Accounts and Developmental Impact* is one of the first publications to provide information on this subject.

In spite of paternal absence, criminality and incarceration, some of our contributors describe an essentially positive relationship with their fathers:

> As a child, I was always attached to my dad. Everybody in my family told me that when my dad was around we were inseparable. I really loved my dad and he was always there for me as a child. He did nice things for me. He made sure there were no spiders in the shower because he knew I wouldn't get in otherwise. He tucked me in at night, or else I wouldn't go to sleep. My brother and I loved potato fries, and my dad was an expert. He cut the potatoes perfectly neat and thin. To this day, I can never cut them as well as he did. He was a good dad.
>
> *Moe-Moe S., adult child of two incarcerated parents*

> [My step-father] … had plenty of free time to play [with me] and he played as if he were a big kid who followed no rules.
>
> *Bruce B., adult child of two incarcerated parents*

> My dad was a wonderful father.
>
> *Jessamyn R., adult child of two incarcerated parents*

Others had less positive experiences:

> [J]ust as [my father] was always absent from my life, his father was absent from his … There had never been any affection shown to him in his entire life, nor was there in mine. I can clearly remember my father telling me, "The last time your grandma hugged me or said 'I love you' to me was when I was eight." He felt lonely and unloved … By him expressing this to me, I am able to see the patterns and their similarities in my life … The only time my father showed affection or told me he loved me was when he was incarcerated.
>
> *James C., adult child of two incarcerated parents*

> My father was an angry man. In sober moments, he could escape the darkness that cloaked him but those were few and far between. As a child I never understood why he lost control.
>
> *Hollie O., adult child of an incarcerated father*

In spite of such experiences, children of incarcerated fathers appear to have a developmental advantage over children of incarcerated mothers. Healthy, appropriate parent–child relationships occur most often among children who receive continuous care from at least one parent. Within the population of prisoners' children, this circumstance is more likely among children of incarcerated fathers, almost 90 percent of whom reside with their birth mothers and have for most of their lives.[33] Among children of incarcerated mothers, only 37 percent reside with their birth fathers and many of these did not reside with their fathers prior to maternal incarceration.[34] Especially disadvantaged in this respect are children who have two incarcerated parents. While there is almost no documentation of long-term outcomes among children of incarcerated parents, preliminary research on risk factors in their lives has clearly established that the relative disadvantage of children of incarcerated mothers (or two incarcerated parents) exists.[35]

Parent and Child Roles among Incarcerated Parents and Their Children

Parent–child relationships within justice-involved families are embedded in a web of complex circumstances that include many adverse influences; in part due to this complexity, there has been very little research on the nature of those relationships prior to parental incarceration or their outcomes. However, the parentification of children – and particularly the children of incarcerated mothers – has long been recognized among children in justice-involved families.[36]

> Naturally, I felt I had to do the job of being Mommy. I cooked whatever I could get my hands on, I got my siblings ready for school and bed daily.
>
> *Aliyah, adult child of two incarcerated parents*

> Mom began to be scarce, to the point where we kids had to cook for ourselves and do the laundry. We also did pretty much whatever we wanted … [Eventually] I found myself acting as a psychiatric nurse/parent.
>
> *Nate L., adult child of an incarcerated mother*

> I usually took care of my mom: cooking, cleaning, and making sure she took her medicine. It was like I took on the mom role, and that was when we got to spend our quality time together. It may not be what most people would consider mother–daughter time, but for me those were the best times.
>
> *Alisha M., adult child of an incarcerated mother*

Among our contributors, about one in four who lived at some time with their incarcerated parents assumed a caregiving role for their parent and/or for their siblings while they were growing up. Studies have suggested that individuals who are parentified in childhood may develop greater competence and self-efficacy, but may also have difficulties in identity development, interpersonal relationships in adulthood, and relationships with their own children.[37]

Parent–Child Relationships in Special Circumstances

Attempts to understand parent–child relationships among the families of justice-involved parents have been severely limited by the almost exclusive focus of researchers on the period of parental incarceration, when parents and children are separated. But recent research provides promising information about prisoners and their children who are living in special circumstances. For example, a recent study of mother–child and infant outcomes among families participating in the Bedford Hills Correctional Facility prison nursery found that the proportion of infants with secure attachments to their mothers was 60 to 70 per cent, a higher rate than what is found in low-risk community samples.[38] These outcomes, among children of mothers in a maximum security prison, suggest that in spite of all of the challenges to parenting and a healthy parent–child relationship, optimal parenting by justice-involved parents is possible.

Relationships with Primary Caregivers

At this time, it is impossible to make definitive statements about the effects of either maternal or paternal incarceration on parent–child relationships. However, the repeated parent–child separations experienced by children of prisoners insure that many children will have other adults in significant, parent-like roles in their lives.

The length of time prisoners' children live with non-parent caregivers and the quality of those relationships has been and is unclear. Examining studies that report on children's living arrangements prior to and during parental incarceration,[39] it can be estimated that at least one in ten children of incarcerated fathers and at least three in five children of incarcerated mothers are being raised by caregivers who are not their parents.

In spite of a relative abundance of publications addressing the caregivers of prisoners' children, the actual relationships between these caregivers and children have not been well examined. An early paper[40] explored some of the relational dynamics between caregivers, incarcerated parents and their children. Two recent studies have found that children of incarcerated mothers who reported feeling less warmth and acceptance from their caregivers demonstrated more behavior problems, while highly stressed caregivers who assessed children's behavior as difficult demonstrated less warmth and acceptance towards the children.[41] Another set of studies examined attachment between prisoners' children and their caregivers, finding that a significant minority of children had secure patterns of attachment to their caregivers.[42]

> I loved my grandmother. She was a kind, caring, beautiful asset to the world and her teachings and way of life live on through her grandchildren, me and my sister.
>
> *David S., adult child of an incarcerated father*

Practice experience and newer research suggest that these caregiving relationships are often complex as the result of multiple factors including the pre-incarceration and current relationship between the incarcerated parent and the caregiver,[43] the anticipated length of the caregiving arrangement, the degree of child and/or caregiver impairment, and the resources that are available to support the caregiver.[44] In some cases, most or all of these factors work against the child's well-being.

> My aunt's rules were normal. Clean your room, do dishes, go to school, etc. However, when my cousin and I didn't comply with those rules, we were beaten badly … I began

to wish I were with my mom to get away from the abuse. Then I began to hate my mom for leaving me in an abusive home. Over the years, I began to rebel.

Marcus R., adult child of an incarcerated mother

I hated the fact that my mother wasn't there to give me the real love and attention that I needed. I used to wet the bed a lot, and when I did, my step-mother would hit me.

Moe-Moe S., adult child of two incarcerated parents

But in other cases, the caregiver has enough support to be able to look after the child and the outcomes of the child's care are good.

I spent a lot of years living with my grandma, and she provided stable, loving care.

Natalie C., adult child of an incarcerated mother

My aunt took me home from the hospital as an infant because my mother was arrested and taken to jail. ... Some might have expected me to end up in jails and prisons just like my mother ... But I am honored to say that I have never been arrested or incarcerated in my life.

Victoria G., adult child of an incarcerated mother

Empirical research on the non-structural elements of relationships between children of incarcerated parents and their caregivers and the content and quality of the care provided is almost non-existent. With a significant minority of the children of incarcerated parents (and a majority of children of incarcerated mothers) in the long-term care of non-parental caregivers, these relationships deserve much additional study.

Relationships with Siblings

Relationships with siblings have the potential to provide substantial developmental supports. The Minnesota Study[45] found that the quality of relationships with siblings is based on the parent–child relationship and that sibling relationships predict a child's competence with peers and the ability to have successful social interactions.

By the time I was five, there were two more kids added to the family and things were worse. I felt that I was the boss and went around the house screaming and hitting my siblings, because I often heard my mom screaming and saw my father hitting her.

Aliyah, adult child of two incarcerated parents

Early research found that separation from siblings was a norm for children of incarcerated mothers.[46] Child custody and placement difficulties were thought to be the reason for these separations. Early studies did not examine the paternity of these children, so it is impossible to know if multi-partnered fertility contributed to those early findings.

Most incarcerated fathers have children by two or more reproductive partners.[47] The children of these unions typically remain with their mothers[48] and therefore live separately from the half-siblings born to their fathers' other reproductive partners.

The Therapeutic Intervention Project (TIP)[49] was one of the first community-based programs of services for children of incarcerated parents. More than 600 families were served; over 90 percent of the families included two or more children. Separation among siblings was the norm, occurring in more than two-thirds of participating families; in addition, a significant number of children had experienced the death of siblings. Sibling issues identified among a minority of families included the utilization of older children as caregivers for younger siblings, and the mutual utilization of siblings for primary emotional support.

> Later my mom … went to jail for 16 months … My main concern was for my little sister, who had just started kindergarten … It was really difficult to work 20 hours a week, attend my college classes and also take care of my sister. There was no financial support from anyone. I couldn't get welfare, or any other assistance … [M]y sister was obviously pretty traumatized by my mom's arrest, and the awful years leading up to it. [She] … acted out a lot during those months. She got in trouble at school and I had no idea how to handle it. We found a therapist for her. I can't even remember how I paid for it, since I had no insurance. … Even though I was young, I was pro-active about getting help.
>
> *Natalie C., adult child of an incarcerated mother*

> My brothers took the place of my dad for me and I did not miss him.
>
> *Betty M., adult child of an incarcerated father*

Among our contributors, 15 percent served as the primary caregiver for one or more of their siblings before, during and/or after parental incarceration.

There is not enough information available to understand the significance of sibling relationships among prisoners' children. However, like parent–child bonds, these important relationships are disrupted among many children of incarcerated parents, depriving them of yet another developmental resource.

Relationships with Peers

> Growing up I would hide the fact that I had a parent in prison … I wanted to be well liked. I worried about what would happen if the kids at school found out that I had a parent who murdered someone … I was unintentionally shy and alienating myself from others outside of my family. I can count on one hand how many times I actually spent the night with a friend through all my school years. I was afraid to make friends who might find out who I was and where I came from. To this day, I noticeably struggle making friends. I attribute that very much to not building that skill when I was younger.
>
> *Carie S., adult child of an incarcerated father*

The Minnesota Study found that the quality of children's peer relationships is based upon their relationships with their parents and their siblings. With disrupted and/or difficult parent–child relationships and separations from siblings, children of incarcerated parents may be expected to have difficulty developing competence in their relationships with peers.

By early childhood, kids who have relationship problems at home have difficulty finding play partners, participating in groups and sustaining interactions – including the negotiation of conflicts, self-regulating in interactions, and enjoying the interactive process – with other children.[50] Indeed, difficulties in early peer relationships have been commonly identified among children at risk for criminal justice system involvement.[51]

By middle childhood, kids should be able to form loyal, lasting friendships, resolve conflicts with peers and function well in groups. Many prisoners' children struggle to achieve these skills, which may have been undermined by parental incarceration and related experiences.

> I was playing with my BB gun in a field when a local kid came up and started annoying me. He was a fat boy who didn't know when to shut up. I got angry and turned the gun against his belly, shooting him with a splinter that lodged in the fat under his skin. It was a great feeling. Later that day, the chief of police came to our house and took the gun away, but he couldn't take away that feeling.
>
> *Michael C., adult child of an incarcerated father*

> [We] ended up moving again ... This was when I got a real big dose of rejection. It was so bad that I stole my mother's .25 caliber pistol and took it to school. The kids at school would ridicule me for the clothes I'd wear and the way I talked. One day I got tired of it and I was going to make them pay for it.
>
> *Kris B., adult child of an incarcerated mother*

In adolescence, children develop the abilities to form intimate relationships, to demonstrate commitment in relationships, and to coordinate multiple relationships, as adults do. However, children who have not had adequate developmental supports do not achieve these competencies.

> My close friendships with kids who were being nurtured by the same criminal atmosphere. Things were easier this way ... And, since I had no extended family, this criminal subculture functioned very much as a type of make-believe family ...
>
> *Bruce B., adult child of two incarcerated parents*

> I met a group of misfits in my eighth-grade year. ... Our little group became Skinheads – anti-Semitism and no interracial mingling were part of our manifesto. We never did actually go out and do any fag-bashing. We never hurt anyone but ourselves. We'd throw parties with our little clique and our girlfriends, get drunk, smoke pot and fight each other.
>
> *Kris B., adult child of an incarcerated mother*

The Minnesota Study found that children who are struggling with adverse circumstances and relationship difficulties are drawn to peers with similar problems. While association with "deviant" peers is often referred to as a risk factor for poor developmental outcomes,[52] it is also an outcome of early difficulties in relationships with parents, primary caregivers and/or siblings. This finding once again highlights the lifelong importance of the quality of children's early relationships and early care.

Romantic and Sexual Relationships

Children who have experienced difficulties in their relationships with parents, siblings and peers might be expected to also have difficulties in their romantic and sexual relationships. This appears to be the case with prisoners' children but there have been no studies of adult children of incarcerated parents to guide us in this area. Early sexual relationships might be expected in this group, especially among children of teenage mothers,[53] children who were sexually abused[54] and children who experienced lack of parental involvement.[55] And, since multi-partnered fertility is an intergenerational phenomenon,[56] with children who have half-siblings more likely to grow up to have children by multiple partners, it might be anticipated that children of prisoners would grow up to have similar relationship behavior patterns. In addition, we might expect relationship conflict and violence to characterize the adult romantic partnerships of prisoners' children, given the high incidence of these behaviors among incarcerated parents and their partners.[57]

The stories of our contributors who provide information about their adult relationships meet these expectations.

> When I was 15, I became pregnant by a man who had once broken into our home and stolen money and jewelry from my mother. When I was four months pregnant, this man started to cheat on me … he [later] became abusive, got hooked on drugs, and constantly cheated on me … There were times when I used drugs with him, because I felt so alone … My son saw all of this … because I did not leave his father … I did not want my son to grow up as heartbroken and fatherless as I had been.
>
> *Danielle C., adult child of an incarcerated father*

> I met my husband when I was 14. He got me pregnant but I had a miscarriage … When I was 17, I got pregnant again and we got married … When I was 26, I got pregnant with twins. I was very irritable in this pregnancy. My husband and I had a fight in my mother-in-law's house and I shot him in the leg. I got out of prison … and went into a treatment program. After that I stayed sober for almost a year and I got off parole. But then I went back with my husband and we started using again.
>
> *Mary, adult child of two incarcerated parents*

However, some incarcerated parents do not have sexual and romantic relationship difficulties, and some children of incarcerated parents have forged positive partnerships. For example, one contributor to this book mentions her successful marriage and her two children who attended college while describing what she learned about relationships from her father's incarceration:

I found out that I was strong. I learned that I could survive tough times. I developed an empathy for the under dog that always existed for me, but now went to new levels. I learned that ... people who cared about others could reach out and take away pain. I learned that sometimes people need things they cannot ask for, and that being kind to everyone is time spent well.

Shari O., adult child of an incarcerated father

It appears that parental incarceration has limited direct effects on the quality of significant life experiences like intimate relationships. This is not surprising from a developmental perspective. Far more important in shaping the sexual/romantic relationships of adult children of incarcerated parents are the quality of their early relationships with their parents and the quality of the care they received.

Relationships with Children

There have been no studies of the way adults who experienced parental incarceration care for their own children. The contributors to this book provide some insight into the ways that parental incarceration might affect parenting.

Some adult children of incarcerated parents are replicating the relational and criminal behaviors of their incarcerated parents.

Between my stints in prison, I somehow managed to impregnate several women and have four daughters. And, sadly, I only had the opportunity to spend time with one of these children before I got locked up to serve a very long prison sentence ... I have recently contacted her on Facebook but she remains very distant with me – very upset that I was not there for her through her young life.

Percy L., adult child of two incarcerated parents

Entering adulthood at 18, I was carrying my second child and my luck was soon to run out. I was arrested and charged with drug sales. My newborn baby and two-year-old daughter became wards of the state ... Every day, I work to better myself. I've gained a relationship with my siblings and I am still working hard to be reunited with my daughters. I ended up where I am by trying to be close to my father and my mother, to manage their lives without being like them. I loved them so much but I no longer want to follow the footsteps of my parents.

Aliyah, adult child of two incarcerated parents

Others are trying to do it differently.

The upside [of our father's incarceration] is that from the painful lessons of our young lives, [my brother and I] paid attention and are probably among some of the best parents on the planet.

Pamela H., adult child of an incarcerated father

It doesn't escape me that I have gone to prison just like my father, but we are very different as parents. He used his child to meet his needs, but I didn't abuse my children. My father never met his child's needs in any way, but I have tried to meet my daughters' needs as my first priority. I do think our problems are linked. I believe that he went to prison as the result of what was done to him, just like I went to prison as the result of what he did to me. I will not allow that to happen to my children. I will break the chain.

Jasmine, adult child of an incarcerated father

How prisoners' children negotiate parenting and parent–child relationships in the face of their own experiences with inadequate parental care and support is among the most critical but unanswered questions about this special population.

Conclusions

Relationships are the most significant developmental resource for children. The majority of children of incarcerated parents are disadvantaged in this area, experiencing extended or permanent separations from their birth parents, attenuated relationships with siblings, and/or troubled relationships with peers and partners.

Clearly, the relationships prisoners' children have with their parents, siblings and families are shaped by the factors that pre-existed and contributed to parental incarceration. Parental violence, drug addiction, criminal behavior and/or mental illness lie immediately behind parent–child separations due to incarceration. In addition, each of these has their own effects on parent–child relationships. Similarly, serial sexual and reproductive relationships among incarcerated parents often lie behind sibling separations. And high levels of stress, economic strain, behavioral problems and mental illness often lie behind unsupportive or traumatic relationships between children of prisoners and their non-parent caregivers.

As a result, it's not surprising that many children of incarcerated parents grow up to have difficulties in their relationships as adults. Some of our contributors continued to have disrupted relationships with their parents into middle age.

My father and I struggle with how to fit into each other's lives. I don't consider his home my home. I feel too intimidated to invite myself for fear of rejection. Although he lives only 15 minutes away, I haven't seen him for years. The last time we had any contact was by text message after a family member passed. I continue to try to give him the benefit of the doubt, knowing that he was institutionalized … The other part of me is not as forgiving. I still continue to be angry that he is absent in my life even now he has his freedom.

Carie S., adult child of an incarcerated father

In addition, the difficult relationships they had in childhood are reflected in contributors' relationships with their sexual/romantic partners and their own sons and daughters.

Yet the picture is not all bleak. Incarcerated parents can clearly go on to right their lives and repair their family relationships. And some children of incarcerated parents come through their experiences with strong relational skills and the capacity for healthy relationships.

Some of my most vivid and meaningful early memories are of my father's comforting touch. If I had run into trouble at school, he would tuck me in and rub my back comforting me until I fell asleep. These moments were special and not uncommon.

Daniel B., adult child of an incarcerated father

[I]n order to move forward, I had to forgive him. He may have been a criminal but he was also my father. And he was loved more than he'll ever know.

Hollie O., adult child of an incarcerated father

Our contributors' stories suggest that many adult children of incarcerated parents carry on, in spite of their circumstances and experiences, hoping for and working toward healthy, appropriate relationships with others.

Notes

1 Sroufe LA, Egeland B, Carlson EA, Collins WA. (2005). *The Development of the Person: The Minnesota Study of Risk and Adaptation from Birth to Adulthood.* New York: Guilford Press.
2 *Ibid.*
3 Carlson BE, Shafer MS. (2010). Traumatic histories and stressful life events of incarcerated parents: Childhood and adult trauma histories. *The Prison Journal*, 90(4): 475–493; Glaze L, Marushak LM. (2008). *Parents in Prison and Their Minor Children.* NCJ222984. Washington, D.C.: Bureau of Justice Statistics; Grella CE, Lovinger K, Warda US. (2013). Relationships between trauma exposure, familial characteristics and PTSD: A case-control study of women in prison and in the general population. *Women and Criminal Justice*, 23(1): 63–79; Johnston D, Gabel K. (1995). Incarcerated parents. In Gable K and Johnston D. (Eds.), *Children of Incarcerated Parents.* New York: Lexington Books; Kjellstrand J, Cearley J, Eddy JM, Foney D, Martinez CR. (2012). Characteristics of incarcerated fathers and mothers: Implications for preventive interventions targeting children and families. *Children and Youth Services Review*, 34(12): 2409–2415.
4 Mincy R. (2002). *Who Should Marry Whom? Multiple Partner Fertility among New Parents.* Fragile Families Publication 2002–03-FF. Available at: http://crcw.princeton.edu/publications/publications.asp.
5 Carlson MJ, Furstenberg FF. (2005). *The Consequences of Multi-Partnered Fertility for Parental Involvement and Relationships.* Fragile Families Publication 2006–28-FF. Available at: http://crcw.princeton.edu/publications/publications.asp; Harknett K, Knab J. (2007). More kin, less support: Multi-partnered fertility and perceived support among mothers. *Journal of Marriage and the Family*, 69(1): 237–253.
6 Carlson MJ, Furstenberg FF. (2006). The prevalence and correlates of multi-partnered fertility among urban U.S. parents. *Journal of Marriage and the Family*, 68(3): 718–732; Hairston CF. (1989). Men in prison: Family characteristics and family views. *Journal of Offender Counseling, Services and Rehabilitation*, 14(1): 23–30.
7 Geller A. (2013). Paternal incarceration and father–child contact in fragile families. *Journal of Marriage and the Family*, 75(5): 1288–1303.
8 Harknett, Knab. *Ibid.*
9 Browne A, Miller A, Maguin E. (1999). Prevalence and severity of lifetime physical and sexual victimization among incarcerated women. *International Journal of Law and Psychiatry*, 22: 301–322; Dutton D, Hart S. (1992a). Evidence for long-term, specific effects of childhood abuse and neglect on criminal behavior in men. *International Journal of Offender Therapy and Comparative Criminology*, 36: 129–137; Wolff N, Shi J, Siegel JA. (2009). Patterns of victimization among male and female inmates: Evidence of an enduring legacy. *Violence and Victimization*, 24(4): 469–484.
10 Davis JL, Petretic-Jackson PA, Ting L. (2001). Intimacy dysfunction and trauma symptomatology: Long-term correlates of different types of child abuse. *Journal of Traumatic Stress*, 14(1): 63–79; DuCharme J, Koverola C, Battle P. (1997). Intimacy development: The influence of abuse and gender. *Journal of Interpersonal Violence*, 12(4): 590–599; National Center for PTSD. (2015).

Relationships and PTSD. Washington, D.C.: US Department of Veterans Affairs. Available at: www. ptsd.va.gov/public/family/ptsd-and-relationships.asp; Roche DN, Runtz MG, Hunter MA. (1999). Adult attachment: A mediator between sexual abuse and later psychological adjustment. *Journal of Interpersonal Violence*, 14(2): 184–207.

11 Ee E, Kleber RJ, Jongmans MJ. (2015, May 11). Relational patterns between caregivers with PTSD and their nonexposed children: A review. *Trauma Violence Abuse.* doi: 10.1177/1524838015584355.

12 Moehler E, Brunner R, Wiebel A, Reck C, Resch F. (2006). Maternal depressive symptoms in the postnatal period are associated with long-term impairment of mother–child bonding. *Archives of Women's Mental Health*, 9(5): 273–278.

13 Banyard VL. (1997). The impact of childhood sexual abuse and family functioning on four dimensions of women's later parenting. *Child Abuse and Neglect*, 21(11): 1095–1107.

14 Lyons-Ruth K, Block D. (1996). The disturbed caregiving system: Relations among childhood trauma, maternal caregiving, infant affect and attachment. *Infant Mental Health Journal*, 17(3): 257–275.

15 Juul SH, Hendrix C, Robinson B, Stowe ZN, Newport DJ, Brennan PA, Johnson KC. (2015, May). Maternal early-life trauma and affective parenting style: the mediating role of HPA-axis function. *Archives of Women's Mental Health*. doi: 10.1007/s00737-015-0528-x.

16 Glaze, Marushak. *Ibid.*

17 Bauman PS, Dougherty FE. (1983) Drug-addicted mothers' parenting and their children's development. *International Journal of the Addictions*, 18: 291–302; Suchman NE, Luthar SS. (2000). Maternal addiction, child maladjustment and sociodemographic risks: Implications for parenting behaviors. *Addiction*, 95(9): 1417–1428.

18 Chaffin M, Kelleher K, Hollenberg J. (1996). Onset of physical abuse and neglect: Psychiatric, substance abuse and social risk factors. *Child Abuse and Neglect*, 20(3): 191–203.

19 Mueser KT, Gottlieb JD, Cather C, Glynn SM, Zarate R, Smith LF, Clark RE, Wolfe R. (2010). Antisocial personality disorder in people with co-occurring severe mental illness and substance use disorder. *Psychosis*, 4(1): 52–62.

20 Kinner SA, Alati A, Najman JM, Williams GM. (2007), Do paternal arrest and imprisonment lead to child behavior problems and substance use? A longitudinal analysis. *Journal of Child Psychology and Psychiatry*, 48(11): 1148–1156; Phillips S, Erklani A, Keeler GP, Costello E, Angold A. (2006). Disentangling the risks: Parent criminal justice involvement and children's exposure to family risks. *Criminology and Public Policy*, 5(4): 688–702.

21 American Academy of Pediatrics. (2014). *Adverse Childhood Experiences and the Lifelong Consequences of Trauma.* Elk Grove Village, IL: Authors.

22 Phillips et al. *Ibid.*

23 Ehrensaft M, Khashu A, Ross T, Wamsley M. (2003). *Patterns of Criminal Conviction and Incarceration among Mothers of Children in Foster Care in New York City.* New York: Vera Institute of Justice; Genty PM. (2003). Damage to family relationships as a collateral consequence of parental incarceration. *Fordham Urban Law Journal*, 30(6): 1671–1684; Smith G. (2000). The Adoption and Safe Families Act of 1997: Effects on incarcerated mothers and their children. *Women, Girls and Criminal Justice*, 1(1).

24 Howard K, Martin A, Berlin LJ, Brooks-Gunn J. (2011). Early mother–child separation, parenting and child well-being in Early Head Start families. *Attachment and Human Development*, 13(1): 5–26; Littner N. (1956). *Some Traumatic Effects of Separation and Placement.* New York: Child Welfare League of America.

25 Robertson J, Robertson J. (1971). *Young Children in Brief Separation.* London: Tavistock Institute; Rutter M. (1971). Parent–child separation: Effects on the children. *Journal of Child Psychology and Psychiatry*, 12(4): 233–260.

26 See review in Johnston D. (1995d). Parent–child visits in jails. *Children's Environments Quarterly*, 12(1): 25–38.

27 Glaze, Marushak. *Ibid.*

28 Johnston D. (1995b). Jailed mothers. In Gable K, Johnston D. (Eds.), *Children of Incarcerated Parents.* New York: Lexington Books; Johnston D. (2001). *Incarceration of Women and Effects on Parenting.* Presented to the Institute of Policy Research, Northwestern University Conference on the Effects of Incarceration on Children and Families; Stanton A. (1980). *When Mothers Go to Jail.* Boston, MA: Lexington Books.

29 McGowan BG, Blumenthal KL. (1978). *Why Punish the Children?* Hackensack, NJ: National Council on Crime and Delinquency.

30 Poehlmann J. (2005). Representations of attachment relationships in children of incarcerated mothers. *Child Development,* 76: 679–696; Shlafer RJ, Poehlmann J. (2010). Attachment and caregiving relationships in families affected by parental incarceration.*Attachment and Human Development,* 12, 395–415.

31 Glaze, Marushak. *Ibid.*

32 Geller. *Ibid.*

33 Glaze, Marushak. *Ibid.*

34 *Ibid.*

35 Dallaire DH. (2007). Incarcerated mothers and fathers: A comparison of risks for children and families. *Family Relations,* 56(5): 440–453; Johnson EI, Waldfogel J. (2004). Children of incarcerated parents: Multiple risks and children's living arrangements. In Patillo ME, Weiman DF, Western B. (Eds.), *Imprisoning of America: The Social Effects of Mass Incarceration.* New York: Russell Sage Foundation.

36 Johnston D. (1995c). The effects of parental incarceration. In Gabel K, Johnston D. (Eds.), *Children of Incarcerated Parents.* New York: Lexington Books; Katarzyna C, Siegel JA. (2010). Mothers in trouble: Coping with actual or pending separation from children due to incarceration. *The Prison Journal,* 90: 447; LaPointe V, Picker O, Harris BF. (1985). Enforced family separation: A descriptive analysis of some experiences of children of black imprisoned mothers. In Spencer A. (Ed.), *Beginnings: The Social and Affective Development of Black Children.* Hillsdale, NJ: Erlbaum; Mazza C. (2002). And then the world fell apart: The children of incarcerated fathers. *Families in Society,* 83(5): 521–529.

37 Earley L, Cushway D. (2002). The parentified child. *Clinical Child Psychology and Psychiatry,* 7(2): 163–178; Macfie J, Brumariu LE, Lyons-Ruth K. (2015). Parent–child role confusion: A critical review of an emerging concept. *Development Review,* 35: 34–57.

38 Borelli J, Goshin L, Joestl S, Clark J, Byrne MW. (2010) Attachment organization in a sample of incarcerated mothers: Distribution of classifications and predictive associations with clinical symptoms, perceptions of parenting competency and social support. *Attachment and Human Development,* 12(4): 355–374.

39 Baunach PJ. (1984). *Mothers in Prison.* Newark, NJ: Rutgers University Press; Dubose DG. (1983). *Incarcerated Mothers and Their Children in Texas.* (Unpublished manuscript held by the Center for Children of Incarcerated Parents); Henriques Z. (1982). *Imprisoned Mothers and Their Children.* Washington, D.C.: University Press of America; Johnston D. (1992). *The Children of Offenders Study: Report to the California Assembly Office of Research.* Pasadena, CA: Pacific Oaks College; McCarthy BR. (1980). Inmate mothers: The problems of separation and reintegration. *Journal of Offenders Counseling, Services and Rehabilitation,* 4(3): 199–212.

40 Glaze, Marushak. *Ibid;* See review in Johnston D. (1995e). Care and placement of prisoners' children. In Gable K, Johnston D. (Eds.), *Children of Incarcerated Parents.* New York: Lexington Books.

41 Johnston D. (1993a). *Caregivers of Prisoners' Children.* Pasadena, CA: Center for Children of Incarcerated Parents.

42 Poehlmann. *Ibid.;* Shlafer, Poehlmann. *Ibid.*

43 Loper AB, Phillips V, Nichols EB, Dallaire DH. (2014). Characteristics and effects of the co-parenting alliance between incarcerated parents and child caregivers. *Journal of Child and Family Studies,* 23: 225–241.

44 Hanlon TE, Carswell SB, Rose M. (2007). Research on the caretaking of children of incarcerated parents. *Child and Youth Services Review,* 29: 348–362; Loper et al. *Ibid;* Turanovic JJ, Rodriguez N, Pratt TC. (2012). The collateral consequences of incarceration revisited: A qualitative analysis of the effects on caregivers of children of incarcerated parents. *Criminology,* 50(4): 913–959.

45 Sroufe et al. *Ibid.*

46 Zalba, S. (1964). *Women Prisoners and Their Families.* Sacramento, CA: Department of Social Welfare and Department of Corrections; Baunach. *Ibid;* Henriques. *Ibid.*

47 Hairston. *Ibid.;* Carlson, Furstenberg. (2006). *Ibid.*

48 Glaze, Marushak. *Ibid.*

49 Erickson KG, Crosnoe R, Dornbusch SM. (2000). A social process model of adolescent deviance: Combining social control and differential association perspectives. *Journal of Youth and Adolescence,* 29: 395–426; Farrington D. (2004). Conduct disorder, aggression, and delinquency. In Lerner R, Steinberg L. (Eds), *Handbook of Adolescent Psychology.* New York: Wiley.

50 Johnston D. (1999). *The Therapeutic Intervention Project: A Report to Funders*. Eagle Rock, CA: The Center for Children of Incarcerated Parents.

51 Olson SL, Lopez-Duran N, Lunkenheimer ES, Chang H, Sameroff AJ. (2011). Individual differences in the development of early peer aggression. *Development and Psychopathology*, 23: 253–266; Trentacosta CJ, Shaw DS. (2009). Emotional self-regulation, peer rejection and antisocial behavior: Developmental associations from early childhood to early adolescence. *Journal of Applied Developmental Psychology*, 30(3): 356–365.

52 See review in Johnston D. (2010). *Intergenerational Incarceration*. Eagle Rock, CA: The Center for Children of Incarcerated Parents; also see Raine A. (1997). *The Psychopathology of Crime*. Houston: Gulf Professional Publishing.

53 Barber JS. (2001). Intergenerational transmission of age at first birth among married and unmarried men and women. *Social Science Research*, 30(2): 219–247; Meade CS, Kershaw TS, Ickovics JR. (2008). The intergenerational cycle of teenage motherhood. *Health Psychology*, 27(4): 419–429; Pogarsky J, Thornberry TP, Lizotte AJ. (2006). Developmental outcomes for children of young mothers. *Journal of Marriage and the Family*, 68: 332–344.

54 Homma Y, Wang N, Saewyc E, Kishor N. (2012). The relationship between sexual abuse and risky sexual behavior in adolescent boys. *Journal of Adolescent Health*, 51(1): 18–24; Jones DJ, Runyon DK, Lewis T, Litrowrick AJ, Black MM, Wiley T, English DE, Proctor LJ, Jones BL, Nagin DS. (2010). Trajectories of childhood abuse and early adolescent HIV/AIDS risk behaviors. *Journal of Clinical and Adolescent Psychology*, 39(5): 667–680.

55 Nettle D, Coall DA, Dickins TE. (2011). Early life conditions and age at first pregnancy in British women. *Proceedings of the Royal Society of Biological Sciences*, 278(1712): 1721–1727.

56 Lappegard T, Thomson E. (2012). *Intergenerational Transmission of Childbearing across Partnerships*. Presented at the Meeting of the Population Association of America, San Francisco.

57 DeHart DD. (2005). *Pathways to Prison: The Impact of Victimization in the Lives of Incarcerated Women*. Available at: www.ncjrs.gov/pdffiles1/nij/grants/208383.pdf; Dutton DG, Hart SD. (1992b). Risk markers for family violence in a federally incarcerated population. *International Journal of Law and Psychiatry*, 15: 101–112; Girshick LB. (1999). *No Safe Haven: The Stories of Women in Prison*. Boston, MA: Northeastern University Press.

PERSONAL STORIES

My Daddy by Betty

My mother was born in 1920. She was the only child. Her name was Johnnie Mae. She was raised in the South where there was slavery and there was still a lot of prejudice. It was back in the time when Black people had to sit at the back of the bus and had to pick cotton for a living.

As a child I guess my mother was lonely because she had no brother or sister. So when she had kids she made sure that they had someone to play with. My oldest brother was born in 1936, and then there were five more. I was born in 1959, and my littlest brother was born after me. We mostly had different fathers.

I never knew my father but my two brothers just older than me called him Daddy. When I was a little girl, they told me he was in jail. My brothers took the place of my dad for me and I did not miss him. When I was in high school, one of my brothers told me that my father was in the Parchman Prison.

Having all these kids was hard in the South. Black people could not get good jobs. But my mother was lucky. Some White people helped her by giving her a job as a maid that paid more money. So it was easier to take care of us.

I was told that I was the most pretty baby in the world and that everybody loved me because I was the only girl. I don't remember much, just what I was told – I was a good girl. My early childhood was great because I was the only girl and my brothers took good care of me when my mother was at work. My school years were OK. I never liked school but I did what I had to do so I could get it over with. As I was getting older, school was getting better because I met people that I really liked and could understand what it was all about. I understood why I needed to learn certain things, why it was important and how it would help me later in life.

Now I am a grown woman. I don't know where I went wrong but I did. I had a lot of children like my mother but the social services took them all when I was homeless. I was using drugs. I got into a program and had my last baby when I was sober. Now all I want to do is keep changing. I want to be a good mother.

I don't know if my father's incarceration affected me. I never saw him, not once. After I got clean, I went back home to see my mother and I asked about him. She said he was a good man who stole money because we were poor. I wanted to go and meet him but she said he had died right after he got out of prison in 1968.

***

My Guardian Angel by David Santiago

My name is David Santiago, and I am someone who has been a witness to the life of a child of an incarcerated parent. My father, David Proulx, has been in jail since I was an infant.

I was raised by my mother, a very beautiful woman who was born in Puerto Rico before coming here. She had three children. My younger brother had a different father than me and my sister. I was very jealous of my little brother because he got a lot of attention and he had a father in his life who would come around on his motorcycle, and they would go out together. I was confused and hurt because I didn't have a father to do things I pictured my brother and his father doing, like fishing and camping. Or just having someone to look up to.

During my younger years, my family – mostly my dad's mom, Gena Proulx – saw to it that my father and I kept in touch through mail and occasionally visits on the holidays, mostly around Christmas time. I don't even remember my father other than the times I've seen him in jail. My grandmother would call it college to protect me from embarrassment, but as I got older my mom told me the truth.

I never knew why he was in jail. The family never spoke of it, they just avoided the subject if it ever came up and that confused me because people would always ask if he was ever going to come home.

I grew up fighting. My little brother looked up to me and I found myself protecting him a lot while we were growing up. In the projects, a lot of older kids would run around starting fights and testing everyone's heart. I never wanted to fight but my mom taught me to never let anyone put their hands on me or my family members. So I was like a magnet for the older kids. They would taunt the vulnerable ones to start a fight with me. If I'd had a father around, maybe things would have been different.

Anger was something that consumed me growing up and I acted out a lot. I started drinking at a young age and smoking cigarettes, hanging around with the wrong crowd, stealing cars and getting arrested. I went to the Department of Youth Services [DYS] after my second offense and had to do time more than once. The last time, the detectives beat me and put false charges on me to take the focus off their actions. No one was going to believe a troubled kid. I spent one year in DYS custody and in order to be released, I had to be put in foster care.

Most foster parents are just interested in the checks they get. The elephant in the room (the foster child) is never really wanted or spoken to. It's like you're invisible but a burden at the same time. It is no way to live. From my loving family to DYS to a house of strangers, my childhood was one really big rollercoaster.

The love of a father was never something I could testify to as I was growing up but my grandmother always spoke the world of my father, so I learned to love him from the love that flowed through her. Of course, I loved my grandmother. She was a kind, caring, beautiful asset to the world and her teachings and way of life live on through her grandchildren, me and my sister. She suffered dearly, more than any of us, having to see her son under the conditions allowed. But she never gave up on him and would tell you that with all the love she had in her heart and all the good she did, she was granted a little piece of what she gave so freely.

Although she received love from me, my sister and my cousins, my grandmother knew pain like no human being should ever have to endure. Her sons, my uncles, both died – one from an overdose and the other from a slow, painful struggle that was caused by drug abuse. My grandmother endured all that only to die a horrible death herself. She smoked for years and was diagnosed with emphysema and finally was forced to quit. She would smoke unlit cigarettes all day long. I remember her cigarettes, with stains of lipstick on them, in her ashtray. I even remember seeing some tape on a few of them. She wanted to live to be there for us kids and her loving son but one day an electrical fire sparked in her apartment. She tried to get some legal documents and personal things she had. I believe that she didn't want to perish in the fire in her hallway. But she had emphysema and any smoke would send her into convulsing spasms of uncontrollable coughing. They say the ceiling collapsed on her and she died in that hallway.

I was with my cousin Magdalena that day when we noticed the smoke in the sky. I had a horrible feeling in my gut. We were only a few streets away from my grandmother's. We quickly drove to her house and jumped out. When I saw the smoke that was coming from her building, I lost it. Then we heard the people from the first floor say that my grandmother was still inside. I tried to run in but I was pinned down by the man who lived on the first floor. He was a very big guy who loved my grandmother and he told me it was too late, not to go in there. I tried to fight him but my emotions and the weariness you get from the pain in your heart dropped me to the floor with a weakness I can't explain. My grandmother, so loving and caring, killed by the thing she gave up – smoke. That incident scarred my heart but I try to live on knowing my grandmother in some way is still with me in spirit, sort of like a guardian angel.

My grandmother never gave up on my father, so I never gave up on him either. I've witnessed him over 30 years of his incarceration try to involve himself in positive education programs to better himself and make way for a chance of being reunited with his children someday. I'm not saying that anything will ever be enough to pay his dues for the life he took but I've witnessed firsthand, through my own mistakes, that being under the influence of a controlled substance changes the way you would normally react to situations. But maintaining self-awareness of one's flaws and mistakes in life and trying to better oneself because of them is what makes us human.

I never knew what it felt like to have a father in my life but I did grow up aware of the effects of forgiveness. My father wrote to me and asked for my forgiveness. He said his drug use was the cause of all the actions that got him a life sentence but that he is the one to blame for letting a drug get a hold of everything that meant so much.

If I could forgive him for all the suffering me, my grandmother and my sister went through, why can't the people who decide whether or not he should be given a second chance see that he is not the man he used to be? He deserves parole. They sentenced him to 25-years-to-life with the possibility of parole and have denied it twice. Now he's really sick and I would love my kids to know him like I knew my grandmother.

There is still life living as an incarcerated parent, as I am today. I am serving seven years. I have two children, one three year old and one two year old, and I have been in jail for two years and nine months – all but a few months of my sons' lives. I only pray I can be there for them and not make them suffer as I did.

My father's name is David Proulx and he is in the prison at Bridgewater. Maybe you can help him in some way or at least hear his story.

★★★

The Unconditional Love by Manuel Reyes Williams

I watched my mother be continually apprehended by Milwaukee police officers. When they'd taken her away, I felt neglected and lonely.

I was a whimpering cub lost for thoughts to protest my mother's absences. I mean, who was I to contest my new environment? I didn't realize the psychological harm that could be done, especially when the adults I was surrounded with expressed a tough love my little heart rejected. It wasn't my mother's love.

I was used to not getting my behind whipped when I was with my mother. But, boy, my grandmother held back not one single blow to my butt. I'd run away with my comrades in the street to avoid my grandmother's punishment. There was nothing like grandmother's punishment. She made me go outside to select a tree branch and if it was too small, she'd reroute me back outside. There was no relief to my anxiety and fear of her. I did not know how scared I was of my grandmother until I started pissing myself in my sleep.

When my mother came to get me I was so happy! I felt a load lifting from my shoulders. But I knew she'd only be with me for a couple of days until she went back to the bar to get drunk again.

Since I couldn't find the unconditional love bouncing from different homes while my mother seesawed through the Milwaukee County Jail doors, I found comfort with the hooligans in the streets. It was like we all understood each other. Despite us deriving from different family backgrounds, we shared a common bond of struggle.

I've seen a lot less of my mother than most, just like I've barely seen my father. Though I had heard rumors about my parents' jail adventures, I did not recognize that my misbehavior would lead me to travel their same journey. I repeated their rhythm with no thought for the consequences.

So, the streets of Milwaukee, Wisconsin, were where I hung out. Since other people couldn't provide me with the love my parents did, I cared less about what they thought of my juvenile delinquency. I began to go to the juvenile court, where they sentenced me to group homes and treatment centers for my violences.

My mother visited me at six month intervals. Our visits concentrated on how she wanted me to be better so I could come home. Though her advice was the best, she didn't see behind my heart to how I had built up the drive to fight like she did. Sometimes, I'd look at her with disgust for betraying who I thought she really was – a hostile force towards authority and not to be messed with.

Anytime I hit the beat I ended up with the same crowd of thugs. Trouble stayed my companion. We did not leave, neglect or abandon one another like I felt my mother was doing to me. I didn't mind kicking it with the dudes in the streets, committing crimes and volunteering for three hots and a cot – at least the system cared.

As I got older and began to deal with the system more, my mother was slowly abstaining from being a jailbird. But it came too late for me. I was too deep into the system to turn back. The neglect and loneliness I felt in the beginning had made my heart a stone.

Now, when I look back, I see the whippings didn't help me. My mother going to jail only put a lasting, invisible distance between us. And hanging out in the streets brought me nothing but trouble.

Now, I seek change from all of that.

★★★

Full Circle by Victoria Greene

I am the last of four children that my mother birthed by the time she reached 21 years of age. Ironically, I was the only one she used drugs while carrying but am said to be the most gifted, intelligent and stable overall. I am humbled by and thank God for such.

My aunt took me home from the hospital as an infant because my mother was arrested and taken to jail following my birth. She was incarcerated on and off from that point until I graduated college at 22 years of age. Most of her arrests were for charges such as theft, forgery, fraud, probation violation and other petty crimes she committed to support her crack cocaine and heroin habits, both of which she used, along with alcohol and other drugs, while she carried me.

Sadly, I, like most young children, loved her blindly as a baby and knew nothing except that she was my mother and there was that natural bond between us in the beginning. That was true until I learned that she was an unstable presence in my life that I couldn't seem to grasp, secure or depend on. While my aunts raised me, she would show up occasionally but her visits were always short and ended in disaster and sometimes emotional trauma to my siblings and me. She actually gave away two of my siblings before I was born and I just reunited with them about seven years ago. At times, before I erected a wall to protect myself, I got excited when she came around, wrote letters to her in state prison and even went to visit at least once, but after so many years of disappointment, broken promises and emotional wounds, I stopped calling her mom and severed the emotional ties between us to the best of my ability.

I loved her with simple Christian "neighbor" love, but nothing more. I considered her an egg donor but not a mother at all. My sister was not as fortunate and prudent as myself and because of the fact that she'd spent more time with my mother and grown more attached, she was detrimentally scarred and still suffers the ramifications of abandonment and negligence to this very day. I always told myself that I harbored no ill feelings toward my mother and would always treat her cordially out of respect, but never allow myself to become too intimate or involved in order to protect myself and my future for the woman, wife, and mother that I would be someday.

That was my plan: to "feed her from a long-handled spoon" since I developed this bit of emotional intelligence as a teenager. However, God, as he often does, had a different plan for me. The year that I received my undergraduate degree, while I was on summer vacation and still basking in the glory of a major goal accomplished in my life, my birth mother was almost killed. My aunt received a phone call from a friend with news that my birth mother had been nearly beaten to death in one of her infamous hang out spots where druggies often congregate. When I saw her in the fatal condition, my heart was tender and I thought she'd die. As a mature Christian, God began to speak to me more about forgiving her and loving her unconditionally to reflect and replicate His relationship with me.

So for the last eight years, I've gone from figuratively "feeding her out of a long-handled spoon" to literally feeding her, as well as bathing, dressing, and grooming my mother in her paralyzed state. It has been a very challenging, growing and testing process because I am constantly reminded that she has not done very much for me since my birth and didn't even care enough for me to stop using drugs while she carried me to ensure that I would have the best possible chance at life. Even with that, I can say that through divine intervention our relationship has progressed, though I do not attempt to forge feelings that are not there.

It's remarkable to me that when I go to the county jail to teach God's word to women, I tell them that it's possible for God to mend their relationships with the kids they have hurt by making bad decisions and turn their children's hearts back to them. What's even more interesting at times is that I've even come across a few inmates who tell me that they have been incarcerated with my mom and that they remember her talking about me. Well, I guess that I can say that life has come full circle, but with a different twist. Some might have expected me to end up in jails and prisons just like my mother and they were exactly right! But I am honored to say that I have never been arrested or incarcerated in my life, but gladly go to jail on a biweekly basis to inspire and empower others that might be mothers like mine. So I stand to say that it's true that roses can grow from concrete, diamonds can be found in the rough and something great can be born out of Nazareth. With God nothing shall be impossible!

★★★

His Children's Conviction by Danielle Chapman

My name is Danielle Chapman, and I am 33 years old. My father is in prison and has been since I was about 13 years old. I am the third to the oldest of my father's children. He has seven children by six different women; my mother is the only woman who had two children with him. I see now how difficult it was for me when I was an adolescent and my father was in prison. Although I did not spend very much time with my father before he was incarcerated, I always thought things would change; I thought there would be a day when we would have a father–daughter relationship. When he was incarcerated, I was shocked about the seriousness of his crime, but I was more upset about what it meant: I would never have a normal father–daughter relationship.

I found out he was in prison one night when my mother came to get me after a school function. She showed me the newspaper article; my father had been arrested for murder. My whole body felt numb. I did not know what to think. My father had been in and out of jail my entire life, but murder was a serious charge. We contacted my grandmother, because we knew she would know what had happened. We learned my three-month-old brother was in the house when it happened, and we learned my father was in the county jail. When we left my grandmother's house, all I could think about was that I might never have my father in my life. It hurt so much, and it hurt to know my brother and I weren't the only ones who would be affected by this. My father's other children would also grow up without their father.

What I think of as my other life, the life where there was no possibility I would have a normal relationship with my father, began the day he was convicted. After he was convicted, I would visit my grandmother's house in San Bernardino, California, and I would walk down the street and cry. I would cry and wonder why I was the kid who was cursed and why I had to be left without a father. I would even daydream about what it might be like if I were not cursed; I would imagine my father was not in jail and the two of us were having dinner together. Or I would imagine him at a school function of mine. I think this was the hardest for me; I never got to experience the father–daughter bond. While all my friends had their dads to take them to the movies or to spend Father's Day with, all I got to do was to see my father in prison and to talk to him on the phone.

During this time my mother struggled to support my brother and me. She did the best she could to make sure we had nice clothes, food in our mouths, and a roof over our heads. We were on welfare, and we did not have a car. We took the city bus to the store for groceries. We lived in an area where there were a lot of gangs, and my brother and I became friends with these people. We went out with them in stolen cars, and we stopped attending school; we just wanted to hang out on the streets. Many of our friends were ultimately killed as a result of their gang activity, and our home was shot at several times. I think a lot of people, including these friends, took advantage of my mother, because there was no man in the house. The man I would become pregnant by was one of these people.

When I was 15, I became pregnant by a man who had once broken into our home and stolen money and jewelry from my mother. He felt like he could get away with hurting my family because we did not have a man in the house. When I was four months pregnant, this man started to cheat on me, but I did not confront him, because I did not want my child to grow up without a father. When I was six months pregnant, I went into premature labor. My child weighed two pounds and four ounces and was 10 inches long. He was in the hospital for 28 days. His father did not help me then or afterward. He became abusive, got hooked on drugs, and constantly cheated on me.

Soon his father and his brother also began to abuse me. Throughout it all, I worked and I went to school. I was trying not to burden my mother with the choice I had made, and I finished high school in 1997. My mother was very proud of me. I continued to work, and I got my first apartment. My son's father lived with us. He became increasingly involved with drugs, and he mentally and physically abused me. It got so bad that in the middle of the night, he would make me walk down the street without shoes on so that people could not hear me cry when he hit me. If I cried, he would hit me again. He would have women in our home and he would take our grocery money to buy drugs. There were times when I used drugs with him, because I felt so alone (he did not allow me to have friends). My son saw all of this, and that was my fault. He saw abuse and drug use, because I did not leave his father. I did not leave my son's father because I did not want my son to grow up as heartbroken and fatherless as I had been.

When I was 21 years old, my son's father broke a sliding glass window on my mother and then he came to work and hit me. I was sick of him being in and out of jail; I was sick of his cheating and his abuse and his drug use, and this episode finally made me realize it. This was not the life I wanted for myself or my son, and I refused to have the problems my mom had. I decided that although my son would be fatherless, I had to leave this man, and I did.

In time I began to date again, and I met my husband. We had a little boy, but I found myself making some of the same mistakes with my husband as I did with my ex. My husband battled with drug addiction, but I never left him, because I did not want both of my children to be from broken families. For ten years, I put up with the fact that my husband used drugs while I worked to support our family. Finally, I had enough, and my husband went to rehabilitation. That was two years ago, and we are still together.

My ex has been in prison for over six years, so my oldest son has grown up without his biological father. His father never attended any events for him; he never went to his son's baseball games, never attended his graduations. He also never financially supported his child. I am a dispatcher, I have not taken drugs in almost 13 years, and I have worked myself into the ground to provide for my family. Although my father has served his sentence, he has been denied parole, so I try to take care of his sons. The three youngest boys have had difficult lives; we older children got lucky, because we had great mothers. I do the best I can to try to help with my younger brothers. I had guardianship of one of them for a while, and I try to provide what I can for the others. I feel as though I have to make up for my dad's absence.

When I think about all this now, I realize that given everything I have been through, I have turned out to be a good mother, daughter, wife and sister. I am proud of that.

★★★

My Parents by Aliyah

I was the second child and the first daughter. My mother thought it couldn't get any better: two beautiful children and a wonderful man who was the love of her life. My father loved hanging out and my mother loved to be the housewife kind of lady. So together my parents, with their two different lifestyles, had one thing in mind: to take care of their children and household.

I was a premature baby, weighing only a little more than one pound. I stayed in the hospital until I was over four pounds. Once I was released from the hospital, the next six months of my life were spent living between my daddy and my grandmother. By the time I was 13 months of age, my mom had given birth to her third child. From what I have been told, I was a happy little girl.

At three years of age, my life seemed great. My parents had had two more children and we lived in three-bedroom house in the city of Compton. But around this time, I can remember my parents arguing, mostly about my father coming in late at night. By the time I was five, there were two more kids added to the family and things were worse. I felt that I was the boss and went around the house screaming and hitting my siblings, because I often heard my mom screaming and saw my father hitting her.

I can remember watching. But as soon as me or my siblings came into view, my mom would wipe her eyes and hug us and tell us she loved us so much. As a child, I got into the habit of crying every time my mother cried. I can still hear her crying, asking herself, "Why me?" So naturally, when pretending or playing make believe I was always the mother and my brother was the father and we did exactly what we'd seen our parents do – scream, fight and cry. I had kind of figured out that this was normal.

By the time I went to school, my life had turned into a living nightmare. By the time I was 10, my parents had nine children together. My father had started to go in and out of jail. We were still living in a three-bedroom house. During those years from 6 to 10, I had been molested three times by two of my paternal cousins and my paternal uncle. I didn't have anyone to talk to about it. My father was always gone in those days and we never had a phone to get calls or went to visit him. And my mother simply wasn't the same Momma. She didn't do anything besides stay up all night and sleep in the day.

Naturally, I felt I had to do the job of being Mommy. I cooked whatever I could get my hands on, I got my siblings ready for school and bed daily, all while getting my innocence ripped away from me. I told my big brother about the abuse and I remember him, at 11 years old, getting a knife and going after my uncle, which led to us telling our parents about the abuse and my mother calling the cops. My father's family was upset, saying I was a liar. Someone called Children's Services regarding my parents' secret life of cocaine use. This turned out to be true and led to my life inside the foster care system.

After being taken from my parents, I spent a year with my grandmother. But the hurt my parents put on me caused me to rebel against everyone. My grandmother sent me to placement by the time I was 13 and I spent the next three years running away from every foster home to catch up to my drug-addicted parents, believing I could make them get clean.

By the age of 15, I was living on my own in a motel and selling drugs to survive and supply my parents, because they were angry without that high. At 16 I had my first baby. She and I were placed back with the Children's Services. Before I was 17, I went on the run again in an effort to save my parents from their addiction, which didn't work. I was still selling drugs to support myself, my child and my parents. If you had asked me back then, I would have said my life was good. I had my parents, which was what I wanted more than anything, my beautiful little girl and enough money to keep all of us happy. But I always had to look over my shoulder, because I was AWOL from foster care. And there were always the cops, although I feared more for my father than for myself, because I had never been arrested.

Entering adulthood at 18, I was carrying my second child and my luck was soon to run out. I was arrested and charged with drug sales. My newborn baby and two-year-old daughter became wards of the state.

Eventually I was released from jail and started to fight for my daughters. I was still addicted to the fast money, so I ended up in prison and did two years. This time, I had it all planned. My father had been murdered, my mother was clean and I thought I was going to reunite with my daughters plus the other children my parents had together and who were mostly in placements. I thought we would all be together. But shortly after my release I was rearrested and this time, I will serve a five-year prison sentence.

Every day, I work to better myself. I've gained a relationship with my siblings and I am still working hard to be reunited with my daughters. I ended up where I am by trying to be close to my father and my mother, to manage their lives without being like them. I loved them so much but I no longer want to follow the footsteps of my parents.

★★★

Blue by Larri Calhoun

Seventeen to life. Those three simple words have made my life a living hell. They've made me suffer every day I've woken up without my dad present. One may not understand how important a father–daughter relationship is, but I do. I never wanted anything more than to have my dad home.

My dad was arrested two months before my twin brother and I were born. Unlike our big sister, we never got to spend time with our dad outside prison walls.

You'd be amazed at what a child can remember. I recall the long drive to the prison; when I saw the windmills on the hills along the side of the road, I knew we were close. During our visits, he was behind glass. All I could do was hold the phone to my ear with Mommy's help, placing my hand upon the glass as if it were actually touching his. It was like looking into a mirror – I'm the spitting image of him, only female. Daddy's little girl.

He got moved to a bigger prison in Vacaville, but we children were too young to enter the visiting room. So instead, we had the time of our lives in the Funhouse. The Funhouse was the area of the prison where the inmates' little children could play. There were small kitchens and all kinds of toys.

Eventually my sister was old enough to go into the visiting room with mom, and then finally my twin brother and I were old enough, too. Most daughters have tons of memories with their fathers. Like hanging outdoors, their first birthday party or what not. But me? The one memory I have that I could never possibly forget was on a dirty blue mat located on the floor of the visiting room. I remember it like it was yesterday. I was jumping on my dad's back, completely happy, despite his situation. I loved my dad; being with him filled the hole in my life that had always been there. The time I spent with him meant the world to me, even though it was never enough.

Sometime around 2003 or 2004, I recall hearing excitement in my mother's voice as if she had just won a million dollars. I walked out of the bedroom my brother, sister, and I shared to see what had made my mother's day. As I got closer, all I could hear her repeatedly saying is: "I'm a free woman, I'm a free woman." Confused as to exactly what that meant I asked her, "How?" She informed me that she and my dad had gotten a divorce, and those were her "free" papers. I walked back to our room for a moment. I was frozen; I didn't understand why she wouldn't want to be with a man as great as my dad.

The day she got her "free" papers was the day I gained my interest in writing. I couldn't express how I felt out loud so I wrote, and right after I was done I sent it to my dad.

We still went to visit him occasionally; Mommy hadn't taken us away from him yet. Though they weren't together, they put their problems aside and didn't let them interfere with our relationship with him. Since Mommy was a free woman, that meant daddy was a free man. I had hope for them to get back together – after all, we were a family.

My dreams of them reuniting as one came crashing down one day in the visiting room when my dad had to make a decision. His new lover and her child had come to visit at the same time my mom, brother, sister, and I had. He was only allowed to see five people, but there were six of us there to visit him. My dad had to choose between seeing us and seeing his new family. I stood on our side with a smirk on my face, because I know my dad was going to choose us. He had to, of course he will! I said to myself. I had no doubt! But to my surprise, he didn't.

Before we left, my mom said to him, "You don't have to worry about me coming here anymore," and just like that, we were out. I cried and cried with confusion swirling around in my head. I asked my mom what was going on and she said, "He chose them over us, Larri." I was hurt and confused about why he didn't choose me, wondering what they had that we didn't. As I looked back at the prison, more tears ran down my face as I replayed my mother's voice saying you don't have to worry about me coming here anymore. That was the last day my mother stepped anywhere near that prison.

My mother met new guys. Some I didn't like at all. I'd say to myself, "He has nothing on my daddy." Until one guy in particular, J.T., started to grow on me; I loved him. He took me everywhere with him. Spoiled me too. But my eyes opened wide one day when they broke up. He taught me that just because a man spoils you and may be present at that moment doesn't mean he'll be in your life permanently. I learned not to get comfortable with any man other than my dad.

After my dad chose another family over his own, our relationship wasn't the same. He stopped showing his affection; he went dark. So I wrote him and I told him how I felt. I didn't appreciate how he was letting others come in between us. He wrote me back, promising that he would never let anyone come between us again. Since Mommy was fed up, she wanted nothing to do with my dad anymore, including taking us to go see him. That's when everything started to fall apart. Just because she had given up on him didn't mean I had to. *Don't I have the right to support as I face my parent's incarceration?*

Since she wouldn't take us to the prison, my siblings and I were stuck riding with his girlfriend and her daughter. As you can imagine, it was awkward. Watching my dad play daddy to another girl started off sweet, but then it got pathetic. They would visit my dad every Saturday and Sunday and would take me with them every blue moon. I always tried to ignore the jealous looks they would have in their eyes while my dad and I were out in the patio section of the visiting room. It's like a tease to the inmates because they're not allowed outside with their family, but at least they can view the sky. The little girl in me also believed he was a few steps closer to his freedom.

When he would walk back to the table after our one-on-one time, his little princess would be all over him calling "Daddy, Daddy." Her mom struck my ears when she opened up her mouth and said to her daughter, "Today's not your day. Let Larri enjoy it, tomorrow's family day and you'll have Daddy all to yourself." Their comments began to get under my skin. I accepted the girl as my little sister, and I was okay with sharing my dad, but in her mind she was sharing him with me.

Eventually my father broke his promise, and again let them come between us. I remember the day my heart skipped a beat and then started beating fast as a drum. I saw a picture on top of my grandparents' fireplace with the three of them: the little princess in the middle with a shirt that read "Miss Calhoun," her mother with one that read "Mrs. Calhoun," and a ring upon my dad's finger. I felt betrayed. It was as if our family had never existed. As I stared at the man in the picture, he didn't look familiar. It made me question if I knew the real him. Guess you can say I still wanted them together: Mommy and Dad. I always dreamed of him coming home to me, to us. I've been waiting for him for eighteen years.

Throughout my years of growing up, there were a few ages that stuck out the most for one particular reason: him. My family would say, "When you're 15, he's coming home." Then it was, "When your sister's 18, he's coming home." By then I was 16. It didn't happen. I didn't lose hope, though. I never lost faith in him coming home to me.

Instead of getting gifts or money on my birthdays or any other holiday, I got cards. They weren't any regular cards either. They were always made by him. So beautiful I kept every one. Occasionally he would send me pictures that he took just for me, and he'd have a message on the back of every one. I loved the little things, like cards and letters, the most. But when you love something, you're bound to notice when it stops. Eventually I stopped getting the cards and those pictures. I guess he figured I was getting too old. Our communication with one another became distant, and that put a dent in my heart. Though he may not have been where I wanted him to be, and times may have been hard on him, he should still have considered my feelings. *Don't I have the right to a lifelong relationship with my parent?* It's not asking for too much. He missed a lot. In fact, he missed everything.

Growing up, blue was my favorite color, but I began to hate it, because that was the only color I saw my dad wear, and I knew what it represented. I noticed that I'd picked up a bad habit from visiting my dad: when I make food, I stand in front of the microwave until it's done, because that's how I'd heat up my dad's food in the visiting room since he wasn't allowed to cross the red line in front of the microwave. Little things like that remind me of his incarceration. I cried on my graduation day because I missed my dad and wanted him there. I thought about sending him a ticket to let him know he had one, but I didn't want to make him sad or feel as if I disrespected him, so his ticket went unused. There are tons of things I wish he had witnessed that he will never have the chance to because of one choice he made. And the outcome of his choice is what I have to live with, what I suffer for. I'm losing my grip on hope, because my dad was sentenced to seventeen-to-life. Although that L sentence behind his name may never end, try telling that to the little girl in me who will always hope for her dad's return.

★★★

All Grown Up by Hollie Overton

My father was an angry man. In sober moments, he could escape the darkness that cloaked him but those moments were few and far between. As a child I never understood why he lost control, forgetting about everything and everyone in his path like he was some sort of deranged science experiment gone wrong.

It wasn't until my early twenties, shortly after his death that my twin sister and I discovered the truth about my father. He was a criminal and an outlaw, an ex-con with a rap sheet as long as my arm. He'd spent his teens and most of his twenties in and out of prison for various drug offenses, robberies and eventually a manslaughter conviction. He never spoke about it but it makes sense now. I'm quite sure his time in prison helped shape him, turned him into the Dr. Jekyll and Mr. Hyde I grew up with.

Of course there were "normal" moments: family dinners, trips to the beach, snapshots taken that hid the tears, the recriminations, the whiskey-fueled tirades. My mother bore the abuse for years, trapped by love and duty. Everyone urged her to break free. But it wasn't until Daddy unleashed his rage and almost strangled her at the local swimming pool that my mother finally had enough. It was an "Us vs. Him" scenario and she chose us.

The divorce was finalized a few months later and Daddy continued to spiral out of control. His arrest at the pool wasn't even his most memorable. I was seven and it was spring break. My mother had reluctantly (after hours of our tearful pleading) allowed my twin sister and I to stay with him in Austin, four hours from her and our home. What was supposed to be a fun adventure with Daddy and his new girlfriend, Pat, soon became a nightmare. Something Pat said or did set him off and a fight broke out. Pat fled the apartment, refusing (at least on this night) to be Daddy's punching bag. Enraged, he followed her, forgetting about my sister and I and leaving us all alone. Hours later, we saw the police lights flashing outside the apartment, but were too scared to open the door. Daddy had driven home drunk after assaulting Pat and was arrested for a DUI, resisting arrest, public intoxication and assault and battery. Despite my mother's frantic calls to the police station, Daddy, in his drunken state, was quite adamant that he didn't have any children. To their horror, the police discovered he was wrong and they threatened to take us into custody. My mother broke every speeding law in Texas to make sure that didn't happen. While she comforted us, Daddy was sent to jail yet again. That weekend ended any unsupervised visits with my father.

It didn't, however, end the merry-go-round of arrests and emotional turmoil he inflicted upon us. There were dozens more DUI's, assault and battery charges and drunk and disorderlies. Daddy spent months in county jail and Mom became an expert at doling out excuses when we didn't hear from him. "Daddy went on a trip." Or "Daddy's working a double shift." Or "Daddy was tired but he loves you girls very much."

Our mother wanted to protect us and she did. In fact, I am grateful for her deceit. I knew my father had been in jail once or twice but the vast array of his offenses remained unknown to me until I was old enough and mature enough to process it. This well-kept secret allowed me to have a normal adolescence. That stigma of having a jailbird father would have dwarfed my childhood and instead I was able to make believe, telling my friends that Daddy was a hotshot construction manager instead of an alcoholic ex-con.

But all of the lies and half-truths couldn't change the fact that I grew up without a father and it affected me in a hundred different ways, big and small. My mother was forced to do the work of two people, which meant we got less time with her. She had to support two kids without a second income or a second support system. She struggled and we felt it. The light bill wasn't paid, the mortgage was late, money was constantly coming in and leaving just as quickly. It wasn't the life Mom wanted and he wasn't the man she thought she'd married.

As for me, I spent my childhood waiting at the door, hoping he'd visit or lingering by the phone hoping he'd call. When he did visit, I spent weekends cowering in the corner, worried that the demons he kept running from would take over and I'd bear the brunt of it. And as I got older, there were all these momentous occasions he missed. The band recitals and school musicals he didn't attend. The homework assignments and tests he didn't help me study for. There were heartbreaks and disappointments he didn't console me through. And in the end, there was a hole in our family, a giant gaping black hole that he left in his wake.

I want to believe that buried under all that rage and anger and hurt my father was a good man. I'm sure if he'd been able to get help or counseling, if someone had been able to reach in and help him fix what was so broken, he'd have been the great man I caught glimpses of. But that didn't happen. And I'm not so evolved that I was never angry. There was a time when I was resentful and pissed and even kind of hated him for not loving me more. But now that I'm all grown up, I realize Daddy was the one that paid the ultimate price. He lost out on knowing his daughters and that is the greatest tragedy. In order to move forward, I had to forgive him. He may have been a criminal, but he was also my father. And he was loved more than he ever knew.

2

SAFETY AND PROTECTION

Denise Johnston and Megan Sullivan

The economic, political and social environments in which children are raised contribute in multiple ways to their development. These environments may offer or lack critical resources and supports. They may provide safety or expose children to hazards. They have a critical influence on all kids, but especially on vulnerable populations like children of incarcerated parents.

Children of Incarcerated Parents and Their Communities

While a significant minority of contributors to *Parental Incarceration: Personal Accounts and Developmental Impact* were raised in working- or middle-class families, two-thirds grew up in low-income neighborhoods and communities.

> Of course, we were dirt poor, always living in the worst part of town or in some rudimentary makeshift home out in the middle of nowhere …
>
> *Bruce B., adult child of two incarcerated parents*

The communities in which the majority of families involved in the criminal justice system reside offer limited developmental resources and supports for children and increase their vulnerability to developmental insults.[1] These communities have high unemployment rates and many families living below the federal poverty line; high-density, poor-quality housing; and inadequate and/or insufficient human services. The ability of these communities to protect and support their residents, especially children, is limited. Every type of risk to children – including prenatal morbidity, premature birth, low birth weight, preventable pediatric health problems, child abuse/neglect, child injuries and child exposures to violence – occurs at a higher rate in these lowest-income communities.

> We started out in this working-class neighborhood where my mom was raised but as my parents got more addicted and they got deeper into crime, we moved closer and closer

to the bad places. At the end, we lived in this neighborhood with cheap apartments, sketchy little stores and long blocks of deserted warehouses.

Jessamyn R., adult child of two incarcerated parents

Within poor communities, parents who will become or have been incarcerated and their children tend to live in neighborhoods with higher crime rates. This kind of neighborhood is characterized by:

- higher rates of poverty (and its contributors, like unemployment, low educational levels and single-parent families) than surrounding areas;[2]
- higher proportions of land zoned for commercial use;[3]
- less residential homogeneity, more major streets, and boundaries that are more traveled than those of low-crime neighborhoods;[4] and
- higher levels of population mobility.[5]

Historically, many of the characteristics of poor neighborhoods have been attributed to their residents[6] but, over the past two decades, researchers have begun to examine the effects of overutilization of incarceration on increasing social disorganization in these communities.[7] This theory suggests that incarceration of many neighborhood residents has secondary effects on neighborhood structure, residential mobility and other characteristics associated with higher levels of crime.

Some practitioners' observations have supported this theory, with one long-term program of services for children of incarcerated parents noting that adult arrest rates in the majority of participants' neighborhoods increased over eight years of program operations compared to adjacent neighborhoods where few or no participants resided.[8] In other words, neighborhood conditions that contribute to parental crime and incarceration are likely to worsen for the children that prisoners leave behind.

[During my father's incarceration] … my mother struggled to support my brother and me … in an area where there were a lot of gangs, and my brother and I became friends with these people. We went out with them in stolen cars, and we stopped attending school; we just wanted to hang out on the streets. Many of our friends were ultimately killed as a result of their gang activity, and our home had been shot at several times.

Danielle, adult child of an incarcerated father

Communities and neighborhoods provide the economic, political and social contexts of child development but the mechanisms by which they cause their effects are complex and most often operate through families.[9]

Families of Incarcerated Parents

The families of prisoners have been described in a number of study reports and publications over the past century.[10] Families involved in the criminal justice system tend to be overwhelmed by multiple needs. This limits their ability to protect and offer other developmental supports to their children, and increases children's exposure to developmental insults like trauma. In addition to family poverty and household economic strain, which are discussed elsewhere, important characteristics of these families include household instability and involvement in substance abuse and/or crime.

Family and Household Instability

Households become destabilized following multiple household member transitions. In U.S. families, transitions typically occur as a result of marriage, marital separation, divorce, or the start/end of a co-habiting relationship; other transitions include departures of family members to the armed services, college or distant employment, as well as additions of other new family members, and the death of family members. Multiple family moves also contribute to household instability.

Incarceration itself has an effect on family structure. Not only are families destabilized by the temporary absence of a family member who goes to jail/prison, the early dissolution of families of incarcerated fathers has also been well documented.[11]

The households of prisoners' children typically experience several other types of instability.[12] Multi-partnered fertility[13] virtually guarantees that many families of prisoners will not have stable structures, as parents transition to new reproductive partners and children are left to be raised by single heads of household.

Other changes in the composition of these families are related to bereavements[14] and high levels of family mobility.

> [M]y mother got connected with a pimp and she'd take me from city to city with this man and other prostitutes, while they turned tricks and lived the street life style … When I was five, my mom and I were living in New York … [after that] my mother married her pimp and we moved to Wisconsin.
>
> *Marcus R., adult child of two incarcerated parents*

> [My step-father] moved us a lot – from Canada to Arizona, from Washington to Wisconsin – ensuring that we lived deranged, anxious, brutal, ignorant, rural lives. I liked the rural part.
>
> *Nate L., adult child of an incarcerated mother*

Lack of family and household stability has been found to have many negative effects on children and child development.[15]

Family Involvement in the Criminal Justice System

The families of prisoners are characterized by multiple members with criminal justice system involvement. More than half of all incarcerated parents have an immediate family member who has been incarcerated,[16] while up to three-quarters of formerly incarcerated persons have one or more relatives involved in the criminal justice system.[17]

A lot of people in our family have been in jail or prison. On my dad's side, there is his father, his uncle, his brother, his cousin and his nephews. On my mom's side, there is her grandmother, her uncle and some cousins.

Jessamyn R., adult child of two incarcerated parents

Parental criminal activity, arrest and incarceration among relatives expose children to increased risks while interfering with the ability of parents to provide adequate care and protection for children. In addition, relatives with a history of arrest and/or incarceration are usually ineligible to become approved caregivers when prisoners' children enter the child welfare system.[18] If their criminal justice system involvement is recent, it also prevents relatives from escorting children to visit their parents in many correctional facilities.[19]

Family Substance Abuse and Dependence

More than a third of all incarcerated parents report that one or more of their parents or guardians abused or were addicted to alcohol/drugs.[20]

My mom grew up with both her parents and three sisters. Her dad was a violent alcoholic … Her mom was a classic enabler. My grandma worked full time, and cared for the household while her husband was drinking. She also enabled my mom's drug addiction for many years … My parents … were both drug users, and my dad was also an alcoholic … I spent much of my teenage years in a multi-generational home living with my mom's parents. It was three addicts and one lifetime enabler under one roof, and it wasn't pretty.

Natalie C., adult child of an incarcerated mother

This is consistent with research on the incidence of substance abuse within families[21] and has additional significance because children of incarcerated parents are often placed in the care of relatives. Addiction to drugs or alcohol has adverse effects on caring for children and may significantly reduce the ability of adult family members to protect the children of prisoners in their care.[22]

Incarcerated Parents

Parents in jail and prison have been the primary focus of research on prisoners' children. Far more accessible logistically, ethically and in terms of study costs than minors, incarcerated parents have been the subjects of large-scale, federal research, as well as many investigations of smaller populations. Historical and current studies of incarcerated mothers and fathers have described a group of individuals who are significantly disadvantaged as parents for a number of reasons, whose activities often present a risk to their children's safety, and whose ability to keep their children safe from other dangers is limited.

Incarcerated Parents Lack Appropriate Parent Models

Many incarcerated parents did not have healthy parent role models while growing up. Unstable parental partnerships, parental alcohol and drug abuse, and parent–child separations characterize the childhoods of incarcerated parents;[23] many also had violent parents or caregivers.[24]

> My father began a life of crime at the age of 15 and, just as he was always absent from my life, his father was absent from his. My father's hurt and pain remained within him silently as if it was a cry that was never heard. There had never been any affection shown to him in his entire life, nor was there in mine.
>
> *James C., adult child of two incarcerated parents*

Appropriate parent models are a critical underpinning of appropriate parenting. Children of parents who had uninvolved or negative parent models are more likely to experience ineffective parenting, with this effect being stronger among children of poorly parented fathers.[25] Ineffective parental protection decreases children's safety and increases the likelihood that they will have harmful experiences.

Incarcerated Parents Have a Lifelong History of Trauma

In many families of incarcerated parents, trauma is an intergenerational phenomenon with the incarcerated parent's parent experiencing abuse as a child or adult.[26]

> [My mom] was one of twelve children and when her father, an Air Force pilot, was severely injured and hospitalized, her mother needed help. The care of the children was taken on by some military personnel who inflicted physical and sexual abuse on my mom, aunts and uncles.
>
> *Nate L., adult child of an incarcerated mother*

> After years of severe beatings by his father, my dad fought back and was put out on the streets of the city when he was 12. From that time forward, he lived by his wits and his fists.
>
> *Michael C., adult child of an incarcerated father*

> My mom grew up in San Diego with Nanna, my great-grandmother … Nanna cared for seven children and abused them all but specially my mom.
>
> *Abel H., adult child of two incarcerated parents*

The majority of incarcerated parents report multiple traumatic experiences in both childhood and adulthood.[27] For example, most incarcerated parents of both genders have experienced childhood sexual abuse[28] and most have been assaulted.[29] In addition to impairing the capacity for self-protection,[30] childhood trauma has been found to adversely affect parenting and offspring outcomes (as described in Chapter One), including the ability to identify and respond to risks to children.[31]

Incarcerated Parents' Lack of Employment Skills and Work Experience

Most incarcerated parents lack employment skills and work experience, and only a minority were employed prior to incarceration.[32] Few contributors to *Parental Incarceration: Personal*

Accounts and Developmental Impact describe parents who had been employed prior to their incarcerations.

[My step-father] never had a job.

> *Bruce B., adult child of two incarcerated parents*

At the time of my first memory, my grandma worked as a seamstress and my grandpa had his own mechanic's shop. My sister was still in school. My mom and dad were not working then, they were both using drugs.

> *Jessamyn R., adult child of two incarcerated parents*

Former prisoners face a worse situation and almost insurmountable odds in finding full-time employment and/or meeting child support obligations following release, even with assistance.[33] In combination with other factors like multi-partnered fertility, lack of employment significantly reduces the economic contribution currently and formerly incarcerated parents can make to their children's lives.[34] This, in turn, increases the children's risk of adverse experiences.

Incarcerated Parents and Parental Identity

The Center for Children of Incarcerated Parents identified parental disempowerment and loss of parental authority as central issues for prisoners with children.[35]

Incarcerated parents typically have a lifetime of disempowering experiences, including experiences with their own absent and/or substance-abusing parents, multiple episodes of childhood trauma, and life-controlling addictions. Involvement in the criminal justice system further undermines their sense of efficacy, with parental incarceration making very specific and concrete assaults on whatever parental authority mothers and fathers retain when they enter jail or prison. Incarcerated parents typically have limited information about and understanding of their children's daily lives, and this reduces their ability to provide parental advice and direction. They are unable to monitor or discipline their children. They are unable to communicate freely or have contact with their children without the involvement of correctional authorities; for example, they are unable to control the type of interaction they have with their visiting children and, during visits, must assume a child-like role, asking permission to go to the restroom, lining up to be counted and/or being prohibited from handling money or using vending machines. These experiences send the clear message that prisoners are in a dependent position and limit their authority as parents.

Loss of the sense of parental authority, efficacy and power is common among prisoners[36] and undermines parental identity.[37] Parental identity predicts parental involvement.[38] Parents who don't feel like parents and who are not involved with their children cannot protect their children effectively.

Lack of Protection and Adverse Experiences among Children of Prisoners

The typical characteristics of their communities, families and parents virtually guarantee that children of incarcerated parents will lack protection. Lack of protection often leads to developmental insults or "adverse childhood experiences" (ACEs). As defined by Felitti[39] and his group, ACEs include:

- emotional abuse or neglect;
- physical neglect;
- physical abuse, including physical assaults or victimization in the community;
- sexual abuse, including sexual assaults or victimization in the community;
- witnessing domestic violence; and
- parent–child separation.

Other harmful experiences, like the witnessing of community violence, were not originally defined as ACEs but have been found to have similar effects and outcomes. Later studies also found that ACEs are usually interrelated rather than occurring in isolation.[40] The large majority of adults who report having one ACE also report others. The ACE model provides a framework for understanding the long-term effects of developmental insults and it also allows for comparison of levels of exposure to such experiences. For example, about one-third of U.S. adults have not had any ACEs.

ACEs are significant because of their well-documented association with early emotional, social and cognitive impairment; "health-risk" behaviors; behavior health disorders like alcoholism and addiction; major disease and disability; and early death. There is a direct correlation between the number of ACEs an individual experiences and these outcomes. Very recently, research has linked a high number of ACEs with the outcome of adult crime and incarceration.[41]

Most children of prisoners experience more than one ACE and some experience many.[42] The contributors to this book are no exception. Some experienced abuse:

[M]y first step-father came into our lives when I was four … [he] beat me with a board that ripped my toenails and left abrasions up and down my legs.

Bruce B., adult child of two incarcerated parents

I was 3 years old when my alcoholic father molested me. It was not a violent experience but it was emotionally devastating.

Jasmine, adult child of an incarcerated father

One of my mother's boyfriends sexually abused me when I was 11. I never told anyone because I didn't understand what happened. When I was 12, I was raped by some men who were visiting my relatives.

Mary, adult child of two incarcerated parents

Many have experiences with domestic violence:

Though I frequently sat crying in some shadowed room while listening to my mom being beaten, crying or choking as my step-father struck her, I would never call the police nor ask anybody for help. This lifestyle lasted until just days after my eleventh birthday, when some neighbors had called the police who made him leave early in the morning. He would never live with us again.

Bruce B., adult child of two incarcerated parents

I often heard my mom screaming and saw my father hitting her … I can remember watching. But as soon as me or my siblings came into view, my mom would wipe her eyes and hug us and tell us she loved us so much … So naturally, when pretending or playing make believe I was always the mother and my brother was the father and we did exactly what we'd seen our parents do – scream, fight and cry. I had kind of figured out that this was normal.

Aliyah, adult child of an incarcerated father

Many experienced permanent separations from their incarcerated parents, and long-term or permanent separations from siblings:

[After several incarcerations], my mom got into a prison program for women with children. Me and [my brother] Sammy went to live with her. (Our other brothers got lost in the shuffle and I don't remember them.)

Abel H., adult child of two incarcerated parents

[When] my mom [went] to prison … [m]y aunt agreed to take me but my brother was … put into the foster care system.

Marcus R., adult child of two incarcerated parents

The majority experienced parental alcoholism or addiction:

My life was hell the second I was conceived. My mother went into premature labor because she was smoking crack … The very next day she had me: three pounds, four ounces. I had to stay in the hospital until I was at least five pounds … Not long after my mother had me she left to go get her next hit. I was a baby fish left to fend for myself.

Moe-Moe S., adult child of two incarcerated parents

When I was growing up as a child, I lived with alcohol pretty much daily. Both my parents were considered alcoholics, I just never saw them that way. Alcoholism to me wasn't an illness, addiction or a bad thing. It was something I saw or felt as normal.

Miranda L., adult child of an incarcerated father

The times with [my dad] were few, and left behind memories of falling asleep on the cold, dirty concrete sidewalks of Downtown Seattle or in a stolen van parked at various places around the city. At the time I did not know that this was wrong, or that he was using drugs.

Jeremy R., adult child of an incarcerated father

A few experienced parental mental illness:

> [My mom] was suicidal and was diagnosed with PTSD, major depression and Multiple Personality Disorder. I found myself acting as a psychiatric nurse/parent and hating life more than any healthy person can imagine.
>
> *Nate L., adult child of an incarcerated mother*

Many witnessed community violence related to crime, drugs and gangs:

> At the age of 11, I was essentially turned loose in the street, free to do almost anything I wanted, and I began to emulate the world around me … I was surrounded almost exclusively by drug dealers, thieves and junkies … periodically [I] watched … spontaneous fights, sudden battles with fists, chains or knives, and I, too, began to get into an occasional street fight.
>
> *Bruce B., adult child of two incarcerated parents*

> One night, one of the pimps stormed into the apartment with a bloody hand from a gunshot wound. Soon after, the pimp my mom was with came in as well, only he was being chased by three other men. His pursuers followed him to the balcony and one of them shot him in the head with a gun and another shot him in the body with a shotgun. My mother's pimp flew over the balcony into the snow … and the snow slowed down his bleeding and he lived.
>
> *Marcus R., adult child of two incarcerated parents*

However, in spite of the traumatic lives of many children of incarcerated parents, it's important to note that some experience a limited number of developmental insults or ACEs. For example, among contributors to this book, several were well protected in early and middle childhood and report few or no adverse experiences other than parental incarceration:

> I grew up as a middle-class Jewish child in Brooklyn, New York. My parents in the 1950s were college graduates. My mother worked part time when money was needed, and my father sold school furniture. We had a small, attached, brick house, but I thought we were rich … In all, I thought I was a very lucky kid.
>
> *Shari O., adult child of an incarcerated father*

Just as in the larger population, the outcomes of our contributors reflect the number and severity of ACEs they experienced. Those who had more adverse and traumatic experiences in childhood have had far worse adult outcomes – including behavioral health problems and criminal justice system involvement – than those who had few. This suggests that parental incarceration, in and of itself, has limited effects on development.

Conclusion

The economic, political, social and family contexts of life for most children of incarcerated parents reduce their developmental supports while increasing the likelihood that they will experience developmental insults. Lack of community, neighborhood and family resources contribute to their inadequate material welfare. Absent parents, unstable households and highly stressed caregivers contribute to their lack of emotional support. The inability of their communities, families and parents to protect them allows their exposure to risk, leading to traumatic and other adverse childhood experiences.

As a result, the outcomes of adult children of incarcerated parents are not surprising. Among contributors to this book, those that had the most adverse childhood experiences also had the most adverse outcomes while those who experienced minimal adversity are doing well:

> Even though my parents used drugs and went to jail, my childhood was not that bad. My parents loved each other and stayed together, we always had a place to live, they didn't beat me or molest me, and nobody in our house was mentally ill or suicidal or homicidal. I got into meth when I was 15 and 16 but then I settled down. I went to nursing school and got married. I work and volunteer. When I think about the worst thing that ever happened to me, I think about when my dad died. I really miss him but I still have my mom, sister and husband, and I am doing all right.
>
> *Jessamyn R., adult child of two incarcerated parents*

This suggests that the outcomes of prisoners' children can be significantly improved by increasing the developmental resources/supports in their lives and reducing the number of developmental insults they experience, rather than by simply attempting to identify and ameliorate the effects of parental incarceration. But since children of parents who will become incarcerated cannot always be identified at birth, this would require deep investments in disadvantaged communities, neighborhoods and families – something that advocates for children say our society has been and remains reluctant to do.[43]

Notes

1 Bruner C, Tirmizi SN. (2004). *Corrections and Making Connections: The Impact of Incarceration on Neighborhoods.* Des Moines, IA: The Child & Family Policy Center; Prison Visitation Project. (1993). *Needs Assessment of Children Whose Parents Are Incarcerated.* Richmond, VA: VA Department of Mental Health, Mental Retardation and Substance Abuse Services; La Vigne DG, Davies E, Brazzell D. (2008). *Broken Bonds: Understanding and Addressing the Needs of Children with Incarcerated Parents.* New York: Urban Institute.
2 Galster G. (2010). *The Mechanism of Neighborhood Effects: Theory, Evidence and Policy Implications.* Presented to the ERSC Seminar, St. Andrews University, Scotland, UK (February 4–5).
3 Wilson RE, Brown TH, Schuster B. (2009). Preventing neighborhood crime: Geography matters. *NIJ Journal,* No. 263. Available at: http://nij.gov/journals/263/Pages/neighborhood-crime.aspx.
4 Greenberg SW, Rohe WM, Williams JR. (1982). Safety in urban neighborhoods: A comparison of physical characteristics and informal territorial control in high and low crime neighborhoods. *Population and Environment,* 5(3): 141–165.
5 Galster. *Ibid.*
6 Shaw CR, McKay HD. (1942). *Juvenile Delinquency and Urban Areas.* Chicago: University of Chicago Press.

7 Rose DR, Clear T. (1998). Incarceration, social capital and crime: Implications for social disorganization theory. *Criminology*, 36: 441–479.

8 Johnston D. (1999). *The Therapeutic Intervention Project: Final Report*. Eagle Rock, CA: The Center for Children of Incarcerated Parents.

9 Galster. *Ibid.*

10 Fenton F. (1959). *The Prisoner's Family*. Palo Alto, CA: Pacific Books; Morris P. (1965). *Prisoners and Their Families*. London: George Allen & Unwin; Schneller D. (1978). *The Prisoner's Family*. San Francisco: R&E Research Associates; Swan A. (1981). *Families of Black Prisoners: Survival and Progress*. Boston: G.K. Hall; Weyand LD. (1920). Study of wage payment to prisoners as a penal method. *Journal of Criminal Law and Criminology*, 11(2): 222–271.

11 Lewis C, Garfinkel I, Gao Q. (2007). Incarceration and unwed fathers in fragile families. *Journal of Sociology and Social Welfare*, 34(3): 77–94; Turney K. (2014b). *Liminal Men: Incarceration and Family Instability*. Fragile Families Working Paper WP 13–12-FF. Available at: http://crcw.princeton.edu/workingpapers/WP13-12-FF-2.pdf; Western B, McLanahan S. (2001). Fathers behind bars: The impact of incarceration on family formation. *Contemporary Perspectives in Family Research*, 2: 309–324.

12 Tasca M, Rodriguez N, Zatz MA. (2011). Family and residential instability in the context of maternal and paternal incarceration. *Criminal Justice and Behavior*, 38(3): 231–247.

13 Carlson MJ, Furstenberg FF. (2005). *The Consequences of Multi-partnered Fertility for Parental Involvement and Relationships*. Fragile Families Publication 2006–28-FF. Available at: http://crcw.princeton.edu/publications/publications.asp; Carlson MJ, Furstenberg FF. (2006). The prevalence and correlates of multi-partnered fertility among urban U.S. parents. *Journal of Marriage and the Family*, 68(3): 718–732; Geller A. (2013). Paternal incarceration and father–child contact in fragile families. *Journal of Marriage and the Family*, 75(5): 1288–1303; Hairston CF. (1989). Men in prison: Family characteristics and family views. *Journal of Offender Counseling, Services and Rehabilitation*, 14(1): 23–30; Harknett K, Knab J. (2007). More kin, less support: Multi-partnered fertility and perceived support among mothers. *Journal of Marriage and the Family*, 69(1): 237–253; Mincy R. (2002). *Who Should Marry Whom? Multiple Partner Fertility among New Parents*. Fragile Families Publication 2002–03-FF. Available at: http://crcw.princeton.edu/publications.asp.

14 Johnston, D. (1992). *The Children of Offenders Study: A Report to the California Assembly Office of Research*. Pasadena, CA: Center for Children of Incarcerated Parents.

15 Sandstrom H, Huerta S. (2013). *The Negative Effects of Instability on Child Development: A Research Synthesis*. Low-Income Working Families Discussion Papers No. 3. New York: The Urban Institute.

16 Glaze L, Marushak LM. (2008). *Parents in Prison and Their Minor Children*. NCJ222984. Washington, D.C.: Bureau of Justice Statistics; Mumola C. (2000). *Incarcerated Parents and Their Children*. NCJ182335. Washington, D.C.: Bureau of Justice Statistics.

17 Barreras RE, Drucker EM, Rosenthal D. (2005). Concentration of substance use, criminal justice involvement and HIV/AIDS in families of drug offenders. *Journal of Urban Health*, 82(1): 162–170; Task Force on the Female Offender. (1990). *The Female Offender: What Does the Future Hold?* Laurel, MD: American Correctional Association.

18 Incarcerated Parents Work Group. (2014, March 18). *Incarcerated Parents and Their Children in the Juvenile Dependency System: A Judicial Training*. Presented to the Los Angeles County Superior Court, Juvenile Dependency Division, Monterey Park, CA.

19 See State of Washington, Department of Corrections. (2015). *Policy: Visits for Prison Offenders* (available at: www.doc.wa.gov/policies/files/450300.pdf) for an example of typical visitation policies regarding justice-involved individuals who wish to visit prisoners.

20 Glaze, Marushak. *Ibid.*

21 Merikangas KR, Stolar M, Stevens DE, Goulet J, Preisiq MA, Fenton B, Zhang H, O'Malley SS, Rounsaville BJ. (1998). Familial transmission of substance use disorders. *Archives of General Psychiatry*, 55(11): 973–979; Rojas JI, Hallford G, Tivis LJ. (2012). Latino/as in substance abuse treatment: Family history of addiction and depression. *Journal of Ethnicity in Substance Abuse*, 11(1): 75–85.

22 Mahoney C, MacKechnie S. (Eds.). (2001). *In A Different World. Parental Drug and Alcohol Use: A Consultation into Its Effects on Children and Families in Liverpool*. Liverpool: Liverpool Health Authority.

23 Glaze, Marushak. *Ibid*; Mumola. *Ibid.*

24 Weeks R, Widom CS. (1998). Self-reports of early childhood victimization among incarcerated adult male felons. *Journal of Interpersonal Violence*, 13(3): 346–361.
25 Belsky J, Jaffee SR, Sligo J, Woodward L, Silva PA. (2005). Intergenerational transmission of warm–sensitive–stimulating parenting. *Child Development*, 76(2): 384–396; Appleyard K, Berlin LJ, Dodge KA. (2011). Preventing early child maltreatment. *Prevention Science*, 12(2): 139–149; Kershaw T, Murphy A, Lewis J, Divney A, Albritton T, Magriples U, Gordon D. (2014). Family and relationship influences on parenting behaviors of young parents. *Journal of Adolescent Health*, 54(2): 197–203.
26 *Ibid.*
27 Browne A, Miller B, Maguin E. (1999). Prevalence and severity of lifetime physical and sexual victimization among incarcerated women. *International Journal of Law and Psychiatry*, 22(3–4): 301–325; Greene S, Haney C, Hurtado A. (2000). Cycles of pain: Risk factors in the lives of incarcerated mothers and their children. *The Prison Journal*, 80(1): 3–23; Weeks, Widom. *Ibid.*
28 Johnson RJ, Ross MW, Taylor WC, Williams ML, Carvajal RI, Peters RJ. (2006). Prevalence of childhood sexual abuse among incarcerated males in a county jail. *Child Abuse and Neglect*, 30(1): 75–86; Messina N, Grella C. (2006). Childhood trauma and women's health outcomes in a California prison population. *American Journal of Public Health*, 96(10): 1842–1848.
29 Carlson BE, Shafer MS. (2010). Traumatic histories and stressful life events of incarcerated parents: Childhood and adult trauma histories. *Prison Journal*, 90(4): 475–493.
30 Pynoos RS, Steinberg AM, Piacentini JC. (2009). A developmental psychopathology model of childhood traumatic stress. *Biological Psychiatry*, 46: 1542–1554.
31 Roberts R, O'Connor T, Dunn J, Golding J. (2004). The effects of childhood sexual abuse on later family life: Mental health, parenting and adjustment of offspring. *Child Abuse and Neglect*, 28: 525–545.
32 Glaze, Marushak. *Ibid.*
33 Pearson, J. (2004). Building debt while doing time. *Family Court Review*, 43(1): 5–12; Pearson J, Griswold EA. (2005). Lessons from four projects addressing incarceration and child support. *Corrections Today*, 67(4): 92–102.
34 Bronte-Tinkew J, Horowitz A, Scott M. (2009). Fathering with multiple partners: Links to children's well-being in early childhood. *Journal of Marriage and the Family*, 71(3): 608–631; Carlson, Furstenberg. (2005) *Ibid.*; Craigie TA. (2010). *Child Support Transfers Under Family Complexity*. Fragile Families Working Paper WP10–15-FF. Available at: http://crcw.princeton.edu/workingpapers/WP10-15-FF.pdf; Geller A, Garfinkel I, Cooper CE, Mincy RB. (2009). Parental incarceration and child well-being. *Social Science Quarterly*, 90(5):1186–1202; Sinkewicz M, Garfinkel I. (2009). Unwed fathers' ability to pay child support: New estimates accounting for multiple-partner fertility. *Demography*, 46(2): 247–263.
35 Johnston D, Gabel K. (1995). Incarcerated parents. In Gabel K, Johnston D. (Eds.), *Children of Incarcerated Parents*. Boston: Lexington Books.
36 Carlin M. (1999). Asserting parental rights from prison. *Family and Corrections Network Report*, 22: 1–3; Carlin M, Johnston D. (2000, September 13). *Incarcerated Fathers and Their Children*. Presented at the North American Conference on Fathers Behind Bars and on the Street, Durham, NC.
37 Chui WH. (2015). Voices of the incarcerated father: Struggling to live up to fatherhood. *Criminology and Criminal Justice*, advance publication online. doi: 10.1177/1748895815590201.
38 Minton C, Pasley K. (1996). Father's parenting role identity and father involvement. *Journal of Family Issues*, 17(1): 26–45; Clarke L, O'Brien M, Godwin H, Hemmings J, Day RD, Connolly J, Van Leeson T. (2005). Fathering behind bars in English prisons: Imprisoned fathers' identity and contact with their children. *Fathering: A Journal of Theory, Research, and Practice about Men as Fathers*, 3: 221–241.
39 Felitti VJ, Anda RF, Nordenberg D, Williamson DF, Spitz AM, Edwards V, Koss M, Marks JS. (1998). Relationship of childhood abuse and household dysfunction to many of the leading causes of death in adults: The Adverse Childhood Experiences (ACE) Study. *American Journal of Preventive Medicine*, 14(4): 245–258.
40 Dong M, Anda RF, Felitti VJ, Dube SR, Williamson DF, Thompson TJ, Loo CM, Giles WH. (2004). The interrelatedness of multiple forms of child abuse, neglect and household dysfunction. *Child Abuse and Neglect*, 28: 771–784.

41 Reavis JA, Looman J, Franco KA, Rojas B. (2013). Adverse childhood experiences and adult criminality: How long must we live before we possess our own lives? *The Permanente Journal*, 17(2): 44–48.

42 Shlafer R, Gerrity E, Ruhland E, Wheeler M. (2013). *Children with Incarcerated Parents: Considering Children's Outcomes in the Context of Complex Family Circumstances*. University of Minnesota, Children's Mental Health eReview. Available at: www.extension.umn.edu/family/cyfc/our-programs/ereview/docs/June2013ereview.pdf.

43 Brooks-Dunn J, Duncan GJ. (1997). The effects of poverty on children. *The Future of Children*, 7(2): 55–71; Children's Defense Fund. (2015). *Ending Child Poverty Now*. Washington, D.C.: Authors.

PERSONAL STORIES

A Life of Crime by Marcus T. Rogers

I grew up with both of my parents being incarcerated and throughout my life I've often needed an outlet to tell my experience.

I was born in Hollywood, California, and by that time one of my two fathers had been sent to prison on drug charges. After that, my mother got connected with a pimp and she'd take me from city to city with this man and other prostitutes, while they turned tricks and lived the street life style. I'm unsure if my mom ever prostituted herself but one can only assume it was possible given the crowd she was around.

When I was five, my mom and I were living in New York and I remember playing card games with prostitutes before they'd go to work the track. Pimps would talk to me in slang, making derogatory comments towards women. To this day, I can't remember where my mom was during all of that. I don't remember being mistreated by anyone, either.

One night, one of the pimps stormed into the apartment with a bloody hand from a gunshot wound. Soon after, the pimp my mom was with came in as well, only he was being chased by three other men. His pursuers followed him to the balcony and one of them shot him in the head with a gun and another shot him in the body with a shotgun. My mother's pimp flew over the balcony into the snow … and the snow slowed down his bleeding and he lived.

After that incident, my mother married her pimp and we moved to Wisconsin with his son and other prostitutes. We weren't in Wisconsin long before my mother had my younger brother.

I'm unsure when this happened but one day my mother got my little brother and I and took us to California to my aunt, my father's sister. My mom was going to prison and had nowhere else to take us. My aunt agreed to take me but my brother was brought back to Wisconsin and put into the foster care system.

I was confused at the time. Not only was I in a strange place with a woman I didn't know, I had to adjust to rules I wasn't accustomed to. While with my mom, I was spoiled by everyone and allowed to do as I pleased. My aunt had rules.

My aunt's rules were normal. Clean your room, do dishes, go to school, etc. However, when my cousin and I didn't comply with those rules, we were beaten badly. I had come from an environment where men beat women and women respected men, to being beaten by a woman. I was confused.

I began to wish I were with my mom to get away from the abuse. Then I began to hate my mom for leaving me in an abusive home. Over the years, I began to rebel. I ran away, I was homeless, got involved with gangs, violence, crime and a very destructive lifestyle.

My involvement in the streets created an atmosphere in which no one was safe and I terrorized many people. I'm not proud of the things I did but I know I did them and daily regret many of them. Back then, I constantly felt like I was alone in this world and I wanted everyone to hurt like I was hurting.

By the age of 17, I had been around the U.S. committing crimes and had been in juvenile halls, jails and prisons in California, New York and Wisconsin. My mom had entered my life again but we had a partner-in-crime relationship more than a mother-and-son relationship.

By the age of 21, my life had completely spiraled out of control. I had been arrested for robbery and went to jury trial; my charge was reduced to burglary, possession of a firearm as a felon and two counts of firearm possession. I was found guilty on all charges. Due to the circumstances of my case and my lengthy criminal record, I was sentenced to 13-and-a-half years in prison and five years of probation.

I've been in prison ten years and in this time I've made amends with my father, who managed to find me, and my aunt. But unfortunately, my relationship with my mom is still damaged.

I have three years left to serve in prison and I've just been trying to get my mind right and my priorities in focus. I've been bitter for too long about being away from my incarcerated parents. It's time to grow up.

I've participated in a lot of programming and acquired trades and skills since I've been in prison. I know I still have work to do but finally I'm ready to do it.

I met my dad in prison. I've been to see my mom in prison and my aunt has been to see me in prison. Incarceration, gangs, violence and emotional baggage have been my life for a long time and I hope it ends here.

I Think About My Father All the Time by Miranda Longo

When I was growing up, I lived with alcohol pretty much daily. Both my parents were considered alcoholics, I just never saw them that way. Alcoholism to me wasn't an illness, addiction or a bad thing. It was something I saw or felt as normal.

My father was abusive. He spent most of his life in prison, for street crime and for domestic violence. My parents separated when I was five and I hardly ever saw him after that. I think he wrote letters to my mother at first, but there were no visits or phone calls. We were too poor.

My mother enjoyed her everyday drinks. Alcohol was pretty much an everyday thing. So, I never saw myself drinking at an early age as wrong or strange. I saw it as normal because so many adults around me were doing the same thing. My mother always seemed to have control over her alcohol and that's what I always thought I did, too.

Even as a child, I would try to hold onto all my responsibilities. I would go to school every day, even if I'd had a drink. I went until I became pregnant with my son at the age of 17. Then I dropped out of high school to start working to support my son. But after working two jobs for a while, I quit. Then I went back to school to learn how to be a medical assistant. I continued my education during my second pregnancy and then finished after having my third child. I worked and took care of my kids while trying to cope with my mother getting ill and being diagnosed with cancer. I took care of her in every way I could. She came to live with me, I paid her doctor's bills and I took her to her appointments while taking care of my children and fighting their father in court for their custody.

After my mother died, my alcohol use increased. Slowly I slipped into the depression that I am in today. I lost control of my drinking. It was now something I needed to forget my problems. It helped me and acted like therapy for me so I could focus on my kids. I was still battling with their dad for them in court. He continuously accused me of having a drug addiction, so I didn't have to address my alcohol addiction in court. They made me drug test and the more I passed the tests and denied the problem, the more they said I was in denial. Then I was driving my friend's car and got pulled over. The police told me it was a stolen vehicle and arrested me. After that, I lost my kids.

At this time, I began to think about my father and wonder if he'd had similar experiences. Because he would fight with my mother and hit her, I had always thought he was bad man and did everything they said he did. But after I got arrested for something I didn't do, I began to think it could have been that way for him, too.

Losing my children broke me. Now I turned to alcohol more than ever before. First thing in the morning until I went to sleep at night, I would drink. Friends told me that I had a problem and I would agree with them and say, "I know it," but that I was not ready to stop drinking. Then I was in a car accident. My Yukon crashed into two other cars on the freeway and three people were hurt. I went to jail for a DUI and they tried to give me ten years in prison. I went to court and began to fight my case. I finally got sentenced to four years.

Till this day I have not seen my kids or heard how they are doing. I will not see them until I get released. Their father has custody and won't allow me to have contact with them. No letters, no phone calls, no visits. My family doesn't know where I am. I've started going to AA meetings and, because my sponsor suggested it, I got medication for depression. My mind is a little clearer now, after so many years.

I think about my father all the time now and wonder if he thinks about me.

★★★

I Wish Things Had Been Different by Moe-Moe Sullivan

Before using drugs, he could sing, he even had a group. And he'd sing to me, in a lovely, high-pitched voice that I'll remember forever. My father and I would be in the car on a nice sunny day; the perfect temperature, not too hot, not too cold, with a cool, gentle breeze. The window would be rolled down and he'd grab the CD holder and shuffle through it. I remember watching, and hoping he wasn't going to put in something I didn't know. Often, he'd reach for The Temptations, which I hated because I never knew any of the words. He'd look at me while turning it on, with an "I know you're gonna hate this but I'm gonna do it anyway" look on his face, singing,

"I know you wanna leave me ..."

"Turn this off, Dad," I'd say. But he'd keep singing, turning it up louder, pretending that he couldn't hear me. I'd giggle. If we were at a stoplight and his hands were free, he would grab my chin gently, and sing,

"Please don't leave me girl, don't you go."

Every now and then my dad will still sing for me today, but because of his drug use, he's had to kiss his lovely voice goodbye. When he tries to hit a note he can no longer reach, he'll cough and say, "I don't sound as good as I used to."

My life was hell the second I was conceived. My mother went into premature labor because she was smoking crack. Shortly after she went into labor, my parents went to the hospital because my mother could not handle the pain. The doctors put her on some type of medicine to stop the contractions; they wanted to keep her in the hospital until I was ready to come out. My father then went to the house to get it ready for me; my mom saw him leaving and wanted to go. My father explained to her that she had to stay, but about an hour after he got back to the house my mother followed suit.

My father says that in the middle of the night my mother started feeling more and more contractions and he remembers thinking, "Dang, why didn't you just stay at the freaking hospital?" They both got up and drove back. The doctors were very angry and told my mother that they were going to induce her labor because she had left. They couldn't take a chance on her leaving again. The very next day she had me: three pounds, four ounces. I had to stay in the hospital until I was at least five pounds. Not long after my mother had me she left to go get her next hit. I was a baby fish left to fend for myself.

Even though my mom left me, my father said that they wouldn't release me to her anyway because they found a lot of crack in my system. My father had to get a court order stating that he was a suitable parent in order to take me home. I used to see this as a victory because I didn't go to foster care. Now I look at it as the social workers and judges taking me from one drug addict and handing me off to another. Even though I didn't know it for a long time, my dad was a functioning drug addict. I was too young to know what was happening, but I'm pretty sure he used regularly. He didn't use around me, though, and he was still able take care of me, until he couldn't.

As a child, I was always attached to my dad. Everybody in my family told me that when my dad was around we were inseparable. I really loved my dad and he was always there for me as a child. He did nice things for me. He made sure there were no spiders in the shower because he knew I wouldn't get in otherwise. He tucked me in at night, or else I wouldn't go to sleep. My brother and I loved potato fries, and my dad was an expert. He cut the potatoes perfectly neat and thin. To this day, I can never cut them as well as he did. He was a good dad, but it always seemed like my father met women who didn't like the fact he had kids, including the wife that he has today, who sometimes tells my father to not let me come over. Until he met my first step-mom, my dad was always someone I could look up to; when he met her, a heavy drug user, their relationship took his addiction to a whole other level.

Before my father met my step-mother, all the bills got paid and, in my opinion, I was well taken care of. After he met her, it seemed like my whole world ended. My father was not the same person. Although I didn't know he was on drugs, I knew things were different in my house. It wasn't the same. Things happened. There were curtains up on the kitchen and living room and if my brother or I walked down the stairs without saying, "Coming down," we would get yelled at or possibly whipped.

I remember this one day. There wasn't anything in my house to eat and this guy named Chris, a close friend of my dad's, made me some beans. I don't even like beans, but they were all we had. After I ate them, I went outside, and sat down on my porch. It was another beautiful, sunny day. My friend came out of her house, and I asked if she wanted to come over. She said, "My momma won't let me because that's a crack house." Right then and there everything started making sense, from the unpaid bills to my father being unable to feed us. It was all drug related. I went into the house and cried my eyes out. When I think about my life, I feel that is when I started getting unhappy. I didn't care if I ate after then. Sadness would stay with me for a very long time.

I hated the fact that my mother wasn't there to give me the real love and attention that I needed. I used to wet the bed a lot, and when I did, my step-mother would hit me. Every morning, I would wake up to her standing in the doorway. She'd ask me if I wet the bed, I'd say "yeah," and she would whip me with a belt. She'd try to kill me. She choked me once, and another time pushed me into the bathtub. My father was never around to see her physically abuse me, and I never mentioned it to him until a few years ago. He was very upset and wondered why I didn't tell him sooner. I didn't tell him because I thought he knew and was okay with it. After all, he left me with her.

In addition to my step-mother beating me, and encouraging my dad to use drugs, her brother was also molesting me. When it finally came out, she despised me even more. One day I told my friend Raven about the molestation, and she vowed to keep it a secret. Soon after that, Jesse, the man that molested me, came down the hill and was coming to my house. Raven started throwing rocks at him, screaming "You rapist!" My step-mother, Michelle, came outside and said, "Why is she calling him a rapist?" I said, "Cuz he molested me." She didn't believe me. She thought that I was just being fast, or that I was lying. Every day after that, if I wore shorts or a tank top, or anything at all exposing, she called me fast.

One day, when I was seven, I got a message from the school office saying to get off at a different bus stop than usual. I was wondering why, but never asked any questions. When I got off the bus, I was looking for my dad because he usually picked me up, but instead I saw one of his friends. I asked her what was she doing, and she told me she was there to get me because my father had something to do. I thought this was weird because my father was always there to pick me up. She took me to her to house, and I played with her daughter, Dextina, who soon became my best friend. I remember everyday asking my dad's friend, Rona, "Where is my dad?" but she never told me. She always had some excuse. After a week, my father was released and he came to pick me up. I ran up to him and gave the biggest hug ever, and told him I missed him. I asked him where was he, and told me that he had had to go take care of something. I knew he was lying, but I was 7 years old – I wasn't gonna tell him he was lying. I later found out he was in jail for possession of crack.

As time went on, the drug use increased, and everything got worse. My dad was physically there, but his mind wasn't. I remember coming home to a dark house because my father hadn't paid the bills. Instead, he spent his money on narcotics, and my step-mom was always there to persuade him to use. I really hated her and wanted her out of his life: I couldn't take any more of the abuse.

Two years went by, and my dad was skinnier than a broomstick. His face was sunken in and his voice wasn't the same. When I was nine, I noticed that my dad didn't have a job. One day I was at school and this lady walked in with a badge on, and told me to come with her. I said no, and then my vice principal, Ms. Sampson, who I was very cool with at the time, came and explained to me that I should go. I trusted Ms. Sampson and I left.

When we got into the car, the lady explained to me who she was and that my brother and I would be placed in a foster home together. As soon as she mentioned CPS, I knew that my life would be over. We then went to my brother's school to get him, and then she took us both to this shelter. The shelter was very clean and had friendly staff members, except I got put in a room with two spiders in it. They scared me. I cried because my father wasn't there to kill them for me. They fed us but I didn't eat. They put me and my brother in different rooms because we were different sexes. The rooms were clean, but the mattresses were so uncomfortable I could barely sleep and I think that's when my insomnia started. When I woke up, I went to go check on my brother, but I didn't see him. I asked one of the staff where he was and she told me that he was placed with a family an hour earlier. I didn't know where my dad was and they had just taken my brother from me. My world was literally over at that point. Everything I knew and loved was gone, and I was now forced to live with strangers.

I later found out that my father was in jail for possession of heroin. That is one of the reasons I went to foster care. I was there from ages 9 to 18. I'm 19 today, and sometimes I feel like I'm still there. I've thought about how if they had drug tested my dad at the hospital, when I was born, maybe they would have just taken me then, and I wouldn't have had to go through so many traumatizing experiences. I also wouldn't have built a close relationship with my dad, and then had the pain of being separated at an older, more painful age. But by the same token, I would never wish that I didn't have a close bond with my father. I would never wish for that to be taken away, because I love him dearly. Today his mind is there, and he's supportive. It's not been easy, though, and my experience has made me hate the system, and also want to help fix it. I want people to know that children with incarcerated parents have a difficult time filling that void while their parent is absent, and that they are not always treated right in other people's care. It's backwards to me that people go to jail for drug charges, instead of going to rehabilitation. I wish my dad *had* been drug tested when I was a newborn. I wish he had been helped. I wish things had been different.

★★★

Life as an Unhealed Wound by Nate A. Lindell

My mom was an attractive woman, raised in a staunchly Roman Catholic community by a working-class family that did its best to play out the roles their society made for them. But she was one of twelve children and when her father, an Air Force pilot, was severely injured and hospitalized, her mother needed help. The care of the children was taken on by some military personnel who inflicted physical and sexual abuse on my mom, aunts and uncles. As a young adult, my mom became a model but was also put in a mental hospital, where she received electroconvulsive therapy for her psychotic depression.

Of course, I had no idea about my mom's past when I was young. All I knew was that she was my mom and I loved her. That's what every TV show, movie, story and person I knew told me about moms. So, it seemed normal to eat the tasty cookies my mom sometimes baked for me and normal for her to push me down the basement stairs, resulting in a severe laceration at the back of my throat and a rush to the hospital. It was normal to watch "Little House on the Prairie" with my mom one day and normal for her to whip me the next day with a wire coat hanger for tracking mud on the floor. It was normal for her to shriek obscenities, red-faced, while tied to her bed and my step-father, Donald, and a phony priest tried to cast the Devil out of her by performing an exorcism as my half-brothers and I prayed for her, kneeling on the spikey side of hard plastic carpets.

This will seem absurd to some, but these things were, or became, normal to me. Our knees bled. Sometimes our stomachs ached when my step-father made us fast (only one slice of sourdough bread, one cup of water and one Vitamin C tablet a day) for up to a week. What was strange was that, no matter what he made us do, the Devil stayed put.

Why would my mom marry such a lunatic? She'd had my older brother out of wedlock by a man my brother never knew and then she became pregnant with me. (She once told me this pregnancy was result of a rape.) These were big No-No's in our family and community, so her parents pushed her into marriage, believing Donald to be a good Catholic and not knowing that he wasn't quite right after being hit by a bolt of lightning that melted a religious medal off his neck. In addition to his religious fanaticism, Donald moved us a lot – from Canada to Arizona, from Washington to Wisconsin – insuring that we lived deranged, anxious, brutal, ignorant rural lives. I liked the rural part.

My mom was stuck with this guy, whose surname I carry, until I was around 6 or 7 years old. Then her brothers (all ex-military) and her sister (a karate expert who brought a .38 with her) busted my mom and us kids out of his house in Nowhere, Montana.

My relationship with my mother was strange and a source of anxiety for me, although I don't think I recognized that until much later in my life. She could be warm and loving, or cold, slamming a door on my finger and refusing to take me to the hospital. I don't recall her ever kissing my wounds, but I could be wrong and I am trying to be fair and honest about her.

After she escaped Donald, we – my older half-brother, me and three younger half-siblings – lived with relatives for some months. I felt like an outcast – my clothing and way of talking were Western and we were in the Midwest, and I had a speech impediment, maybe related to my throat injury. My mom and her parents did their best to mold us into good Catholic children, as if our crazy past was dead and gone. She worked two or three jobs and got us our own place to live. I don't remember seeing her much during that time, but I distinctly recall her beginning to drink brandy in the evenings.

Mom wasn't a robot and she began to crack from her past traumas. Cocaine was hip at the time and she began snorting it. Then she began snorting heroin and drinking heavily. One of my warmest memories from that time was staying up late with her, watching "Buck Rogers" and eating vanilla ice cream mixed with brandy. Sometimes all of us sat around the kitchen table with our mom and played Uno or listened to some books-on-tape. Our mom began minimizing our contact with her family at that time, telling us that they were very abusive, evil and dangerous – to her addictions, I now believe.

Mom began to be scarce, to the point where we kids had to cook for ourselves and do the laundry. We also did pretty much whatever we wanted. We often fought about who was in charge, sometimes chasing each other with knives, tying each other up and forming shifting alliances. We found a bunch of bullets and gunpowder in the basement of our building and tried to make bombs or set off the bullets with hammers and by throwing them at the sidewalk. When we had nothing to eat, we would raid our neighbors' gardens and fruit trees, and even plotted to kill and eat a pet rabbit.

Although I was curious and deeply interested in nature, the feral nature of my home life didn't provide me with the confidence to explore socially, among other people. What I did, I did alone or with no more than two other kids, or with my siblings. All through this period – around the time I was in third grade – we rarely saw our mom and had no adult supervision. Mom was working and partying with a group of bikers in our small Wisconsin town.

Then one day I came home from St. Patrick's School with the rest of my siblings (an older half-brother, two younger half-brothers and the youngest, my half-sister – each of us about a year apart in age) and found our mom unconscious in her recliner, frothy drool oozing from between her lips. As hard as my siblings tried, they could not wake her from her stupor. One of them called 911 and an ambulance came, picked up our mom, then drove away with her. It was all perfectly normal. After all, I hadn't lived a previous, nicer life.

Later I learned that our mom had OD'd on heroin and cocaine. The only thing I knew about these drugs was that they were part of every episode of "Miami Vice," which was then one of my favorite TV shows. But we lived in a small river town, not on the ocean in Miami.

After our mom was wheeled off, there is a blank space in my memory. I don't know how it happened but my siblings and I were placed in two different foster homes. My oldest brother and I wound up living on a farm in rural Wisconsin. The vanishing of my mom was probably more traumatic than I realized because the blank memory – called "dissociation" – is known to be a defense mechanism against severe psychological pain.

My mom went to jail for possessing narcotics and was court-ordered to do a nine-month inpatient drug and alcohol dependency program. The foster home my half-brother, Tom, and I were in was decent. It was on a farm near a small town, with our nearest neighbor in sight but beyond shouting distance. I was worried that the foster family – an older couple and their pudgy only son – were going to abuse us, but they were square. Tom and I picked on this kid (how could we not?) but we also protected him at school, which he loved. In spite of how normal these people were, I never relaxed in that foster home for the nine or so months we spent there. I knew we were just passing through. I think I had a vague longing for my mom and was even concerned about my three youngest half-siblings, with whom I had no contact. I think I maybe had some letters from my mom during her incarceration.

After my mom completed jail and rehab, a social worker brought us kids back to the same house and the same room where we'd found our mom OD'd nine months previously. It still hurts me to think that the court let our mom have custody of us again. Did they know about addictions to multiple substances, relapses and the correlation between single moms like ours and children who become mentally ill, addicted, criminal, etc.?

My mom really tried to stay sober and, mostly, she did. She hung out with a lot of scuzzy people she met at her NA and AA meetings. Some of them beat us – with 2×4s, wire hangers, whatever was handy – and one raped my mom. After about a year, my mom moved us to a bigger Wisconsin city, on the Mississippi. She was, again, often busy. She fed us and took better care of us than before, but we were still poor and ran wild in the neighborhood. Yet, compared to what was to come, our time in this new setting was amazingly stable. There was a Boys & Girls Club where we spent time and a library where we went to read; we could all read really well, and my brothers and I loved books.

After about a year in our new home, my mom moved us to a much nicer neighborhood and enrolled in a technical college to become a dental technician. She also married an ex-con named Bill, a half-German, half-Native American guy who loved the outdoors. Bill and I got along great. I got a paper route, did well in school and began to come out of my shell, socializing with less dysfunctional kids than previously.

But there were problems developing in the marriage, which really cut me since I looked at Bill as an acceptable step-father. My mom and Bill argued and Bill began to stay away from home, coming back angry. Then $85 disappeared from my paper route money; my mom and siblings suggested Bill was to blame and I asked him, in an accusing manner, if he took it. He knocked me down, banged my head on the floor, and then kicked me in the butt. A few tense days passed and then Bill slapped my mom during an argument. My siblings and I plotted, got knives and a broom, called the police and then confronted him. He left.

My mom got her degree and things looked possibly hopeful, but then her psyche collapsed. She was suicidal and was diagnosed with PTSD, major depression and Multiple Personality Disorder. She was deemed disabled, put on anti-psychotics and repeatedly tried to kill herself with overdoses and once with a cleaver (which she turned on me when I tried to stop her). I found myself acting as a psychiatric nurse/parent and hating life more than any healthy person can imagine.

I also received services. It might seem weird, but I was in Upward Bound, a program for smart kids with the potential for college. I liked it but my mom hated my tutor, thinking that he was a gay predator (which was not true). All of us kids also attended Al-Anon for people who had loved ones with alcohol/drug addiction. That program had the benefit of scaring me off from cocaine and heroin, which were unavailable in my community, anyway.

My whole family was well known to the local psychiatric community and all of us kids were seeing one or more therapists or shrinks. I couldn't concentrate at school, became more of a loner and developed a hair-trigger temper; at the urging of my mom, I was diagnosed with Attention Deficit Disorder and put on Ritalin. That pisses me off to this day because I've learned enough about PTSD to realize that was what the problem was; the therapists, social workers, psychiatrists and other professionals who dealt with me should have known that, too. I saw a therapist every week for my "anger problem" but then had to go back and live in a home with a mother and brother who were flagrantly and violently mentally ill.

Although I still feel agony at the thought of us kids being left in our mom's custody after her overdose and jailing, I now believe that I was probably already fatally injured in my personality by that point in my life. As an adolescent, I got in a lot of fights and began committing petty crimes, often just to lash out at a stupid world. I got caught in the juvenile justice system's web and sent to juvenile detention, as judges tried to intimidate me into being a good boy. Apparently, they didn't realize that, compared to my home, detention was like going on a vacation. Never had even the worst delinquents come at me with a cleaver!

Due to setting a toilet on fire at my high school, I got in serious trouble and was sent to a foster home run by a prison sergeant (who hated me so much that he accused me of trying to burn down his house so that he could get me removed from the placement immediately). Next I went to the Rawhide Boys Ranch where I stayed for seven months. Although I was always in trouble there, always on discipline, everyone said the Ranch did have a positive influence on me.

But back at home, I began to fall apart. My mom and younger brother were much more stable and my mom tried to act like a mother. But I didn't respect that, although I had to put up with it because I had no other family to speak of (my mom had hidden us from her family for many years by that time) and no real friends.

As a way out and with the intention of becoming a nuclear tech, I enlisted with the Navy. I planned to do my stint then go on to a prestigious university, which the Navy would have paid for. I was ecstatic about the hope this offered. But then an acquaintance snitched on me and on himself, reporting to the police some thefts we'd done as minors, and it shipwrecked my enlistment. I reacted by going on a crime spree. Arrested but given another chance, I went on a second spree in Kansas and Missouri. In the Wyandotte County Jail in Kansas, I desperately turned to God. I was given a third chance, got out and stayed true to my newfound faith.

Back in Wisconsin, my Catholic family rejected me for my Pentecostalism. All I had was my church community. But after a conflict over my schooling, they pulled away from me and I severed all ties with them. Although I was doing well in school, I had no safety net and no moral checks. When I needed money for restitution and rent, I burglarized a man's home to get it.

My younger brother and I had resumed our relationship and he proposed we rob a bank. My counterproposal was that we rob and kill the guy who I had burglarized because he was selling S&M child pornography. We did, and months later we were arrested. My mother and brother testified against me so that he could get a deal leaving him eligible for parole in 25 years. He also told the cops that he'd stolen my paper route money years before. I was given a sentence of life without parole.

Such, I believe, is likely the case with many incarcerated people who had incarcerated parents. Parental incarceration at one or more points in our lives is only a minor part and maybe the best (yet worst) part of our making. My mom's incarceration was a good thing in that it separated me from the abuse and trauma, but it was a terrible thing because she was my mom, the only mom I had. Foster care was a good thing in that I was at least fed regularly, wasn't beaten by strange men who came home with Mom, and had some supervision, albeit by people who were decent but who didn't love me and whom, by then, I couldn't love nor trust even if they had loved me. But it would have been better if there had been a permanent separation and I'd been given the long-term, loving, honest, non-religious rearing I needed. However, that would have required concern and money that society couldn't spare.

Now I sit in a supermax prison, where I've been for the last 11 years, serving my life sentence for homicide, deemed "highly psychopathic," afflicted by knowledge of scars that I apparently can't heal but which sure hurt and are added to daily. Now society is concerned and has money to spare for me.

Maybe this story will help prevent others from being so wounded.

★★★

Betty Boop by Percy Levy

Back in July of 1970, my mother went into labor while serving time at a California women's prison; I was allowed five minutes in my mother's arms before being whisked away to a foster home. I can only assume that Child Protective Services ran a much looser operation in those days, because surely in this modern era it would be very difficult to imagine a child being so easily returned to a drug-addicted, alcoholic and criminally oriented mother prior to some sort of counseling, drug testing or a period of supervised visitation. But back in 1971 my mother was released from prison whereupon she immediately collected me from foster care and hit the highway headed for Seattle, Washington.

I don't know why my mother decided to move to Seattle. Although I have tried to piece together a true and honest version of events from different sources, I must concede that those sources are questionable. I can't ask my mother because any answers elicited from her would simply leave me chasing my tail. From what I have gathered, it appears that my father, a mid-level drug dealer from Northern California, had actually been waiting at the prison gate for my mother to be released. But she had intentionally given the poor man an incorrect release date. So after several hours of waiting in the parking lot, my duped father was informed by the guards that my mother had been released the day before and had been picked up by a lesbian lover she had befriended while in prison. It must have been heartbreaking for my father to find out that he had been rejected by the woman he loved and lost the chance to get to know his new son – all on the same day. (My father and I would not meet until 24 years later.)

My early years in Washington are blurry, yet I know certain, incontrovertible facts about my dear mother. Betty Gore, AKA Betty Boop, was an extremely beautiful, raven-haired, well-proportioned White woman. Her beauty allowed her to have her pick of men, and her choice always happened to be the local African American drug dealer. I do recall her being involved in prostitution at times, but I never remembered her having a pimp, at least not in the classical sense that is portrayed on television and in the movies. I remember Betty Boop as simply an alcoholic, drug-addicted free spirit who always did whatever she wanted to do in life. Even when her violent alcohol binges led her to become injured or jailed (which happened often), she was fortunate enough to maintain a following of men who flocked to her rescue to bail her out of whatever messed-up situation she found herself in.

I suppose that in a weird way I benefited from my mother's ability to wrap men around her finger. There was never a shortage of drug dealers who would step forward when she went to jail to take care of me until she was released. They would drive around selling their product while I sat in the back seat and ate copious amounts of soda, chips and candy. Such treatment actually made me look forward to the times when my mother went to jail. I can honestly say that not a single one of Betty Boop's men ever abused me physically or mentally and at least one, John Lee, constantly rescued me from Betty Boop's extreme physical abuse.

As I grew older, Betty Boop's violence dramatically increased – not only towards me but towards John Lee. When I was about 10 years old, I recall her stabbing him in the chest during an argument. Even worse, two weeks later, after he refused to press charges against her and accepted her back into his home, he had to sit and watch as she ran around his house in an alcohol-induced rage, punching out his windows.

I still wonder what caused her behavior to escalate so quickly. I would swear at one point that she had given up on living. I definitely know that she had given up on dragging a child around with her everywhere she went. Things might have worked out if she had chosen to live with John Lee, who I accepted as my father figure, but Betty Boop did not choose this route. She simply left me with whatever dope dealer she was with at the time as she tore through life on a perpetual drug- and alcohol-fueled binge. The situation was bound to come to a head, and it did.

Once, when she was beating me, she accidentally hit me across the face with a stick. The bridge of my nose all the way across my eye was split open and swollen, and it looked grotesque. For some reason, my mother believed that the particular dope dealer she was with at the time was going to put up with her running off on a binge while he cared for a small child who obviously needed medical attention. It was not happening with this fellow. He immediately took me to the Department of Social and Health Services [DSHS] and dropped me off. The social workers seemed genuinely shocked as they took photographs of my injury.

This marked the beginning of a long and convoluted relationship between myself and the foster care/juvenile institutional system – in other words state child care. The first few foster homes I was placed in were a shock to me. No matter how kind and considerate they might be, I did not appreciate strangers taking care of me. I actually ran away from foster homes to seek out my mother. As a child, I had no grasp of the concept that Betty Boop was a terrible mother. For me, her presence had a calming effect. No matter what her mental or physical condition when I located her, it always created a comfortable, womb-like sense of protection inside of me.

At some point, I became an expert at manipulating the foster care system. I knew which foster homes were good and which ones were bad. I would check in and out of them as if they were motels. My social workers became accustomed to having me appear at their work desk requesting food and clothing vouchers and giving ridiculous excuses for why I had run away from my last foster home.

One day my social worker surprised me by telling me that a woman named Joan wanted me to live with her. All I knew about Joan was that she was a White woman who had hired me a few times to mow her grass. I also remembered that she had been extremely nosy about the fresh wounds that she observed on my body. To this day, I have very fond memories of Joan as a person. What I remember most about living with her was her love of reading and her desire for me to share that love. She read to me for hours every day and took me to all the children's events around the greater Seattle area. I wish I could explain what I'm about to say but I cannot. For some reason, I never felt comfortable around Joan. Something inside of me made me question her reason for being kind to me. My mind simply could not accept the idea that she did not have ulterior motives. In retrospect, I see that my mother had not prepared me to deal with a woman whose ultimate goal was not to take advantage of the people around her. Joan may as well have been a creature from outer space when it came to her kindness towards me.

My discomfort with Joan would never get a chance to work itself out because Betty Boop managed to cut her drinking and drugging enough to con the state of Washington into returning her child. But even though she had slowed her drug and alcohol use to a manageable level, things were not much better. The fact that she only went on binges every once in a while seemed to make her all the worse. Her violence against me and John Lee increased tenfold.

This time, instead of stabbing John Lee, she stabbed me.

The events are branded in my mind for eternity – the enraged look on her face as she came forward, the glint of steel from the steak knife, and the slow motion movement of John Lee rushing forward to stop her. However, what I remember most about that day was the drunken sobbing of my mother as she cleaned my wounded arm and told me she was sorry ... but added that it was my fault because I should have made it back into the house before the street lights had come on. She had the nerve to tell me that she feared that if I ever got caught outside after dark that a stranger might harm me.

That was the last time my mother ever hurt me. A friend of mine talked his reluctant mother into taking me in. Although she was very uncomfortable interfering with another woman's child, my unstitched stab wound convinced her. My friend has two brothers and a sister. With very little supervision, our days were mostly spent smoking weed, drinking beer and practicing a new fad called break dancing. But one day, returning to the house, I found my friend's mother standing on the porch with a box full of my clothes. She was crying as she told me my mother had sent the police to her house and threatened to have her arrested if she did not cease and desist in allowing a runaway to live in her home.

Nothing was ever the same after that day. I am not sure of the exact emotion I felt – frustration, anger, or just a general sense of defeat – but my new weed and alcohol abuse combined with a deep depression and led me to hang out with a different crowd than the first time I had lived on the streets. Instead of showing up and begging for food and clothing vouchers from social workers at DSHS, I now shoplifted and snatched purses, which ultimately led to the larger crime of burglary.

My first few stays in juvenile hall introduced me to a more serious criminal element. The older boys' influence drastically changed my thought processes. The cultivation of deviant behavior firmly took root. I may have begun crime with the general concept of survival, but it slowly morphed into the "Money is God" concept that is so much a part of the urban criminal subculture. I began to choose girlfriends who were prostitutes. It was a very natural thing to become involved with girls who were social rejects, like me.

When I was between 13 and 15 years old, my mother turned her life around and became very religious. Although she asked me back into her home, the stabbing incident would never allow me to trust her again enough to live with her. I started staying at the YMCA Youth Shelter. During some of those visits, I began forming a relationship with the director of the place, Chris. To this day, I respect this man more than any person who has been in my life. I believe that in my times of great sadness and depression, his words have been all that carried me through.

Chris, who lived in the suburbs, eventually took me into his home. But after spending the majority of my life hustling and fighting to stay alive, it was now a serious shock to find myself in such a calm, serene environment. Life in the suburbs seemed lonely to me, and I yearned for the city life. Sadly and predictably, I took the new car and the designer clothes that Chris provided for me and commuted on a daily basis back to the city. I even had the nerve to bring street friends back from the city to hang with me. Eventually, some of the criminal activities from the city made their way out to the suburbs. I eventually discovered that the suburbs had a juvenile hall just like the city and after a while I knew most of the staff on a first name basis.

Chris made every attempt to help me change the destructive path I was on. Unfortunately, back in 1986 the crack epidemic was just starting to hit hard and I became one of its first casualties. Although I heard Chris's words trying to save me, my decline into addiction was fast and hard.

Within only a short time, I wound up traveling up and down the West Coast between Washington and California, involved in narcotics sales and the promotion of prostitution. The prison system became my second home. Between my stints in prison, I somehow managed to impregnate several women and have four daughters. And, sadly, I only had the opportunity to spend time with one of these children before I got locked up to serve a very long prison sentence. I have now been locked up for ten years. My daughter Jordyn is a beautiful 15 year old who grew up with her aunt and uncle. I have recently contacted her on Facebook but she remains very distant with me – very upset that I was not there for her through her young life.

At 42 years of age, I have now come to the stage of my life where I must examine my daughters' lives and question what they must feel about having a father like me – the child of Betty Boop.

★★★

The Chain by Jasmine

I was 3 years old when my alcoholic father molested me. It was not a violent experience but it was emotionally devastating. When I was five, I told my mother and my father went to prison.

My father and I never lived together again but I've always felt that I knew him well, probably because of our unhealthy intimate relationship. He wrote to me from prison but I never received his letters. We didn't have any communication again until I was an adult.

You might expect that a woman who marries a child molester would not be emotionally healthy and my mother wasn't. She used too much medication and was a workaholic. We lived in a motor home behind my grandparents' house. It was easiest for me to focus on external things and get along on a superficial level. I got good grades and I was pretty and popular. As teenager, I liked alcohol more and partied harder than the other girls.

I never told anyone about my father. I actually tried to forget about him and what he did. Not because he was incarcerated, but because I knew people would ask why he was in prison. Some of my family members knew, but that was all. When people asked about him, I just said that I hadn't seen him since my parents divorced. There were a lot of kids in that situation.

I met my husband when I was 17. Even though he drank too much, he was really good to me and he was very good-looking. His parents had a car dealership that he began to manage after we got married. I got pregnant immediately.

It seemed like I had the perfect life. I was a housewife and we had a beautiful home. My in-laws were like the parents I should have had. They were very loving and helpful to me. I really liked my sister-in-law, who was the wife of my husband's brother. We became tight friends and partied together. She would stay over at my house with the kids when the guys went out.

Both my husband and I drank; it was a big part of our social life. He had a lot of issues about my behavior and the domestic violence started after my first daughter was born. He assaulted me during my second pregnancy and abused me verbally and physically when he was drunk. I was more careful about my drinking because of my children. I drank mostly when they had gone to bed or when I went out, and I started to have the casual sexual relationships my husband had accused me of.

When my daughters were still little, I got arrested for a DUI and, very soon afterwards, for a second one. They sent me to the county jail for a year on that case but I only served six months. My mother-in-law took care of my girls while I was gone.

I handled a lot of things by not thinking about them, just like I didn't think about my father. After I got out of jail, I tried not to think about my DUI's and went back to my regular life. I kept on drinking. When I was 24, I was driving drunk and got in an accident with another car. The woman driving the other car died from her injuries. The only thing in my favor was that she had been under the influence, too. I was sentenced to 12 years in prison for manslaughter. My daughters were four and six.

While I was incarcerated, my in-laws drove 150 miles each way to the prison almost every week to visit me, bringing my daughters. My husband continued to work at the family business and continued to drink.

I was popular in prison. It was like high school. I worked and took community college classes. I didn't have romantic relationships on the yard, but did have something with my cellie, who was also from the northern part of the state. I played and partied just enough to be accepted. I got drugs for depression and to help me sleep but I used them to get high.

After I had been incarcerated for a couple of years, my father wrote to me. In his letter, he told me about his molestation as a child, apologized for everything he did to me and said he wanted us to try to have some kind of parent–child relationship. I started using drugs on the yard after I got the letter. I was in AA and the group called me out for the way I was acting. I denied it but I realized that other people could see there was something wrong with me. I began to straighten up and got sober. After asking people I trusted and respected, I decided not to correspond with my father.

While I was in prison, I did everything I could to maintain my relationship with my children. I phoned them every night, wrote to them every day and had visits with them three or four times a month. My daughters grew from middle childhood into adolescence while I was incarcerated. When I looked at other incarcerated mothers, I realized that I was lucky that my family supported everything I wanted with my kids.

My husband didn't visit me, so I didn't have to work on my marriage during my first few years in prison. During my third year, he told me he was in a relationship with another woman and we separated. Later, he filed for divorce with my consent.

I served 75 months in prison and got out when my daughters were 11 and 13; I discharged my parole after two years. It doesn't escape me that I have gone to prison just like my father, but we are very different as parents. He used his child to meet his needs but I didn't abuse my children. My father never met his child's needs in any way but I have tried to meet my daughters' needs as my first priority.

I do think our problems are linked. I believe that he went to prison as the result of what was done to him, just like I went to prison as the result of what he did to me. I will not allow that to happen to my children, I will break the chain.

My teachers and advisors have told me it is possible for my kids to overcome the effects of my incarceration and our separation and grow up normally, as long as they have the supports they need and don't have any more trauma. More than anything, I want that and will try to make it come true.

★★★

Nothing Like My Dad by Aaron Godinez

When I was a child, I had an incarcerated father. I was asked to write this essay about my experience with him and that part of his life.

My father was an asshole. His father was violent, a drunk and married to my demented grandmother. I'm sure both of them had been incarcerated. My father was one of eight children. All of his brothers and two of his sisters have gone to jail. They were all juvenile delinquents and went to juvenile hall. My father was first incarcerated at 15. He was in a gang and subject to all of that nonsense, and he was also pretty violent, so he got locked up. He had violent arguments with his friends and was violent to my mom and to us.

He got my mother pregnant with my oldest brother when she was 16. She lost a set of twins after that because my dad hit her in the stomach. He was gone a lot of my childhood, mostly because he was in jail or prison, but he always came back. Then we would have a couple of nervous days and a week of dread, followed by some violent explosion. My father would beat my mom down while my brothers and I tried to hide, but he would eventually come after us. One time when I was seven we were hiding on a little second story balcony when he finished with my mom, and I was so scared I jumped over the wall. (No broken bones.)

When I was nine, my father got a long sentence to state prison. Our lives got much better after that. My mom started running a daycare center and my brothers went to school and got jobs. We got a better apartment and my mom got a car. I always excelled at education, so they let me skip grades. I was thinking about becoming an engineer because math and science have always come easy to me.

My dad got out when I was 16. He just showed up one day. My mom almost fainted when she opened the door. My oldest brother and his wife had already had their first baby and there were six of us living at home when my dad came and we all stopped talking for the next two weeks. He was pretty calm the first days but then my uncle came over and they started drinking. After he'd been there a week he beat my mom up. That went on for a few days and then the cops came and arrested him for domestic violence, a violation of his parole on domestic violence charges.

That time, the last time, he was gone for a couple of years. When he got released, he didn't come around. Fourteen days after he got out he was killed by some guy on the street. To me, his life was a total waste. Every effect he had on me was bad. I'm glad he's gone.

I graduated from high school last year and got a job at the company where my oldest brother works. He has three kids with his girlfriend and they're trying to buy a house in Pajarito. He works hard and he's never been in trouble. My youngest brother still lives with my mom, too, but he works for the cable company. He's never been in trouble, either.

I'm taking a couple of theatre classes and I think I want to be an actor. I myself have never used hard drugs, had anything to do with gangs, been arrested or been incarcerated. I used to get drunk on the weekends but lately I have stopped drinking. I don't want to do anything like my father did.

★★★

My Parents' Incarceration by Mary

My name is Mary and I am Cahuilla. I was raised on the reservation for the first part of my life. My father was in jail most of that time. They took me to visit him but I don't remember it. He got killed in jail when I was three. I don't remember that or anything about him except that he was a very big man and when he picked me up it felt like I was high up in the air.

When I started school we moved to a small town called Banning. It was just my mother, me and my brother, who was younger. Sometimes my mother's boyfriends would live with us. All of them beat us kids up.

My mother had an alcohol problem at that time. She always drank too much and there was always liquor in our home. On occasion she was arrested for being drunk or driving under the influence. Those nights that they kept her in jail, me and my brother stayed with my aunts.

I don't remember what I thought about my mom being in jail. A lot of people we knew had been arrested. I never visited her in jail, because she was never there very long, at the most only a few days. I think I was 11 the last time she went.

One of my mother's boyfriends sexually abused me when I was 10. I never told anyone because I didn't understand what happened. When I was 12 I was raped by some men who were visiting my relatives on the rez. No one called the police but my uncles tracked them down and gave them some rez justice.

I started drinking when I was 10 but didn't drink heavy until I was 13. Later I started smoking marijuana and using methamphetamine. Meth is the drug of choice in my community. I thought the drugs and alcohol helped me stay calm so I wouldn't fight all the time. But sometimes I fought when I drank too.

I met my husband when I was 14. He got me pregnant but I had a miscarriage. When I was 17, I got pregnant again and we got married. My son was born when I was 18. They took him away from me at the hospital because he had meth and alcohol in his system but I got him back after about a year.

When my son was three, I went to jail for possession. The CPS didn't find out so there was no problem with his custody. My mother kept him while I was in jail. Two years later I was arrested again and that time they reported it to CPS. My son went back into the system but they put him with my husband's mom so I didn't have to worry about losing him.

When I was 26, I got pregnant with twins. I was very irritable in my pregnancy. My husband and I had a fight in my mother–in–law's house and I shot him in the leg. The CPS took my son and put him with a foster family. I got arrested and went to prison. My twins were born at the prison and my mother took them home and got guardianship for them.

I got out of prison four years ago and went into a treatment program. After that I stayed sober for almost a year and I got off parole. But then I went back with my husband and we started using again. I ended up pregnant. In my third trimester I gave the CPS a dirty test. They terminated my parental rights for my oldest son and they took my baby when he was born. These were the most painful experiences I ever had.

If I have to say something about my parents' incarceration I would say it didn't affect me that much. There are worse things that can happen to a child.

3

CARE AND GUIDANCE

Megan Sullivan and Denise Johnston

Chapter 2 examined how children's safety and protection is compromised by the communities where they live, the family structures that impacted their parents and in turn impact them, and by their parents' characteristics. This chapter examines how the care and guidance children receive before, during, and after a parent's incarceration affects them. Almost every aspect of this care is related to economic strain.

Economic Strain and Instability

The poverty experienced by prisoners' families in the U.S. has been widely recognized since the early years of the twentieth century;[1] historical and current research suggest the majority of prisoners' families have always been poor, with many dependent upon public charities for support while the parent was incarcerated.[2]

A number of reports have recently addressed economic strain in the households of incarcerated parents.[3] Contributors to this book have also written about economic strain, both the kind that occurs in all low-income families and the kind that occurs when a breadwinning parent is suddenly incarcerated. The economic status of the families of incarcerated parents is a major determinant of children's care before, during and after parental incarceration. The characteristics of these parents that most determine their children's outcomes – lack of education, untreated mental illness and/or substance abuse[4] – are all income-related. Family income in turn has a great influence on how members manage the events and experiences of parental criminal justice system involvement, including incarceration and reentry.

Lower income is associated with a higher risk of behavior problems in children, juvenile delinquency, adult criminal behavior, arrest and incarceration.[5] Most incarcerated parents had a pre-incarceration income at or below the poverty level.[6] So even prior to parental incarceration, many children of criminal offenders live in very low-income households.

Of course, we were dirt poor … Other than my mom's welfare check we'd get money from [my step-father's] petty drug deals or selling stolen property. But we'd also periodically scrap cars as a family, selling the metal; or [he] would sometimes buy cars, clean them up and sell them for a profit … Our lives were an endless day-to-day hustle, never knowing where our next meal might come from, living always on the edge of chance and opportunity.

Bruce B., adult child of two incarcerated parents

Having all these kids was hard in the South. Black people could not get good jobs in the 1950s. But my mother was lucky. Some White people helped her by giving her a job as a maid. So it was easier to take care of us.

Betty M., adult child of an incarcerated father

Several studies have attempted to quantify the economic impact of incarceration on families and children. The Fragile Families and Child Wellbeing Study compared children of incarcerated parents to other low-income, urban children and found that if a child's father is incarcerated the child is 25 percent more likely to experience material hardship than a child whose father has never been incarcerated and 19 percent more likely to receive public assistance. The same study found if a mother is incarcerated a child is 11 percent more likely to receive public assistance.[7] Other studies have reported that children of incarcerated parents are more likely than other kids to live in households characterized by economic strain.[8]

Especially if a parent has been contributing to or providing for the family's income, his/her incarceration will affect the family's financial life.

[After my father's incarceration] we were immediately plunged into poverty and my mother reluctantly went to work.

Pam H., adult child of an incarcerated father

My mother struggled to support my brother and me … we were on welfare, and we did not have a car. We took the city bus to the store for groceries.

Danielle C., adult child of an incarcerated father

The light bill wasn't paid, the mortgage was late. Money was constantly coming in and leaving just as quickly.

Hollie O., adult child of an incarcerated father

The change in a family's financial status is often not only devastating, but also long-lasting. The story of one contributor to this book suggests how difficult it is for children and families to emerge from the poverty that accompanies parental incarceration.

[When my father got incarcerated] our economic state collapsed. My mother had to find a full-time job. She could not tell anyone she had a college degree, or she would be seen as over-educated … I was a very good student, so the plan [had been] that I would go away to college … [But] I immediately had to find a job, and became an after school and weekend nanny.

Shari O., adult child of an incarcerated father

Regardless of its cause, the adverse effects of family poverty on child development have been well documented.[9]

Basic Care

Although many of the risks they face are well recognized, there are almost no empirical studies that examine how children of prisoners are sheltered and fed, or how their physical health is maintained before, during and after parental incarceration. Research on previous generations of prisoners' families identified undesirable living conditions, including older, poor-quality, high-density housing; lack of transportation; increased child health problems like anemia and asthma; and lack of adequate health care services.[10] We need to know more, however.

Food and Nutrition

Beyond what is known about poor children, we have very little information about the diet and nutrition of the children of incarcerated parents. Our contributors' stories suggest some children of prisoners may receive inadequate nutrition *prior to* parental incarceration.

Nikki was my best friend, and we played with Whopper. Their parents used drugs and went to jail, too. Nikki's house was little but it was clean and there was always food there because her mother sold drugs. But Whopper's parents were what my dad called "hope-to-die dope fiends." At their apartment, there was never any food except a package of hot dogs in the refrigerator.

Jessamyn R., adult child of two incarcerated parents

I remember this one day [while living with my father]. There wasn't anything in my house to eat and this guy named Chris, a close friend of my dad's, made me some beans. I don't even like beans, but they were all we had.

Moe-Moe S., adult child of an incarcerated father

However, many children also face inadequate nutrition, food insecurity or hunger during a parent's incarceration.

There was never a shortage of drug dealers who would step forward when [my mother] went to jail to take care of me until she was released. They would drive around selling their product while I sat in the back seat and ate copious amounts of soda, chips and candy.

Percy L., adult child of two incarcerated parents

Though we narrowly avoided losing our house, we did lose our car. Pancakes were often what we had for dinner, for meat was too expensive.

Shari O., adult child of an incarcerated father

Housing

Wherever a child is placed when a custodial parent is incarcerated, that child will probably experience emotional and material instability.[11] Yet research and our contributors' reflections provide insight into the exact nature of some of this material instability.

Women whose partners are incarcerated face an elevated risk of housing insecurity.[12] If a child's mother is living with a partner who becomes incarcerated, that mother and child's housing is often jeopardized, especially if the housing is subsidized and even if the mother has not been involved in any criminal activity.[13] Mothers report "missing" or "skipping" rent or mortgage payments, and are at an increased risk of losing public housing as a child ages.[14]

One of our contributors speaks to longstanding housing insecurity that seems tied to criminal activity, poverty and incarceration.

[My family was] … always living in the worst part of town or in some rudimentary makeshift home out in the middle of nowhere.

Bruce B., adult child of two incarcerated parents

Another contributor recognizes the more direct link between housing insecurity and criminal activity and/or incarceration.

Luckily my grandma was stable enough to keep her house in a nice working-class neighborhood until my Mom's legal bills forced her to sell it.

Natalie C., adult child of an incarcerated mother

The risk of housing insecurity often continues after parental incarceration.

[After her release] my mom was living in a shelter in Livermore, which meant that I was also staying in a shelter for the summer. When I got there, my mom was so happy to see me … The happiness soon came to an end, though, when my mom and I were kicked out of the shelter. After staying in a motel in Livermore, we moved to Richmond, to another shelter.

Alisha M., adult child of an incarcerated mother

In 2004, Human Rights Watch estimated that over a five-year period, more than 3.5 million people with criminal convictions would be denied access to housing assistance as a result of "one-strike" policies, and their partners and children might also lose access to public housing.[15]

Many other aspects of the basic care of prisoners' children also remain unexplored. For example, children's general health status and their utilization of pediatric services are unknown, while most of the few existing studies related to their health care address mental health services for behavioral problems.[16] The need for investigation in this area is highlighted by a recent study that found an association between parental incarceration and physical health disorders – including high cholesterol, asthma and migraine – in young adults.[17]

Caregivers and Placements

Almost all research on the living arrangements of children who have experienced parental incarceration has addressed the periods when their parents are locked up. Except for reports by jailed and imprisoned parents on their own living arrangements in relation to their children, there are few reports of where these children lived before their parents were incarcerated and virtually no information on where they live after their parents are released.

Prior to Parental Incarceration

National research has found that almost half of imprisoned fathers and almost two-thirds of imprisoned mothers report living with at least one of their children immediately before they were incarcerated.[18] However, the high prevalence of multi-partnered fertility in this population suggests that few of these parents will have been living with *all* of their minor children. This suggestion is supported by smaller studies that examined pre-incarceration parent–child living arrangements by child and found that only about half of the children of incarcerated mothers and about two out of five children of incarcerated fathers reported living with those parents prior to parental incarceration.[19]

In fact, many children of prisoners have never lived with their parents who have been incarcerated. Among contributors to this book, more than one in four never lived with their parent who was incarcerated. The Fragile Families Study found that at least 15 percent of ever-incarcerated fathers are no longer in a relationship with the mothers of their children at the time of the children's birth.[20] This proportion appears to increase with children's age. A study of randomly selected middle and high school students compared children of ever-incarcerated parents with all other children and found that about 40 percent of the children of ever-incarcerated fathers had never lived with their fathers, in contrast to about 9 percent of other children.[21] This study also found that about 20 percent of the children of ever-incarcerated mothers had never lived with their mothers, compared to less than 1 percent of other children.

This body of research tells us that since most children of prisoners were living with another caregiver before their parents went to jail or prison, only a minority experience a change of living arrangements when their parents are incarcerated.

During Parental Incarceration

When a parent goes to prison or jail, the degree to which children experience disruption of their care and placement will depend upon the prior parent–child living and caregiving arrangement. For example, when children have never lived with their arrested and incarcerated parents, the effects of parental arrest and incarceration on their care and placement may be negligible.

> I don't know if my father's incarceration affected me. I never saw him, not once.
>
> *Betty M., adult child of an incarcerated father*

The majority of the children of prisoners live with their other birth parent during parental incarceration, just as they did prior to the incarceration. Nearly nine out of ten imprisoned fathers and four out of ten imprisoned mothers report having at least one child living with the child's other parent.[22]

Up to 15 percent of imprisoned parents report that at least one of their children lives with a grandparent, including about 12 percent of imprisoned fathers and about 45 percent of imprisoned mothers.[23] Some children in this group will have lived with their grandparents all or most of their lives, while others will have been placed in their grandparents' care as the result of their parents' arrest/incarceration.

> My grandmother has pretty much taken care of me my entire life.
>
> *James C., adult child of two incarcerated parents*

> I was primarily raised by my paternal grandparents but I also had full access to my maternal grandparents, as their households were separated by a mere two blocks.
>
> *Willard J., adult child of two incarcerated parents*

More than half of the children of incarcerated mothers are cared for by grandparents after their mother's arrest.[24]

> While I was incarcerated, my in-laws drove 150 miles each way to the prison almost every week to visit me, bringing my daughters ... I was lucky that my family supported everything I wanted with my kids.
>
> *Jasmine, adult child of an incarcerated father*

In general, kinship care provides more stability for children, increases their satisfaction with their placement and reduces their behavioral problems; for children in foster care, it also reduces the rate at which they return to out-of-home care.[25] However, in the case of grandparent caregivers, there are concerns that they are older, poorer, more often single, and less formally educated than non-relative caregivers.[26] This can often mean difficulty in caring for troubled children.

A smaller number of prisoners' children live in other kinship settings. About 6 percent of imprisoned fathers and 23 percent of imprisoned mothers report that they have at least one child living in the care of non-parent, non-grandparent relatives.[27] Typically, these are female relatives, including aunts and older sisters.

I'm unsure when this happened but one day my mother got my little brother and I and took us to California to my aunt, my father's sister. My mom was going to prison and had nowhere else to take us. My aunt agreed to take me.

Marcus R., adult child of two incarcerated parents

Later my mom was arrested again and this time went to jail for 16 months. I was in my second year of film school and doing very well there. My main concern was for my little sister, who had just started kindergarten … I brought my sister to live with me in my college apartment … It was really difficult to work 20 hours a week, attend my college classes and also take care of my sister … [but] somehow it all worked out, and I was glad we could be together.

Natalie C., adult child of an incarcerated mother

However, the extended families of prisoners' children may share the strain and instability that characterize the households of incarcerated parents.

Some prisoners' children live with personal or family friends during parental incarceration. Very little is known about these settings or their effects on children. Several of our contributors turned to peers or adult friends for support.

Since I couldn't find the unconditional love bouncing from different homes while my mother seesawed through the Milwaukee County Jail doors, I found comfort with the hooligans in the streets. It was like we understood each other. Despite us deriving from different family backgrounds, we shared a common bond of struggle.

Manuel R.W., adult child of an incarcerated mother

However, living arrangements with friends are unstable at best, and many children in these settings – like our contributors – become essentially homeless.

[After my mother's arrest] … I ended up moving in with one of my closest friend's cousins. She soon became like a second mother to me, and I told people she was my god-mom. She treated me like I was her own daughter. I always felt very lucky to have found someone like her in my life. Still I missed my mom, but tried not to think about her … One day … I got in trouble for stealing from Target. Because of this, my god-mom said I needed to [leave].

Alisha M., adult child of an incarcerated mother

[My mother and I] ended up moving from motel to motel, staying with her druggie buddies while she prostituted herself to buy more crack. I finally got fed up with it and left. I stayed with a friend of mine and his family. Back before my mother lost control of her addiction Josh had got into a fight with his father. She let him stay with us until he and his father could patch things up. Josh's father remembered that and took me in … I got a job at McDonald's. Things were going alright for a little while until Josh had to go to some youth program mandated by the court and dad and his brother were going on a trip. I was back out on the streets.

Kris B., adult child of an incarcerated mother

Another small group of prisoners' children live in foster care during parental incarceration. Although children of incarcerated parents are four to five times more likely to have contact with the foster care system than other low-income urban children,[28] only about 2 percent of imprisoned fathers and 11 percent of imprisoned mothers report having a child in foster care.[29] There are no studies that identify the proportion of these children who enter the child welfare system as the result of parental incarceration and the proportion who are already in the system when their parents are arrested. For incarcerated mothers, at least, there is good evidence that child removals are typically related to maternal drug addiction and precede maternal incarceration by one to two years.[30] Among our contributors, about one in five spent some time in foster care. While this might seem like a relatively high proportion compared to published data, it is a "lifetime rate," something that has never been measured among children of incarcerated parents.

> The first few foster homes I was placed in were a shock to me. No matter how kind and considerate they might be, I did not appreciate strangers taking care of me. It may be hard to believe, but I actually ran away from foster homes to seek out my mother at bars and drug haunts I knew her to frequent.
>
> *Percy L., adult child of an incarcerated mother*

Once settled, some contributors found positive aspects to foster care:

> [The foster mother] got enough money from all of us to have some housekeepers and the house was always clean. It was too far from the prison to visit my mom. She wrote letters and I wrote back until she stopped writing when I was 10. [My brother and I] stayed in that foster home until I was 14.
>
> *Abel H., adult child of two incarcerated parents*

> When I was starting second grade, my mom went to prison for stabbing someone. I don't know where my father was at that time … I didn't see my father again until I was an adult but now I know he was incarcerated in prison for most of that time. While they were both gone, my sister and I lived with my aunt, but a couple of times they took us away from her and we were in foster care. The first place they put us was with this Mexican couple that didn't speak English. My sister ran away and left me there. Then they moved me to a white lady's home; her name was Mrs. Vann, and she was very nice to me. They let me go back home when my mom got out.
>
> *Shadow, adult child of two incarcerated parents*

But others had a harsher experience.

> I went to go check on my brother, but I didn't see him. I asked one of the [shelter] staff where he was and she told me that he was placed with a family an hour earlier. I didn't know where my dad was and they had just taken my brother from me.
>
> *Moe-Moe S., adult child of an incarcerated father*

Among both incarcerated parents and their children, involvement in the child welfare system is often seen as a catastrophe.

> When we got into the car, [the social worker] explained to me who she was and that my brother and I would be placed in a foster home together. As soon as she mentioned CPS, I knew that my life would be over.
>
> *Moe-Moe S., adult child of an incarcerated father*

While this last statement might seem melodramatic, in fact families involved in both the criminal justice and child welfare systems are almost twice as likely to experience termination of parental rights as other families with children in foster care.[31] So, placement in foster care may mean that a child will never again live with his or her incarcerated parent.

Finally, a very small proportion of prisoners' children live with "others." This designation refers to children whose living situation does not fall within the category of family, friends or foster care or whose whereabouts are unknown.

> I started staying at the YMCA Youth Shelter … [The director] eventually took me into his home.
>
> *Percy L., adult child of an incarcerated mother*

Clearly, where children live during parental incarceration may be critically important to their well-being and future development. There are also implications of placement during this period for parent–child contact, which in turn has implications for parent–child reunification.

After Parental Incarceration

There is almost no information available about where children live after parental incarceration or the rate at which incarcerated parents reunify with their children. Among public school students who have experienced parental incarceration, rates of parent–child reunification are disturbingly low, with only 13 percent of the children of ever-incarcerated fathers studied living with their dads, compared to more than half of children whose fathers had never been incarcerated.[32] Among children of ever-incarcerated mothers, the same study found 50 percent were living with their moms, compared to more than 90 percent of children whose mothers had never been incarcerated. These findings are somewhat consistent with other reports in the literature, which found rates of full mother–child reunification of 25 to 70 percent for formerly incarcerated mothers,[33] and very consistent with the experience of contributors to this book: about half of those with an incarcerated mother lived with her after incarceration while less than 15 percent of those with an incarcerated father resided with him after paternal incarceration.

Changes of Placement

While research suggests that many children of incarcerated parents live with their other birth parent and do not change placement *as the result of parental incarceration*, there is strong evidence that residential instability[34] and multiple placements[35] are norms for this population. For example, an early study of the children of urban families involved in the criminal justice system found that less than one in nine had lived continuously with a single primary caregiver since birth – including those who had never known or lived with their incarcerated parent.[36] Similarly, among the contributors to this book, more than two-thirds experienced multiple placements, many of those unrelated to parental incarceration. The association of multiple placements with child behavioral problems is well documented[37] and undoubtedly contributes to negative long-term outcomes among children of prisoners.

Guidance

As a result of multiple factors, including lack/loss of resources and changes in placement, the direction, guidance and supervision provided to children of incarcerated parents become particularly important. However, the same factors that reduce the quality of their material care also affect the guidance these children receive.

Family Support

The Fragile Families and Child Wellbeing Study reveals that it is not just the loss of income that makes families of incarcerated parents vulnerable. In households with two parents, families may be doubly stressed when one parent loses his/her partner and co-parent to incarceration.[38] Describing her mother's reaction to her father's incarceration, one contributor suggests how many levels of loss a child may feel after a parent goes to jail or prison:

> Years later [after my father was arrested], within a counseling setting, a therapist observed that it must have been really traumatic losing both parents on the same day … I missed [my father] to the point of paralyzing grief and there was no one to talk to about it.
>
> *Pam H., adult child of an incarcerated father*

Children's reactions to and recovery from losses are dependent upon the emotional support they receive in those circumstances.[39] But parental incarceration often removes supports from children's lives. For example, while maternal grandparents are ubiquitous when mothers are incarcerated, paternal incarceration has been found to decrease the frequency of children's contact with their paternal grandparents.[40] For these and other reasons, children of prisoners may receive minimal support while their parents are locked up, leaving them disadvantaged in their attempts to address and overcome loss.

> That first time, [my mom] was only in jail a few days. I don't remember her being gone; no one really told me what was going on … To make things worse, my sister was only 2

years old, and my dad was drinking very heavily. A lot of childcare fell on me. I remember many nights around that time when I was trying to do my homework and take care of my sister with my father drunk and berating me.

Natalie C., adult child of an incarcerated mother

You might expect that a woman who marries a child molester would not be emotionally healthy and my mother wasn't. [After my father's incarceration] she used too much medication and was a workaholic ... It was easiest for me to focus on external things and get along on a superficial level.

Jasmine, adult child of an incarcerated father

But many families carry on and do well for their children after a parent's incarceration, providing strong, positive direction and guidance.

Since my mom was a single mother, she raised me to be a very independent woman.

Sharika Y., adult child of an incarcerated father

My grandmother always spoke the world of my father, so I learned to love him from the love that flowed through her ... She suffered dearly, more than any of us, having to see her son under the conditions allowed. But she never gave up on him.

David S., adult child of an incarcerated father

I used to question my mom about my name ... [and she said] "Tony, I understand you believe it's not fair to be named after your father. At the same time, don't let his actions make you think you're less of a person. If you don't want to go down the same road your dad is on, then you set a new meaning for Tony Shavers III. Set a positive example for Tony Shavers IV, so that he may take ownership and speak with purpose that he is named after a great father."

Tony S., adult child of an incarcerated father

Children's Models

Children's natural role models are their parents. However, when parents are absent, children will seek guidance from others. The disadvantaged communities, rough neighborhoods and highly stressed families of the majority often offer unsuitable models for prisoners' children to emulate.

Cliff was an unconventionally fun step-father. He never had a job, but he had plenty of free time to play and he played as if he were a big kid who followed no rules. He would take us fishing late at night at the fish hatchery, where the fish were so eager to eat that they would take a baitless hook as soon as it touched the water's surface. We'd drive around raiding people's gardens for vegetables to go with our fish dinners. We'd break into warehouses and steal cases of food; we'd catch hundreds of pigeons, filling pillowcases full as we'd pluck the birds from their nightly roosts beneath restaurants that hung over the Columbia River; and we'd smoke lots of marijuana.

Bruce B., adult child of two incarcerated parents

The void that a father's absence creates in a boy's life has to be filled in the ways that children fill their unmet needs, often by reaching out to people immediately available to them ... Many of the older guys that were accessible to me were struggling with problems created by their own deprivations. My attachments to them were made out of desperation to be accepted by older male figures. By my early teens, I was cutting school, hanging around bars, delivering weed and drinking. My mother had completely lost control of me and I came and went as I pleased.

Mike C., adult child of an incarcerated father

Education

Formal guidance for children is provided by our educational institutions. In addition to instruction, schools provide a wealth of relational and social resources for children, many of which also provide guidance.

Historically, schools have not been effective in providing guidance and resources for children of prisoners. Beginning with a 1965 study,[41] many researchers have found children of the incarcerated have lower academic achievement and/or are more likely to fail or drop out of school.[42] Less than half of the children in one study expressed interest in school, and a third reported failing a grade.[43] Murray and Farrington's examination of delinquent behavior found large differences between the truancy and school failure rate of boys whose parents are incarcerated and those who did not have incarcerated parents.[44] Stories from our contributors support these findings.

School was not a positive experience for me. I hated it and didn't want to go.

Jessamyn R., adult child of two incarcerated parents

I would go to school very sad because I didn't want my friends to know where my dad was. Instead of me being focused on books and maybe dating I was thinking of my dad. It was hard to feel complete as a teenager because in the back of your mind you always want to be with your dad.

Sharika Y., adult child of an incarcerated father

[My family's] lifestyle was incredibly unstable and there was always a lot of moving around, house to house and school to school. None of us kids graduated. I myself attended at least two separate schools for every grade. I did not complete the sixth grade and still attended three different schools; I spent a half a year in the seventh grade and attended two schools; I did a few months in eighth grade and two schools; and I spent a few months in the ninth grade at two regular schools and one alternative school. After the sixth grade, I did not do any schoolwork and I ditched class at least two days a week ... By the time I was 15, I had completely quit school, become a full-time meth user, and frequently carried a gun.

Bruce B., adult child of two incarcerated parents

Towards the end of my eighth grade year, I got the chicken pox and missed months of school. When I got better, there might have been two-and-a-half months left of the year. I never went back. I know my report card listed 152 days absent. But they passed the entire eighth grade that year, sending them on to high school just to get rid of them then three weeks into my ninth grade year, the county opened a new high school. I ended up having to leave all my friends and attend this new school. I dropped out instead. At this time, my mother's crack addiction was so consuming that she didn't care. All told, from kindergarten through the ninth grade, I went to a total of ten different schools.

Kris B., adult child of an incarcerated mother

Yet, in a more recent meta-analysis of 40 studies, Murray and colleagues found that parental incarceration does not appear to *cause* poor educational performance.[45] This suggests that most children of prisoners who don't do well in school have academic problems for the same reasons as similar children who don't have incarcerated parents.

Conclusions

Care and guidance are critical experiences in children's lives and have a profound effect on their developmental outcomes. Most children of prisoners are disadvantaged in this arena, experiencing economically strained households, the effects of poverty on housing and nutrition, highly stressed caregivers, multiple changes of placement and/or lack of appropriate guidance. It is not surprising that a large minority follow in the footsteps of their incarcerated parents.

Yet, while negative outcomes of poor quality care and guidance are disturbing, they are also a source of hope because these elements of children's lives can always be improved.

They let me out [of the Youth Authority] when I was 17 and my probation officer helped me get emancipated. I tracked down my uncle in Carson and moved in with him and his family. I have stayed out of trouble since then.

Abel H., adult child of two incarcerated parents

I got released in 2001, after 16 years in Pennsylvania and federal prisons. ... I visited my son and granddaughter, who live in another state, and they came to visit me. At first, we were very careful with each other and my son was emotionally distant. But over the past ten years, our relationship has become more normal and we now disagree, have arguments and even ignore each other for periods of time like other fathers and adult sons. I never had a chance to do it this way with my own dad. My father was a tough sonofabitch and a bad man by society's standards. I still get mad at him. I still wish I'd gotten more of him and from him. He shouldn't have been gone all the time, I needed him. But the time he spent with me was spent trying to educate and protect me and those are some of the most important things a parent can do.

Michael C., adult child of an incarcerated father

The stories with the best outcomes and the best endings are those of children whose mothers and fathers changed their lives and returned home to parent their kids. Reflecting on his family's reentry story as the lawyer he has become, contributor Daniel B. writes:

> Looking out into that crowd of youthful faces, I was besieged by feelings of pride, sadness, and shame. Alongside these emotions, though, was the prevailing sense of resiliency that still defines our family.

Daniel's story provides hope for others.

Notes

1   Gemmill WN. (1915). Employment and compensation of prisoners. *Journal of the American Institute of Criminal Law and Criminology*, 6(4): 507–521; Weyand LD. (1920). Study of wage payment to prisoners as a penal method. *Journal of Criminal Law and Criminology*, 11(2): 222–271.

2   Aronovici C. (1913). Punishing the innocent. *Annals of the American Academy of Social and Political Science*, 46: 142–146; Fenton F. (1959). *The Prisoner's Family*. Palo Alto, CA: Pacific Books; Morris P. (1965). *Prisoners and Their Families*. London: George Allen & Unwin; Schneller D. (1978). *The Prisoner's Family*. San Francisco: R&E Research Associates; Swan A. (1981). *Families of Black Prisoners: Survival and Progress*. Boston: G.K. Hall.

3   Phillips S, Erklani A, Keeler GP, Costello E, Angold A. (2006). Disentangling the risks: Parent criminal justice involvement and children's exposure to family risks. *Criminology and Public Policy*, 5 (4): 688–702; Schwartz-Soicher O, Geller A, Garfinkel I. (2011). The effect of paternal incarceration on material hardship. *Social Service Review*, 85(3): 447–473; Wildeman C. (2014). Paternal incarceration, child homelessness and the invisible consequences of mass incarceration. *Annals of the American Academy of Social and Political Science*, 651(1): 74–96.

4   Phillips et al. *Ibid.*

5   Davis JB. (2006). Distribution of property crime and police arrest rates across Los Angeles neighborhoods. *Western Criminology Review*, 7(3): 7–26; Henry B, Avshalom C, Moffitt TE, Silva PA. (1996). Temperamental and familial predictors of violent and non-violent criminal convictions. *Developmental Psychology*, 32: 614–623; Sampson R and Lauritsen J. (1994).Violent victimization and offending: Individual, situational, and community-level risk factors. In AJ Reiss, JA Roth (Eds.) *Understanding and Preventing Violence*, 3: 451–481. Washington, D.C.: National Academy Press; Zilanawala A, Pilkauskas N. (2012). Material hardship and child socioemotional behaviors. *Children and Youth Services Review*, 34(4): 814–825.

6   Glaze LE, Marushak LM. (2008). *Parents in Prison and Their Minor Children*. NCJ222984. Washington, D.C.: US Department of Justice, Bureau of Justice Statistics.

7   Center for Research on Child Well-Being. (2008). *Parental incarceration and child well-being in fragile families*. Fragile Families Research Brief 42 (April, 2008). Available at: www.fragilefamilies.princeton. edu/briefs/ResearchBrief42.pdf.

8   LaVigne N, Davies E, Brazzell D. (2008). *Broken Bonds: Understanding and Addressing the Needs of Children with Incarcerated Parents*. Washington, D.C.: The Urban Institute Justice Policy Center.

9   Brooks-Dunn J, Duncan GJ. (1997).The effects of poverty on children. *The Future of Children*, 7(2): 55–71.

10 Johnston D. (1992). *The Children of Offenders Study: A Report to the California Assembly Office of Research*. Pasadena, CA: Center for Children of Incarcerated Parents; *Prison Visitation Project*. (1993). Needs Assessment of Children Whose Parents Are Incarcerated. Richmond. VA: Department of Mental Health, Mental Retardation and Substance Abuse Services; Schneller. *Ibid;* Swan. *Ibid;* Zalba S. (1964). *Women Prisoners and Their Families*. Sacramento, CA: Department of Social Welfare and Department of Corrections.

11 Hairston CF. (2007). *Focus on Children with Incarcerated Parents: An Overview of the Research Literature*. Baltimore: The Annie E. Casey Foundation.

12 Geller A, Franklin AW. (2014). Paternal incarceration and the housing security of urban mothers. *Journal of Marriage and Family*, 76(2): 411–427.

13 *Ibid.*

14 *Ibid.*

15 Carey C. (2014). *No Second Chance: People with Criminal Records Denied Access to Public Housing*. New York: Human Rights Watch.

16 Murray J, Farrington DP, Sekol I. (2012). Children's antisocial behavior, mental health, drug use and educational performance after parental incarceration. *Psychological Bulletin*, 138(2): 175–210; Phillips S, Burns BJ, Wagner HR, Kramer TL, Robbins JM. (2002). Parental incarceration among youth receiving mental health services. *Journal of Child and Family Studies*, 11(4): 385–399.

17 Lee RD, Fang X, Luo F. (2013). The impact of parental incarceration on the physical and mental health of young adults. *Pediatrics*, 131(4): e1188–1195.

18 Glaze, Marushak. *Ibid.*

19 McGowan BG, Blumenthal KL. (1978). *Why Punish the Children?* Hackensack, NJ: National Council on Crime and Delinquency; Walker C. (2003). *Parents Behind Bars Talk about Their Children: A Survey of Allegheny County Jail Inmates*. Pittsburgh, PA: Pittsburgh Child Guidance Foundation; Zalba. *Ibid.*

20 Western B, McLanahan S. (2000). Fathers behind bars: The impact of incarceration on family formation. *Contemporary Perspectives in Family Research*, 2: 309–324.

21 Johnston D. (2002). What works: Children of prisoners. In Gadsden V. (Ed.), *Heading Home: Offender Reintegration in the Family – What Works*. Lanham, MD: American Correctional Association.

22 Glaze, Marushak, *Ibid.*

23 *Ibid.*

24 *Ibid.*; Walker. *Ibid.*

25 Conway T, Hutson R. (2007). Is kinship care good for kids? *Center for Law and Social Policy*. www.clasp.org/publications/is_kinship_care_good.pdf; Winokur M, Holtan A, Batchelder K. (2014). Kinship care for the safety, permanency, and well-being of children removed from the home for maltreatment: A systematic review. *Campbell Systematic Reviews*, 10(2).

26 Ehrle J, Green R, Main R. (2003). *Kinship Foster Care: Custody, Hardships, and Services*. Snapshots of America's Families III. No. 14. Washington, D.C.: The Urban Institute.

27 Glaze, Marushak. *Ibid.*

28 Center for Research on Child Well-Being. *Ibid.*

29 Glaze, Marushak. *Ibid.*

30 Ehrensaft M, Khashu A, Ross T, Wamsley M. (2003). *Patterns of Critical Conviction and Incarceration among Mothers of Children in Foster Care in New York City*. New York: Vera Institute of Justice.

31 D'Andrade AC, Valdez M. (2012). Reunifying from behind bars. *Social Work in Public Health*, 27(6): 616–636; Incarcerated Parents Work Group. (2014, March 18). *Incarcerated Parents and Their Children in the Juvenile Dependency System: A Judicial Training*. Presented to the Los Angeles County Superior Court, Juvenile Dependency Division, Monterey Park, CA.

32 Johnston. (2002). *Ibid.*

33 Arditti JA, Few-Demo AL. (2006). Mothers' reentry into family life following incarceration. *Criminal Justice Policy Review*, 17: 103; Hunter, SM. (1984). The relationship between women offenders and their children. *Dissertation Abstracts International*. University Microfilms No. 8424436; Johnston D. (1995a). Child custody issues of women prisoners: A preliminary report from the CHICAS Project. *The Prison Journal*, 75(2): 222–239; Kubiak SP, Kasiborski N, Karim N, Schmittel E. (2012). Does subsequent criminal justice involvement predict foster care and termination of parental rights for children born to incarcerated women? *Social Work in Public Health*, 27(1–2): 129–147.

34 Tasca M, Rodriguez N, Zatz MS. (2011). Family and residential instability in the context of maternal and paternal incarceration. *Criminal Justice and Behavior*, 38(3): 231–247.

35 Baunach PJ. (1984). *Mothers in Prison*. Newark, NJ: Rutgers University Press; Johnston. (2002). *Ibid.; Zalba. *Ibid.*

36 Johnston. (1992). *Ibid.*

37 Newton RR, Litrownik AJ, Landsverk JA. (2000). Children and youth in foster care: Disentangling the relationship between problem behaviors and number of placements.*Child Abuse and Neglect*, 24 (10): 1363–1374.

38 Wildeman C, Schnittker J, Turney K. (2012). Despair by association: Mental health of mothers with children by recently incarcerated fathers. *American Sociological Review*, 77(2): 216–243.

39 Kalter N, Lohnes KL, Chasin J, Cain AC, Dunning S, Rowan J. (2002–2003). The adjustment of parentally bereaved children. *Journal of Death and Dying*, 46(1): 15–34; Wyman PA, Cowen EL, Work WC, Parker GR. (1991). Developmental and family milieu correlates of resilience in urban children who have experienced life stress. *American Journal of Community Psychiatry*, 19(3): 405–426.

40 Turney K. (2014c). The intergenerational consequences of mass incarceration: Implications for children's contact with grandparents. *Social Forces*, 93(1): 299–327.

41 Friedman S, Esselstyn TC. (1965). The adjustment of children to parental absence due to imprisonment. *Federal Probation*, 29: 55–59.

42 Stanton A. (1980). *When Mothers Go to Jail*. Lexington, MA: Lexington Books.

43 Trice A, Brewster J. (2004). The effects of maternal incarceration on adolescent children. *Journal of Police and Criminal Psychology*, 19: 27–35.

44 Murray J, Farrington D. (2007). The effects of parental imprisonment on children. *Crime and Justice: A Review of Research*, 37: 133–206.

45 Murray J, Farrington DP, Sekol I. (2012). Children's antisocial behavior, mental health, drug use and educational performance after parental incarceration. *Psychological Bulletin*, 138(2): 175–210.

PERSONAL STORIES

Man of the Year by Pamela Hayes

He was the fair-haired boy of every company he ever worked for. He read three newspapers a day. He had been a high school sports hero. He was movie star handsome. And, he was a con man. His stylized armed robbery was embezzling and writing bad checks. His drug of choice was gambling. He swept my Indiana farm-girl mother off her feet and less than six months after their fairytale wedding at a Methodist Episcopal church, I was born. We began life well, the three of us. He was the national manager for a chain of department stores and we lived in great apartments and hotels all over the country until I started school. That was 1951. My brother was born the following June in the same year that my father was named the Chamber of Commerce's Man of the Year.

It began shortly after – long absences from home, my mother crying on the phone. Then there came a miraculous reconciliation that moved us across the country to California where my father already had a job and a house. Life was good. My mother and father purchased and operated a couple of small department stores in the surrounding towns and our family became relatively high-profile – being new and shiny – in the community where we lived. My father's first arrest hit the papers and life came to an abrupt halt. He went to prison and my mother moved into her own survival mode. She angrily explained (we were ages nine and four) that we were now from a "broken home" and everyone would expect us to fail. Therefore, we must excel at everything we did.

Despite the press coverage, I did not know that my father was incarcerated until I was bullied by some classmates. My mother never spoke of it. Years later, within a counseling setting, a therapist observed that it must have been really traumatic losing both parents on the same day. That is precisely what happened. Although she provided for our basic needs, there was not a shred of humanity left in my mother. Oddly, our father had been the one to teach us jokes and songs and games, and had also been the ultimate listener offering sage advice. I missed him to point of paralyzing grief and there was no one to talk to about it.

We were immediately plunged into poverty and my mother went to work. Even at our young ages, we had no childcare once my brother started kindergarten. We readied ourselves for school and at the end of my school day I picked him up on the school playground where he had been unattended for a couple of hours. In the summers, we were on our own with a chore list that would rival that of a stay-at-home mom. When I think now of how we were left without any oversight, it scares me to death.

Four years later, my father was released to a nearby honor camp. My mother was newly engaged to a wealthy local businessman and was decked out in furs and a three-carat diamond when she arrived with us in tow to visit my father. He, in contrast, was decked out in prison garb – quite the departure from the custom-made suit I'd seen him in on that last day. In a futile attempt to mask her rage, my mother came off as looking silly and self-righteous.

It was not his last incarceration. There were others to follow. My mother married the businessman who, as it turns out, was a remarkably wonderful step-father. Together, they had a child eleven months to the day after they married. My mother constructed a new family of three who shared the same name and, after my father's final release, sent us across the country to him while she and her new family traveled the world. But for food and shelter, my brother and I supported ourselves until high school graduation when we bolted.

For good or for ill, my brother and I had done what she ordered, mostly because our mother was both verbally and physically abusive. Between us there were few less-than-perfect report cards as we became more-than-perfect children. In the end, my brother managed to work his way through an accelerated PhD program at a major university in the Midwest and become the Director of Institutional Research at one of the most highly regarded private universities in the nation. I managed to get myself through college, earn an MBA, and enjoy what could be called a charmed career. Ironically, much of my professional life was centered on the *inside* of the juvenile justice system working in child protective services, delinquency, and adoptions. The "call" to do this work was no doubt fueled by my own abandonment experiences. To the kids I worked with I could say with a high degree of integrity, "I get it." But for all the success of my brother's and my professional lives, our personal lives suffered through a string of bad marriages. The upside is that from the painful lessons of our young lives, we paid attention and are probably among some of the best parents on the planet.

As for my father, by some quirk of fate, we ended up living near one another. Following his final prison term – which was still in the pre-background-check days – he was once again the fair-haired boy of the company he worked for. He retired at 77. He still read three newspapers a day and was recognized as a former football hero; he was still handsome, and he was still a con man. He lived into his eighties and my brother and I were with him in his hospital room when he drew his last breath. From his estate, we inherited 123 spotless neckties and a bowling trophy.

★★★

A Rocky Start by Willard C. Jimerson

I am currently incarcerated and I have been judicially penalized for over 18 years. I am in the last stretch of a 20-year sentence for the unfortunate crime of murder. I have been incarcerated since my thirteenth year of existence and I am now 31 years of age.

My family knows me as Little Willie, my childhood friends know me as Willard, and my recent acquaintances refer to me as Willie Jay. The State of Washington Department of Corrections knows me as Inmate #727804.

I am an African American male who grew up in an economically deprived section of the City of Seattle called the Central District. Known as the "CD" by its residents, it is referred to as the "Crime District" or "Criminal District" by myself and my cohorts.

I was primarily raised by my paternal grandparents but I also had full access to my maternal grandparents, as their households were separated by a mere two blocks. I did not live with my grandparents due to an untimely death of one of my parents or another disaster. No, this was not the case. I lived with my grandparents because my parents were more concerned with the hustle and grind of the streets than they were with parenting.

At the time of my birth, my mother was incarcerated at a correctional facility known as the Washington Correctional Center for Women. It was also called Purdy, after the small unincorporated community where the prison is located. Because there was no maternity ward in Washington Correctional, my mother was sent to a local hospital to give birth.

I imagine that right after I was delivered, I was whisked away by family members while my mother was escorted back to the prison cell where she would remain for the rest of her sentence. It would be three years before she spent one actual free day in the world with her newest addition to the family. By the time of my mother's release from prison, I had already grown fond of my paternal grandmother and viewed her as my mother.

My parents were active participants in the criminal underpinnings of the city's street life. They were often incarcerated for numerous violations of the law. Around them, I found myself actively engaging in the processes of street life, as well. I became an early participant and, as a result, I got caught up in the juvenile judicial system. I began going to the King County Youth Detention Center by the age of 10.

I was born into this world with more minuses than pluses, a rocky start. The pipeline to prison was definitely made easily accessible to me and others like me, whether they were relatives or members of my community. Many of the valuable lessons I have learned throughout life, and which will remain with me forever, came from this journey.

I was provided with the platform I had to learn from. They say hard-learned lessons are never forgotten. Many of the life-altering changes in my life have been a direct result of the many hardships I have encountered, whether they were the by-product of erroneous teachings, skills, coping mechanisms and/or social disorders that were provided to me.

There are some days in a person's life that they wish had never happened, and the incident that led to my incarceration definitely happened on one of those days. However, I can say that what I have gained in experience and valuable knowledge as the result of that day put things into perspective for me.

My hopes, dreams and aspirations are very well defined now, more real and attainable. I realize that I now must assist and help others in areas where my new-found knowledge has made me most effective.

★★★

The Culture of Incarceration by Bruce Bennett

My name is Bruce L. Bennett, Jr., and a culture of incarceration has dominated my entire life, from my earliest childhood indoctrination against law enforcement to my step-father's frequent incarcerations, from the criminal subculture I knew as family to my own imprison-ment. I have been in prison since December 31, 1993 and, at age 41, I have spent nearly my entire adult life locked in a cage. During my incarceration, I have repeatedly encountered my step-father, I have been cellmates with my nephew, and I have missed my daughters' childhoods.

I was born on August 25, 1970 to inexperienced teenaged parents who did not have supportive families. My parents separated when my earliest memories were just beginning to develop. I spent most of my childhood with my mom.

My first step-father came into our lives when I was four. He was a large and aggressive man who frequently beat my mother until she was bloody, bruised and broken. He moved us around, from town to town, so often that I attended at least two different schools every year, if not three or four. The police discovered my step-father's pot plants one afternoon after I was caught shoplifting. I was eight, and my step-father later beat me with a board that ripped my toenails and left abrasions up and down my legs. I was not being punished for shoplifting; I was being punished for bringing the police to my home, something I would never intentionally do again.

Though I frequently sat crying in some shadowed room while listening to my mom being beaten, I would never call the police nor ask anybody for help. This lifestyle lasted until just days after my eleventh birthday, when some neighbors called the police, who made my step-father leave early in the morning. He would never live with us again.

My second step-father, Cliff, moved in with us a couple of months later. Cliff was 22, an independent outlaw biker (not a club member), and freshly released from prison. His possessions consisted of a motorcycle, one box of clothing and a five-foot boa constrictor. I thought he was one of the coolest guys in the world.

Cliff was an unconventionally fun step-father. He never had a job, but he had plenty of free time to play and he played as if he were a big kid who followed no rules. He would take us fishing late at night at the fish hatchery, where the fish were so eager they would take a baitless hook as soon as it touched the water's surface. Afterward we would drive around and raid people's gardens for vegetables to go with our fish dinners. We'd break into warehouses and steal cases of food; we'd fill pillow cases with pigeons that we'd pluck from their nightly roosts; and we'd smoke lots of marijuana.

But not everything we did was illegal. Cliff would let me drive cars, ride motorcycles, and shoot guns. We'd spend our summers floating on inner tubes in the river. We'd spend our winters making ice rinks by spraying water in layers across the blacktop. Of course, we were dirt poor, always living in the worst part of town or in some rudimentary makeshift home out in the middle of nowhere. Other than my mom's welfare check, we'd get money from Cliff's petty drug deals or selling stolen property. But we'd also periodically scrap cars as a family, selling the metal; sometimes Cliff would buy cars, clean them up and sell them for a profit. We often stole gas, traveling at night and stopping to siphon fuel from random vehicles. Our lives were an endless day-to-day hustle, never knowing where our next meal might come from, living always on the edge of chance and opportunity.

At the age of 11, I was essentially turned loose in the street, free to do almost anything I wanted, and I began to emulate the world around me. I smoked pot every day with Cliff and my mom, and I was welcome at the homes of various drug dealers. I was surrounded almost exclusively by drug dealers, thieves and junkies, so nobody really asked any questions when I'd steal bikes or toys from wealthier kids, and nobody paid much attention when I'd stay out late at night. I periodically watched Cliff get into spontaneous fights, sudden battles with fists, chains or knives, and I, too, began to get into an occasional street fight. Even though we sometimes had no food or money for school supplies, we had all sorts of pets, including giant snakes, lizards and other oddities. Our pets might have been some sort of ironic reflection of the people around us, a human jungle of wild life.

This lifestyle made law enforcement and incarceration a constant presence in our lives. The police would often intrude upon our criminal freedom by raiding our various homes for drugs, taking my mom to jail a couple of times but frequently – if they could catch him – taking Cliff. Whenever Cliff got arrested, he would call constantly on the phone, talking for hours upon hours (this was before jails put time limits on phone calls). Even when there was nobody for Cliff to talk with, we'd just leave the phone off the hook and he could listen to our day or talk to anyone who came by, until the phone would get turned off. My mom visited Cliff at least three days a week and many times I accompanied my mom and little sister to the jail. I grew up visiting Cliff in jail.

My mom was so committed to this incarcerated relationship that she once made a large sign that read "I (heart) you, Cliff" and posted it on a street sign outside the jail. The love sign made the newspaper, *The Columbian*, in 1983. Eventually, Cliff would get out of jail and our wild lives would continue as if he had never been gone.

Cliff hated the police, and my mom never trusted them. Though Cliff's parole prohibited him from associating with other felons, drug dealers, junkies and thieves were almost exclusively the types of people who occupied our social circle. It was a tight circle that only cautiously welcomed newcomers and most of us were constantly worried about criminal consequences and incarceration. Yet instead of functioning as a deterrent, this concern operated more as a positive reinforcement.

My close friendships were with kids who were being nurtured by the same criminal atmosphere. Things were easier this way. It spared me the hassle of making new friends or having to leave the house every time there was a drug deal or some other illicit activity. And, since I had no extended family, this criminal subculture functioned very much as a type of make-believe family for me, my sister and my mom.

This lifestyle was incredibly unstable and there was always a lot of moving around, house to house and school to school. After the sixth grade, I did not do any schoolwork and I ditched class at least two days a week; I attended two or three different schools each year. The other kids in this subculture were doing the same, and we all progressed through a list of drugs from marijuana, alcohol, psychedelic mushrooms, LSD and methamphetamine to just about every street drug imaginable. By the time I was 15, I had completely quit school, become a full-time meth user, and frequently carried a gun. I got arrested for stealing a car, carrying a concealed weapon, and possession of other stolen property.

Eventually, these experiences culminated in a state of utter chaos. My step-father, Cliff, became increasingly deranged from his drug use. When I was 16 and babysitting my little sister, he stormed into our dilapidated trailer and began shooting our pets with a 9mm handgun, leaving the room filled with the odor of gun smoke, blood and dead animals. Before he left, he chopped the phone up with a hatchet, chopped holes in the walls and gave me a small baggie of cocaine as an apology. This was an example of the madness that would later lead to his arrest and return to prison, where my mom and I would hitchhike more than 100 miles to visit him one last time before she separated from him. But Cliff's impact on my life was far from over.

My mom's home and the meth house where I stayed were raided for drugs. My friends and I lived in a constant state of extreme intoxication, and we fired guns so frequently that the home's interior sometimes sounded like a war zone. We used steel pipes to smash most of the kitchen, putting holes in the walls and ceiling and various pieces of furniture. Motorcycle parts were piled in one room, garbage in another, and damaged lives came and went. Many of the people I knew were getting arrested, shot, seriously assaulted or even killed. All but the closest of us began to mistrust one another. After my eighteenth birthday, most of the people I thought of as family were in jail, dead or scattered. My mom moved in with a new boyfriend and found a healthier and more wholesome environment for herself and my step-sister, and I wandered off to another town and fell in love.

I moved in with a girl and her mother. The truth is that I had fallen in love with a girl who came from a tough outlaw family, a girl who had a background similar to my own. This girl and I would struggle to clean up our lives as we became parents but, ultimately, I would fail. At the age of 20, while running around with a couple of old friends who were frequently in and out of jail, I was arrested and sent to prison.

When I first arrived, I saw my step-father, Cliff. At the time, I thought it was good to see a familiar face as I sat next to him in the loud chow hall or the Orientation Room. I didn't give much thought to all those years of visiting him in jail. After orientation, Cliff and I were sent to different prisons and it would be a few years before I saw him again.

Upon my release, I returned to my girlfriend and my two daughters. I got my old job back and I worked hard to be a good dad. I completed an alcohol treatment program, paid all my fines, and made my parole officer happy. But it's difficult to escape a lifestyle and a subculture when it's all you've ever known and it's still surrounding you. My girlfriend and I shared an apartment with her mom and other family members, and many of the people hanging around were ex-prisoners.

At age 22, I was preparing to start my own business (drain cleaning and plumbing). I was trying to be a good father, but I had started drinking again, and my girlfriend and I were struggling in our relationship. We loved each other very much but there were many dysfunctional forces tugging on us from all different directions and I moved out. As I grappled with all these challenges (my outlaw subculture, fatherhood, work, addiction, love), a new and disastrous set of circumstances was about to completely destroy me and leave my daughters with an imprisoned father. For the first time in my life, I was about to meet members of my mom's real family – her sister and my two little cousins.

My aunt came to Washington State with her two daughters, fleeing a man who had beaten and often hospitalized my aunt, once even attacking her with a baseball bat. When they arrived, I empathized with them and promised I would never allow anybody to hurt them again. A few weeks after I turned 23, my aunt's boyfriend, Eric, discovered where she was and followed. Eric had previously spent time in prison and had an anti-establishment personality. Shortly after his arrival, he began to regularly threaten the lives of my aunt and her daughters, as well as the lives of my mom, my little sister, my girlfriend and my two daughters.

On December 22, 1993, at a small social gathering in the apartment shared by my aunt and my girlfriend, Eric began assaulting my aunt. With assistance, I stopped the assault and persuaded Eric to leave with me and two other men. My intent was simply to get Eric away from the women and children; however, within the following two hours, due to my own horrible and immensely misguided decisions, I stabbed Eric to death.

I was arrested for Eric's murder on December 31, 1993, and spent several months awaiting trial. As I sat in the jail visiting room, looking through the glass at my mom, my aunt, my cousins, my girlfriend and my daughters, I very clearly remembered visiting Cliff and looking through the exact same glass, but from the other side. It caused me enormous heartache to see my mom cry and my daughters (ages five and two) cry because they wanted me to come home. I also spent many hours on the phone, calling and calling until people's phones were turned off due to an inability to pay the bills. And no matter how much my loved ones cried, I would not be coming home. I was convicted of second degree murder in August of 1994 and I was ultimately sentenced to 33 years in prison.

My step-father Cliff would make many appearances throughout my incarceration. During one of my pretrial hearings, Cliff was assigned to the same public defender representing me. While Cliff and I were escorted out of the courtroom with the other prisoners, he laughed and joked to the guards, "Bruce didn't do this shit. I taught him better. He wouldn't have left no witnesses."

I would see Cliff again two years later in the Washington State Penitentiary in Walla Walla. A couple of months after Cliff's arrival at Walla Walla, I was transferred to the McNeil Island Correctional Center. Everywhere in the system, I often encountered people who knew him and recognized me as his step-son. During this time, almost everybody I knew on the outside was fading out of my life, as tends to happen during long prison sentences, and each time somebody spoke to me about Cliff and that outlaw subculture, I just felt deserted. I felt that all of those people who professed to love me like family, all those people for whom I would literally have given my life, abandoned me to my prison sentence. It hurt especially bad as I realized that the people that I loved so much, the people that were forgetting about me, were the same people who taught me the behaviors that contributed hugely to my incarceration.

After many moves, a prison race riot and allegations of an escape attempt, I was placed in the maximum security unit at Clallam Bay Corrections Center. I had been in isolation for two weeks, staring at the walls, when I resolved myself to two things: one, I was going to be in solitary confinement for a long time (ultimately, 18 months), and two, I was going to write my life story.

Since I had no education and I had never read a book before coming to prison, committing myself to writing a book about my life was a much bolder venture than I had originally anticipated. I stayed the course. I spent my mornings meticulously writing down almost every major life event I could remember, and I spent the rest of the day studying magazines about writing, studying my small pocket dictionary and reading every book I could get with my extremely limited privileges. I hoped my story would serve as both an apology (to my daughters, family and society) and as a warning for others.

After 18 months in solitary confinement, I was transferred back into general population and continued my writing. Though prison libraries had never before meant anything to me, they became the greatest treasure chests available in my incarcerated life.

In late 2004, my nephew (actually, the nephew of my children's mother) was moved into my prison cell. He was a part of the new generation of prisoners, following after his father and uncles. He was my cellmate for about three months. During his stay, I postponed my studies and instead talked with him about life. I did everything I could to encourage him to stay out of prison. I nearly had tears in my eyes as he was released and we said goodbye.

After spending time with my nephew as a cellmate, I refocused on my studies and my writing with a rekindled fury. I completed a 200,000-word autobiography, *The Sunset Confessions*; I wrote short stories and a novel exploring how addiction destroys families. In 2009, I applied for and was awarded two scholarships from the Prison Scholar Fund, which I used for correspondence courses in English and Psychology through Adams State College. In 2010, I was transferred to Coyote Ridge Corrections Center and was afforded the opportunity to earn an Associate of Arts degree through Walla Walla Community College. During my college studies, I discovered a passion for sociology.

Although I am still trapped physically and emotionally, my mind feels healthier. I have some wholesome family and friends who have rejoined my life, supportive of my direction and my accomplishments. But the past is a difficult thing to escape.

Just a month ago, I learned that Cliff was here in the same prison. He reached out to me, sending his love. Though I was affected profoundly, I was also bitter and did not respond. Then Cliff was moved into my housing unit and I now see him almost every day. He's prematurely old, ravaged by heavy drug abuse and his unchanged outlaw lifestyle. As I talk with him at yard, I am profoundly repulsed by most everything he still embraces and represents, and I simultaneously ache with childhood memories, both good and bad. I am keenly aware of the people he has stabbed and beaten on the street during the decades I have spent in prison trying to repair damage partially caused by him. I am tortured as I listen to him describe his recent crimes, knowing he will soon be released to continue his path of destruction and pain. Yet here I am, aching to return to my daughters, but with a minimum of 12 years to serve on my sentence.

All I can hope for is that one day my daughters will see that I am truly sorry for failing them. I'm sorry for not giving them a life away from that culture of incarceration, addiction and despair. I know that they quit school very early, just as I did, largely due to the unstable lifestyle around them. I know their adult lives today are filled with seemingly insurmountable challenges. I accept blame for these conditions, and with the pain of my guilt, I will continue to write.

★★★

My Mother's Incarceration by Natalie Chaidez

When I was 16, my mom was arrested. I don't know the details because she never sat down and explained to me what was happening legally. Her arrest came as no surprise, because I knew she'd been using drugs for years.

My mom grew up with both her parents and three sisters. Her dad was a violent alcoholic and, unbeknownst to her while growing up, had a second family on the side. Her mom was a classic enabler. My grandma worked full time, and cared for the household while her husband was drinking. She also enabled my mom's drug addiction for many years.

My parents met in high school. They grew up in a suburb of Los Angeles. Both were drug users, and my dad was also an alcoholic, with many arrests and incarcerations of his own. They were, however, both well educated and very intelligent – in fact my dad was accepted to UCLA on scholarship and my mom attended Ivy League schools.

I have one younger sister who is adopted. I spent much of my teenage years in a multi-generational home living with my mom's parents. It was three addicts and one lifetime enabler under one roof, and it wasn't pretty.

My mom worked as a physician for a few years before things fell apart for her – and her family – because of her addiction. It was tragic and heart-breaking to see her take such a big fall, from idealistic young doctor to someone whose every waking moment was devoted to either getting drugs or getting out of the trouble the drugs had caused her. Luckily my grandma was stable enough to keep her house in a nice neighborhood until my mom's legal bills forced her to sell it.

Despite their addictions, my mom and dad were decent parents. They encouraged me academically and made me believe I could do anything. Unfortunately, this went hand-in-hand with lots of horrible drug-related incidents, and a household that centered completely on their addictions and later, their legal troubles. I spent a lot of years living with my grandma, and she provided stable, loving care – as long as it didn't interfere with my mom's needs, which always came first.

When my mom was arrested, I was doing extremely well in high school. I was getting good grades, and was involved in many extracurricular activities. My household went into complete crisis mode after her arrest. An attorney was hired, and she went to court. Again, I don't know all the details because she never bothered to sit me down and talk me through what was going on. I did overhear her conversations with my father, and I knew that she may have beaten her charges but she was guilty.

That first time, she was only in jail a few days. I don't remember her being gone; no one really told me what was going on, nor did I speak to my mom by phone. To make things worse, my sister was only 2 years old, and my dad was drinking very heavily. A lot of childcare fell on me. I remember many nights around that time when I was trying to do my homework and take care of my sister with my drunk father berating me and my mom nowhere to be found.

I only told a few close friends about her arrest. I was completely humiliated. There was an article in the newspaper, and some people – even a few teachers – found out though I hadn't told them. I had one teacher in particular who was very kind to me. When our AP English class took a field trip and I couldn't afford it, he paid for me to attend. He later sat me in the classroom seat where the first Latina Rhodes scholar had sat years before, to encourage me. He was an amazing teacher, an older gay man who knew what it was like to have a secret, and he helped me tremendously.

My friends really didn't care. If they looked down on me because my mom got arrested, they didn't show it. But still I felt so much shame and embarrassment. I was running for student body office at the time, and I remember feeling very surreal and phony, standing up there giving a speech and knowing some people may have been snickering about me behind my back.

The financial blowback from my mom's arrest was even worse. Within a year, we had no car and no home phone. All our money was going to legal bills and my mom's on-going addiction. I developed bulimia during high school, no doubt a result of all the family stress. I had terrible cavities because I was throwing up all the time, and yet no one took me to the dentist. I remember a few nights literally banging my head against the wall in pain to try and help me sleep. I wondered why she had an attorney to get her out of a crime she had committed, while my basic medical needs weren't being met.

Needless to say, my relationship with my mom was horrible. She was completely consumed by her addiction and legal troubles. My grandma was in complete denial, and even when I managed to take the drugs from my mom's purse and showed them to her, she looked right at them and said I was lying. My mom made no effort to tell her I was right, and instead would call me a bitch for calling her out. I lost all respect for her, and saw her as a dangerous, selfish, manipulative and dishonest person who would use anyone and anything to serve her own needs, while being completely unconcerned with her children's. Now that I have kids of my own, it's hard for me to understand how a mother could treat her kids that way. I believe addiction is a disease, but one you can choose to fight. And until her arrest, my mom never admitted her problem to her family, or tried to get treatment.

My first year in college, I took myself to the free college counseling center. I had never received any kind of counseling or therapy. I went for a few months, meeting with a graduate student getting her Master's in Psychology. We talked through a lot of issues, and I think it helped me a lot.

Later my mom was arrested again and this time went to jail for 16 months. I was in my second year of film school, and doing very well there. My main concern was for my little sister, who had just started kindergarten. My dad's alcoholism made him incapable of providing for her, either financially or emotionally. He basically got falling-down wasted every day. I decided to bring my sister to live with me in my college apartment.

It was really difficult to work 20 hours a week, attend my college classes and also take care of my sister. There was no financial support from anyone. I couldn't get welfare, or any other assistance. Luckily people were very generous. Thankfully my college roommate loved my sister and was very supportive. She helped with baby-sitting and whatever else I needed. A local YMCA gave us childcare and summer camp for free when I told them my situation, which was great since my sister got to go to Knott's Berry Farm, Disneyland, and all kinds of fun kid places my mom couldn't afford before her arrest and that I couldn't afford either. Neighbors left me bags of groceries and my church really helped also.

Somehow it all worked out, and I was glad we could be together, since my sister was obviously pretty traumatized by my mom's arrest and the awful years leading up to it. My sister acted out a lot during those months. She got in trouble at school, and I had no idea how to handle it. We found a therapist for her. I can't even remember how I paid for it, since I had no insurance. It was a very nice female doctor at an excellent local hospital, Cedars Sinai. I took my sister there once a week. At the least, I thought, therapy would make her feel like her feelings were important. I don't know if it helped, but it was something.

Even though I was young, I was pro-active about getting my sister help. I knew how to ask people for what I needed, and because I was in college I lived in a wealthy part of town with a lot of resources. It was a really tough time, but I'm sure it must be even more difficult for caregivers who don't have the resources I did.

I only went to see my mom once or maybe twice in jail. I was just too angry at her for what she'd done to me and our family. My grandma visited regularly and took my sister to see her, which was good for all of them. Honestly, I was a little relieved my mom was locked up, because then at least she couldn't keep draining my grandma's resources, or keep using drugs. (I know that's possible in jail, but I was hoping she would stop.)

As far as the long-term effects of her incarceration, it is difficult to separate them out from the effects of everything else. From all the bad experiences, my relationship with my mom is still strained. I don't trust her, I don't respect her, and there is no way for her to take back the years and years of pain she inflicted on our entire family. When I was a teenager, I was deeply ashamed of my parents' drug and legal troubles. As I became a successful writer as an adult, my backstory made me interesting and marketable, so I feel less shame about it now.

The time my mom spent in jail did make my sister and me closer, so I'm grateful for that. It seemed to help my mom get clean, and start a new life. But overall, her incarceration was an awful and difficult time.

★★★

Life Without by Kris William Benson

My name is Kris Benson and I am inmate in the Florida Department of Corrections, currently serving a natural life sentence for a murder I committed in 1995 at the age of 17. This is my story.

I was born in Sacramento, California. I've never known my father except from a couple of photos. By the time I was 3 years old, my mother had left him. We moved to Daytona Beach, Florida to live with my grandmother, my aunt Julie and my uncle Alex. We lived with them until my mother had found a steady job and we moved out. I'd only see my grandmother on the weekends; we'd go to the beach and church on Sundays. My grandmother was the religious pillar in our family, even though it was only me and her going to church. She instilled in me a deep love of God and faith.

Around the time I turned eight or nine, my mother got real bad into drugs and got sick; she had to go into the hospital. My grandmother put me into the care of my aunt Julie while my mother cleaned up her act – at least until my aunt's drug addiction forced her into rehab. The only thing I looked forward to was the weekends with my grandmother, going to church and just spending time with her.

When I turned 10, my mother convinced my grandmother that the only way to break her addiction was to leave Daytona Beach. So we packed up and left with my mother's boyfriend. We moved to Fort Ann, New York, a small country town. I started fifth grade and it was the first time I ever had trouble adjusting to change. It was the combination of my mother fighting with her boyfriend and the advanced curriculum of the northern schools. My teacher suggested I should repeat the fifth grade.

Needless to say, I didn't have many friends. The one friend I did have was kind of an outcast. He was four years older than me and his family was poor. We'd go fishing and hunting with BB guns; the fish we caught and the rabbits we killed went on his family's dinner table. I smoked my first cigarette, drank my first beer and skipped school for the first time with Tim. I got caught by the sheriff for being out of school and he brought me home.

My mother's boyfriend decided to punish me by beating me with his belt. When my mother got home from work, she went ballistic and chased him out of the house with a tire iron.

We ended up moving again further out into the country. We were living with a widower who was retired and had a son a year younger than me. This was the best year of my life. Ernie was like the father I had never had and his son Tory was my best friend and a brother. There were plans for my mother and Ernie to get married, but I guess my mother got cold feet and couldn't go through with it. I don't really know.

I do know that my mom met some guy during that summer. We packed up and drove across the country with him to San Pedro, California, which was fun. I again started a new school, trying to finish the sixth grade, trying to fit in and not really succeeding.

I met Jacob one day when the Mexican kids thought it would be great to have the only two gringos in the sixth grade fight each other. I broke his fist with my nose. After we left the nurse's office, we had to see the principal. He suspended us from lunch, which was fine – I lived only two blocks away.

This was also the first time racism was brought to my attention. Our principal was Black and he explained to us that we were two of the dumbest White boys he had ever seen, fighting each other. He explained to us about the gangs in SoCal and steered us away from them. Needless to say, Jacob and I became the best of friends. We even convinced our parents to let us take Tae Kwan Do together.

That summer, my mother took me to a friend's ranch in Shingle Springs. I stayed there all summer, helping to tend to the couple of horses that were boarded there, while my mother and her new boyfriend tried to work things out. By the end of the summer, things had changed. We moved in with the manager of the apartment complex where we had been living, but ended up moving again to Oceanside, California, and then to Carlsbad, California.

This was where I got a real big dose of rejection. It was so bad that I stole my mother's .25 caliber pistol and took it to school. The kids at school would ridicule me for the clothes I'd wear and the way I talked. I was going to make them pay for it. But while sitting in English class, something stopped me from pulling that gun out and blowing them all away. What helped save those snobbish, stuck-up kids is that they didn't have a school bus system. Students used the city bus lines and could ride for free. At the end of class, I left school, got on the bus and never went back there.

But it turned out that I wouldn't have had to. My grandmother was sick and had lung cancer. My mother flew back to Florida to take care of Grandma. I stayed in California and rode the bus all day instead of going to school. Then my mom's boyfriend drove me to Florida.

When I saw the state my grandmother was in I prayed to God. Oh, did I pray for Him to heal her, for Him to take me instead, everything.

My mother decided she wasn't going back to California. I went back but wouldn't return to school and those terrible kids. I ended up flying alone and met a girl a couple of years younger than me on the plane. She was flying alone, too, coming from Louisiana by way of Texas. We talked and I let her play with my Gameboy. I told her about my grandma being sick and she comforted me; it was like we were soulmates, we had an instant connection. We exchanged addresses and a kiss before deplaning. I wrote that girl once, I think, and never wrote back after she answered my letter because this was the final stage of my grandmother's life. After Grandma went into the hospital, I never saw her again.

The realization that my grandmother was never coming back struck me halfway through her funeral service. It totally and completely devastated me. I ran out of our church, crying. That day I hardened my heart and turned away from God.

My mother contested my grandmother's will and got everything. We moved to South Daytona, where my mother started her downward spiral back into drug addiction. There, I met a group of misfits in my eighth grade year. I lost my virginity, smoked lots of pot, took lots of acid, huffed anything that would get me high. Our little group became skinheads – anti-Semitism and no interracial mingling were part of our manifesto. We never did actually go out and do any fag-bashing. We never hurt anyone but ourselves. We'd throw parties with our little clique and our girlfriends, get drunk, smoke pot and fight each other. We had the neighbors call the cops on us a few times but nothing ever came of it.

Towards the end of my eighth grade year, I got the chicken pox and missed months of school. When I got better, there might have been two and half months left of the year. I never went back. I know my report card listed 152 days absent. But they passed the entire eighth grade that year, sending them on to high school just to get rid of them. Then, three weeks into my ninth grade year, the county opened a new high school. Rather than having to leave all my friends and attend this new school, I dropped out instead. At this time, my mother's crack addiction was so consuming that she didn't care. All told, from kindergarten through the ninth grade, I went to a total of ten different schools.

My mother wasted the money she had inherited and we ended up moving from motel to motel, staying with her druggie buddies while she prostituted herself to buy more crack. I finally got fed up with it and left.

I stayed with a friend of mine and his family. Back before my mother lost control of her addiction, Josh had got into a fight with his father. She'd let him stay with us until he and his father could patch things up. Josh's father remembered that and took me in. I grew out of being a skinhead and got a job at McDonald's. Things were going alright for a little while until Josh had to go to some youth program mandated by the court, and his dad and his brother went on a trip. I was back out on the streets.

At this time, my mother got arrested for possession of a controlled substance and introduction of contraband into a county facility. She got sentenced to 11 months and 29 days. I had nowhere to go. My uncle Alex and his wife allowed me to stay with them. I quit Mickey D's and helped out my uncle with his tree service business.

Since the time I was 14, pot and inhalants were the only solace I got from this world. Almost everyone I knew smoked pot – my mother, all my friends, Josh's father and his brother, my uncle. But his wife gave him the ultimatum – either I had to go or she was going to go. I didn't really blame him with the choice he had to make. She was pregnant with his son at the time.

I left and lived on the streets for a couple of weeks. I met a guy when I applied for a job at Wendy's; he lived with his parents and they let me crash on their couch for a while. Then I ran into my mom's friend Mary. Mom had been writing her from jail. She found me a place to stay. This would've been perfect; the woman was hot, in her twenties, and her husband was older. I could tell she was into me. The only problem was that her husband owned a lot of guns and could probably kill us both if he found out. That scared me. I stayed there for two weeks and left before things could get out of hand.

After this, I worked up the courage to ask my aunt Julie if I could stay with her and her husband. The pain of her rejection almost drove me to suicide. I had nowhere to go, so I slept under bridges, on the beach, all the time trying to keep my job at Wendy's. I ended up living back with Josh and his family, paying rent. His father worked as a bartender at a new blues club and got me and Josh jobs as parking lot security.

This was around the time my mother got out of jail. She came to see me, explaining that she was getting married and moving to Virginia. It was the beginning of 1995 and I was 16. I told her that I wasn't going to go with her and she respected my decision, so I stayed. I had no type of adult supervision. Josh's dad had moved in with his girlfriend and her two daughters and we only saw him at work. I worked hard, partied harder, turned 17 and met a girl who I thought was "the one." Everything was going pretty good until it all came crashing down when Kristen smashed my heart to pieces.

Her rejection was the straw that broke the camel's back. I gave up. The only problem was that I was too much of a coward to implode. I decided to explode and let the State kill me, instead. At 17 years, 3 months and 4 days of age I decided to kill someone. I made it random, because I didn't think I could have done it if I had any type of personal relationship with the individual.

After getting caught and going to trial, I found out that the victim was Jewish, which at the time held no significance for me because I wasn't a skinhead anymore. I went to trial not caring, hoping for the death penalty. I was sentenced to life in prison without the possibility of parole. After my direct appeal, I never challenged the Court's ruling. I was found guilty of the crimes I'd committed.

I eventually found remorse for what I had done. I found God again after studying the Kabbala and then Judaism. I discovered that I'd killed my victim on Yom Kippur, the Jewish Day of Atonement when God writes the names of the living in the Book of Life and the names of the dead in the Book of the Dead.

I've come to understand a lot of things God has shown me. One of them is that the Florida justice system is flawed regarding juveniles. I put in for clemency this year. I've had as much time in prison as I lived free in the world. If I'm granted clemency by the governor, I hope to get out and help troubled teens, and petition the Florida Legislature to change the juvenile justice system.

***

Everyone in My Family Has Been in Prison by Shadow

My mother is part Apache, part Mexican and part Samoan. She grew up in foster care in Los Angeles. They abused her in foster care and it made her very angry and violent. She was in McLaren Hall, Los Padrinos and camp. People were afraid of her because she carried a knife.

When my mom was 17, she had my sister, then a couple of years later she had me.

Our dad is Sioux and has a chief's name, but he goes by the English name Joe. His family was from the Midwest but they came to California, so he grew up an urban Indian.

When I was small my parents split up. My mom had always been a drinker and pretty violent, but she got worse after my dad left. She would go to the clubs in South Gate and leave us with my aunt. When she got home she would beat us if my aunt told her we had been bad.

My sister got very wild after my dad left. She got put in foster care and then the juvenile system because she was so violent. Even though I was bigger than her, I was always calmer. I always tried to stay close to my mom and I would even follow her to the neighborhood bars. I stayed so close to her they called me Shadow Girl.

When I was starting second grade, my mom went to prison for stabbing someone. I don't know where my father was at that time. We went to see her two times and I remember those visits so clearly that I recognized the buildings the first time I went to prison myself. My mom introduced us to her partner and that was very confusing. Her partner was Michie, another American Indian woman.

I didn't see my father again until I was an adult, but now I know he was in prison for most of that time. While they were both gone, my sister and I lived with my aunt, but a couple of times they took us away from her and we were put in foster care. The first place they put us was with this Mexican couple that didn't speak English. My sister ran away and left me there. Then they moved me to a White lady's home; her name was Mrs. Vann, and she was very nice to me. They let me go back home when my mom got out.

I started getting in trouble when I was a teenager and got sent to camp. I did my first prison sentence for assault when I was 18, at the same prison my mother had been at. My sister was already there, so I didn't have any trouble.

I got out when I was 19. I was using speed and drinking and running around. My parole officer violated me twice, the last time when I was 22. When I got to the prison and had the physical, I found out I was pregnant. My son was born at the prison. My mom and I weren't speaking so I didn't have a place for him to go. My friend Alice helped me; her mom had been a foster parent, so she got cleared and took my daughter to her home.

After that I started going to parenting classes and they let me call my daughter and call my mom. Me and my mom started working on our relationship. But she has a very mean mouth. After a few calls, she started asking about the baby. Then we had an argument about where the baby was living. Pretty soon we weren't talking again.

While I was still in prison, they let me call my dad. He was in the hospital in Chicago and he wanted to see me. We made some plans and met up when he came out to LA.

Everyone in my family – my mom, my dad and my sister – has been in prison. I didn't know my dad was incarcerated when he was gone. My mom's incarceration was a bad time because we couldn't see her very much. Of the times I have gone to prison, I would say that I only actually broke the law once – the first time. Every time after that, I have been incarcerated for a violation of my parole. When I got out after my last incarceration, my son was 26 months old.

***

About My Mother by Abel Hawkins

I am the child of incarcerated parents.

My mom grew up in San Diego with Nanna, my great-grandmother. No one knew it but Nanna was schizophrenic. My great-grandfather went up to LA in the 1960's. He was rolling and never came back to San Diego and Nanna.

Nanna cared for seven children and abused them all but specially my mom. Nanna was White and my mom is part Black and dark-skinned, so she got the worst. Nanna made her wear rags to school and she had to take care of her brothers and sisters and all the cousins. My light-skinned aunts had it better.

My mom was good in school until she got molested by family "friends." It was a regular thing that started when she was eight. She took it 'til she was 11 and then ran away. She would get caught and sent back to Nanna, so she started stealing from stores to get money for the Greyhound. She finally got arrested when she was 15 and sent to juvenile hall.

It's crazy, but they let her go home from juvenile hall with this older man. She ran away from him, too, but they brought her back until she was 17 and got arrested as an adult. When she met her father, my grandfather, for the first time she thought she was saved. She was 19 at the time. She had her own room in his apartment and got a job and her GED. But my grandfather was a dog and tried to molest her, too, so she ran away again and got involved with drug addicts. She did not use drugs then but needed a place to stay.

When she was 23, she moved in with a man who became the father of my oldest two brothers. He was a working man and he supported her. She smoked marijuana with him but stopped stealing and had a good life for about six years. Then he started using hard drugs and they broke up. My mom got her own place and started taking care of my uncle who was still in school.

When she was 32, my mom started using drugs, too. She had to start stealing again to pay for them. A few years later she met my father, an older man who was also a drug user and a criminal. They lived together for two years and had my brother. Then, just after my mom got pregnant with me, my father was arrested and sent to state prison. Their relationship was not very good and they lost touch. My mom never took me to see him.

When I was one year old, my mom was arrested. My uncle, my brother Sammy and I went into foster care. They tell me I was a happy, well-adjusted baby. When I was two, my mom got into a prison program for women with children. Me and Sammy went to live with her. (Our other brothers got lost in the shuffle and I don't remember them.) Sammy and I lived in the program until our mom was released and then she got an apartment for us. We all lived together for about two years but then she got arrested again.

Sammy and I went back into foster care. I was seven. We got sent to live way out in the desert with a family related to my father. The house belonged to an old lady who took care of other foster kids and two retarded adults. It wasn't too bad there, she got enough money for all of us to have some housekeepers and the house was always clean. It was too far from the prison to visit my mom. She wrote us letters and I wrote back until she stopped writing when I was around 10. We stayed in that foster home until I was 14.

My mother had gotten out of prison earlier, but she never came to get us. You might think that someone would wonder about that and try to find her, but they never did.

On my fifteenth birthday, I got in trouble with my brother and got sent to the California Youth Authority. One of the counselors was trying to find my mom and found that she had been murdered in 1998 while I was living in foster care. Later I found out she was strangled and raped and left behind a dumpster in El Monte.

They let me out when I was 17 and my probation officer helped me get emancipated. I tracked down my uncle and moved in with him and his family. I have stayed out of trouble since then.

I never visited my parents in prison and never got a phone call from them. I have looked for my father in the prison system but there is no one by his name. He would be in his seventies now, so maybe he died there.

When we were living in the desert, my mom sent me a picture of her sitting in the shade at the CCWF prison up north. She didn't look like I remembered her but I kept the picture for years until the color film chipped off. When I got older I started to wish my mom had gone to prison forever like my dad. She would still be alive and I could have visited her and got to know her again.

★★★

In His Footsteps by Jeremy Mark Read

I recently read a statistic stating that over 50 percent of boys who have had an incarcerated parent would find themselves incarcerated at some point during their lives. Unfortunately, I am a member of this not-so-esteemed group.

I am 30 years old and I have been incarcerated since I was 16 years of age. When I was seven, my dad, Mark Read, was sent to prison for a series of robberies. By the time my young, shackled feet first stepped off a chain-bus and shuffled through a heavy steel door into a dirty concrete building called prison, my dad was still incarcerated at the Walla Walla State Penitentiary.

I can recall the only Christmas that I ever received anything from my dad. I was eight years old and my grandparents, his parents, brought me some gifts to open on Christmas morning, including one from him. The box contained a very cheap Walkman radio and a toy car carved from wood. It was not until much later, when I was in prison, that I came to realize that the Walkman was one that you could purchase from the prison commissary and the toy car was crafted by a wood worker in some prison hobby shop. My dad, more than likely, had to pay a significant amount of money in prison terms to send me these gifts. At the time, I hated them.

It was no big astonishment that I made my way to prison. I was in and out of juvenile facilities since the age of 12. In fact, I was fresh out from doing an 18-month stint in a juvenile prison when I caught my present case. The last thing that I told my cellie as I left the institution was, "See you at Walla Walla!"

From a young age, I was convinced that my purpose in life was to follow in my dad's footsteps; everyone seems to expect it. Every time I found myself in trouble, many hastily made me aware that it was not my fault, that I acted out because my dad was gone and in prison. Soon, I heard, "Do you want to end up like your dad?" and finally, "You're just like your dad." As the old adage goes, "Like father, like son."

I did not know my dad while he was in prison. I never visited him, not once. Someone thought that it would not be a good idea, so to me that's exactly what he became – an idea. The idea of my dad materialized from the highly dramatized prison movies I had seen. I had no clue how prison actually was. For years I carried this idea of my father and prison. Together with people's expectations, it created my image of myself as well.

Once, while in a juvenile group home, I had a kind counselor who thought it was best for me to re-connect with my dad and so a phone call was arranged. During the call, I enthusiastically bombarded my dad with questions about prison life. I asked him about his sleeves (a term used for arms that are fully covered in tattoos) and I proudly told him of my criminal exploits. I thought he'd share my pride. Instead, he sounded disappointed as he attempted to explain to me that prison was not like in the movies and it was not cool. I did not want to hear that and I'm sure he could tell. From then on there were no more calls.

At first, having a parent in prison was a source of shame, anger and pain. I can remember telling kids on the playground that my dad played for the Seattle Seahawks. That's the truth that I wanted, that I imagined so intensely I almost believed it myself. As I got older, the fairy tales could no longer suspend reality. The shame, anger and pain quickly re-emerged and at about ten or eleven years of age, I began to seriously act out. When it all became too unbearable, I learned that if I cut myself, the physical pain would dull the emotional pain.

One time, after a heated argument with my mom, one in which I was asked if I wanted to end up like my dad, a dark, ominous cloud of despair overcame me. I ran into my room and slammed the door. Feeling nothing but an extreme desire to cease to exist, I found a black leather braided belt and looped it around the pole that you hang the clothes from in the closet. I placed the other end of the belt around my neck and attempted to hang myself. On the verge of losing consciousness, I felt the bracket holding the pole to the wall begin to break. I fell asleep crying on the floor of my closet. I couldn't even kill myself right.

By the age of 12, I'd had enough. Instead of continuing to bury the shame, I embraced it. I started to wear my circumstances as a badge of honor and I would challenge anybody who attempted to belittle me because of them. "So what if my dad's in prison … got a problem with it?" This led to fighting, a lot of fighting. This attracted the attention of kids similar to me, and this soon led to me joining a gang. In the gang, I found a place of acceptance, a place where having an incarcerated parent was not only common, but something to boast about. Soon the trips to juvenile hall commenced.

Prison at any age is hard. At 16 years old, it is abominable. Do you remember how slowly a school year would drag by at that age? Now imagine that, as a juvenile in an adult prison.

During a short stint of freedom when I was 15, my dad's father, my grandad, took me out to lunch. He wanted to show me something that he had been helping my dad with. It was the beginning phase of a book titled *Steel Bars & Dirty Concrete: Poems & Illustrations from Inside America's Gulag*. I was slightly amused but not very interested. I was more interested in the food.

Shortly after getting to prison myself, I received from my grandad a finished copy of my dad's book. Although full of dark and depressing poetry, half about his life on the inside and half about his life of addiction, this book provided me with the most transparent view of my dad that I'd had up to that point. Being in a dark place, I was able to relate to the trepidation in his words. I was inspired.

With the help of a very kind and encouraging teacher at Clallam Bay Corrections Center, I set forth working on my own book. The book, a collection of stories, poetry and artwork by inmates under the age of 18, is titled *Young on the Inside: Young Minds in Hard Times*. This was my first positive accomplishment.

I do not remember much about my dad from before he went to prison. What I do remember is not great. He was extremely violent towards my mom and would beat her up in front of me. She left him when I was 3 years old. After that, the times with him were few and left behind memories of falling asleep on the cold, dirty concrete sidewalks of Downtown Seattle or in a stolen van parked at various places around the city. At the time I did not know that this was wrong or that he was using drugs. Needless to say, his poetry was very enlightening.

Two and a half years into my sentence I found myself in the Intensive Management Unit [IMU] for assault. There I received a letter from my dad telling me that he was out. He inquired as to how long I had left and informed me that he was getting married. He told me that when I got out I could go live with him in England. I promptly wrote back, telling him how long I had left. I never heard back from him.

One time, while in transportation between prisons, I met a guy who knew my dad from Walla Walla. He told me stories of my dad continually assaulting the officers and spending much of his time in the IMU. He referred to my dad as a "snap-case." In prison, they have a solution for "snap-cases." It involves large doses of psychotropic drugs. I like to call them the "walking dead pills," because they leave you nothing more than a zombie, wandering aimlessly around in a cloud. Pharmaceutical paradise.

A poem by Mark Read, my dad:

Not a Spade in the Fresh Earth

This hole is not permanent

in my case

not like a hole in the earth

never to be released

when the final gate opens

my mind will be reborn

into a world where

nothing

nothing will drive me to

open my flesh

brooding over my last wounds

which hammer persistently

with a vision where

all things are black

dying

decaying

lost

burnt spoons

I will not surrender

you must dig elsewhere.

In October 2001, two years after his release and at the age of 38, my dad, Mark Vernon Read, was found dead in his flat in England. He died from a heroin overdose. At the time, I was 19 years old and only in the third year of a 28-year sentence. Needless to say, I was devastated.

Time went by, I grieved, I hurt, and I resolved that I would no longer follow in my father's anguished footsteps. To do so would be pure insanity. The irony is that through his death he finally found success as a parent. His death became the catalyst of my desire to change, and change I have. I am nothing like my dad, I am me. I am Jeremy Mark Read, and my odyssey will no longer be characterized by steel bars and dirty concrete. It can now only be defined by redemption.

★★★

This Indescribable Butterfly by Alisha Murdock

Another normal day. I was in the sixth grade and had just moved to Oakland, California. I woke up and to my surprise the smell of freshly cooked eggs and bacon filled the house. My mom did not normally cook so I was very happy. I sat down at our small kitchen table and began to eat.

"I love you, baby," my mom looked at me and smiled.

"I love you too, Mommy," I said. Then I glanced at the clock and noticed that I was almost late, so I pushed some more food in my mouth, gave my mom a kiss, and ran off to school.

She stood at the door and yelled to me, "Be safe, I love you."

I arrived at school just as the bell rang. My second period class, PE, was my favorite. Right before I went to kick the ball, Coach Brown came to me and told me someone was here to talk to me. It was my neighbor.

"Alisha, your mom was arrested today after you left for school and she is in jail. I have to take you home to pack the apartment," she said.

My eyes started to water, but I quickly sucked it up because I was always told "tears are a sign of weakness."

"Okay," I said simply, and we were on our way home.

When I got to the house, the door was smashed in, and the living room was destroyed. My room was a mess, mom's room was horrible, and everything was everywhere. My mom's mattress looked like it had been attacked by an angry dog. On the floor, stuff was scattered all over, including foil, burnt spoons and needles. I fell to the floor and just stared blankly at the walls. My neighbor asked if I wanted her to stay, but I said, no. I felt this was not her mess to clean up; I was not my neighbor's responsibility. It was not her job to fix my mother's mistakes. I knew that I was going to have to leave the apartment sooner or later, so I packed stuff up, grabbed what I needed, and left. With nowhere to go to, the first night was the hardest. I slept in a park close by the school so that I wouldn't be late the next morning.

After the first night in the park, I bounced from friend's house to friend's house. I ended up moving in with one of my closest friend's cousins. She soon became like a second mother to me, and I told people she was my godmom. She treated me like I was her own daughter. I always felt very lucky to have found someone like her in my life. Still I missed my mom, but tried not to think about her.

When my mom was clean, we were very close. She was like my best friend. I always told my mom everything, no matter how good or bad. For me, just being in my mom's presence made me feel close to her. I usually took care of my mom: cooking, cleaning, and making sure she took her medicine. It was like I took on the mom role, and that was when we got to spend our quality time together. It may not be what most people would consider mother–daughter time, but for me those were the best times. But when she was on drugs, it felt like our connection disappeared. Because of her drug use, we had a very on again–off again relationship, especially after she went to jail.

One day during that time period, I got in trouble for stealing from Target. Because of this, my godmom said I needed to stay with my family for a while, so my aunt and uncle came to pick me up. Then they sent me to live with my big sister in Washington State. I only remember meeting my sister once, when I was about three or four. I was now in the seventh grade. I felt like an unwanted child being shipped off to live with a stranger. All I wanted was my mom. Even though we didn't have the best relationship, she was my whole world; she was my everything, my heartbeat.

When I was living with my sister, I purposely didn't do what I knew I should do. I always had an attitude, and didn't try in school. My sister would always tell me I was fat and ghetto. She cut my hair short and made me wear dressy clothes. My sister calling me fat really got to my head, to the point where I stopped eating. I remember one day I came home from school, and she started yelling at me about the dishes. As she was yelling at me, I passed out because I had not eaten. When I woke up, my sister was looking at me. She slapped me, sent me up to my room, and told me I made myself pass out to get out of trouble. I felt like an outcast around my own family. Didn't I have the right to be well cared for during my mother's incarceration?

I lived with my sister for almost a year and a half, and then she said I was going to go visit my mom in California. I didn't know yet that I was going back for good, but I was excited. When I got to Cali, my mom was staying in a shelter in Livermore, which meant I was also staying in a shelter for the summer. When I got there, my mom was so happy to see me, and it showed all over her face, like a halo over an angel. The happiness soon came to an end, though, when my mom and I were kicked out of the shelter. After staying in a motel outside of Livermore, we moved to Richmond, to another shelter.

By this time I was a freshman in high school, and my mom enrolled me into John F. Kennedy High School. It was about two months into the school year, but for me it was another first day at a new school. Richmond soon became home to me. Outside of our place, I had a happy life, lots of friends, and too much freedom. At home, however, my mom was starting to use again. One day after school, I went up to our room and found my mom drunk and high. I was so angry. I knew I had to make sure that the staff didn't see my mom like this, because then we would be asked to leave. The next day we were kicked out.

My mom went to a motel, but I went to stay with a friend from my after-school program. Her name was Danielle, and she soon became my little sister, and her family became my family. After staying with Danielle for a little over a year, I went back to live with my mom. She said she was clean and had her own place. It turned out that it was true she was clean, but she did not have her own place; we were in yet another shelter. After a couple of months, the staff told my mom they had a place for her but that the apartment was only for single people. I told my mom to take the apartment, and I enrolled myself in Treasure Island Job Corps.

I went to Job Corps so that my mom could keep going down the right path. But as soon as I left, she went right back to her old ways. Soon, we had a big fallout about her constant lies and bad habits. I knew I was what kept her going, but for once, I felt like she needed to do something on her own. And when she couldn't, it broke my heart. I was angry at her, and I also felt partially responsible for the direction her life was going in. I felt that if I had stayed with my mom, I could have kept her on the right track. My mom and I didn't talk for a little over six months.

In August 2010, I completed Treasure Island Job Corps and transferred to Los Angeles Job Corps. During that time, my mom and I would speak every other week. It was still very difficult to talk with her, but I was happy that my mom was at least trying to come back into my life. Then, in October 2010, I received a phone call from my mom. She informed me that she was in Carson City Jail, in Nevada. I had so many questions, but her time on the phone was up. My eyes filled with tears, but my heart was filled with much more anger. I felt like her drugs and street life would always come before me.

I left LA Job Corps in November 2010, and I moved in with my pastor and his family in Richmond. Ever since my mom and I first moved to Richmond, they had been my support system. Living with them gave me a sense of what a real family might look like: yes, they had problems, all humans do, but they always showed that they loved each other, and I could see it. I was truly happy.

January 28, 2011 was one of the biggest days of my life. It was my graduation day from Job Corps! I was receiving my GED and a certificate in Painting. As I walked to my seat, my eyes glowed with joy as I saw my pastor, his wife, Sister Marshelle, and their daughter, Mikaela, sitting in the crowd. It felt great to know I had people I loved there to support me on such a big day. Finally, they called my name. I think I jumped across the stage! I was so excited and proud of myself. The only thing missing was my mom. I always imagined her being there the day I graduated. Her absence is just the reality of my situation.

For me, hardest parts are still the holidays. Last July Fourth, I spent the day with my pastor. The day was great; we had a barbeque. Later my pastor was taking his son to see the fireworks and asked if I wanted to go. I chose to stay home. That night I lay in my bed and listened to the fireworks, and I thought it was just another holiday that my mom was not there with me. I love and truly miss my mom. More than anything I miss her unneeded lectures, her long bear hugs, and the way her eyes glow every time she looks at me. All I want is for her to see me moving forward. I know she would be proud of me.

These days my mom is in prison in North Las Vegas, Nevada. It's impossible for me to see her, since I'm all the way in Richmond, California. The price of a phone call from prison is too expensive to afford, and my mom seems to never write back to my letters. I feel that if she was still out here with me, and I could actually see and talk with her, then we would have some sort of relationship. Don't I have the right to see, touch, and speak with my mother during her incarceration?

Today I am 19 years old and I still live with my pastor. I'm working two jobs and getting ready to go to college. My pastor has pushed me to do my best. I never had a father, and he has helped me in the ways a father should. Sister Marshelle is like a second mom to me. She is always there to listen and to give honest advice. I am finally moving forward and becoming a young woman. I don't regret anything that has happened in my life, because it's all made me the person I am today: I'm independent, loving, faithful, brave, self-motivated, and a young lady of God. I simply wish my mom could have been around to watch her caterpillar become this indescribable butterfly.

4

THE EXPERIENCES OF PARENTAL ARREST, INCARCERATION AND REENTRY

Megan Sullivan and Denise Johnston

While all children of prisoners have a parent who has been arrested and incarcerated, and many will have a parent who reenters society, children's family structures and social supports will determine their experiences of parental arrest, incarceration and reentry. This chapter examines how children undergo and are affected by each phase of a parent's criminal justice system involvement. It explores whether and how children are told about a parent's incarceration; the circumstances that facilitate children's contact with incarcerated parents, including visits to prisons and jails; and children's experiences of a parent's return to society and the family.

When a Parent is Arrested

There were about 11.3 million arrests in the U.S. in 2013, representing a decrease in the annual number of arrests since 1990 in every major offense category except drug abuse violations.[1] Based on national samples of state and federal prisoners, it can be estimated that at least half of the adult arrests in this population were arrests of parents.[2]

Witnessing Parental Arrest

Some 20 to 40 percent of incarcerated parents report their children were present at the time of their arrest.[3] The basic concept of arrest – involuntary removal of an individual from the community by armed, uniformed strangers – suggests that it would be upsetting and even frightening to children.

> I watched my mother be continually apprehended by Milwaukee police officers. When they'd taken her away, I felt neglected and lonely.
>
> *Manuel R.W., adult child of two incarcerated parents*

I saw [my mom] arrested for the first time when I was four. The marshals came in the morning while it was still dark and got her. I was frightened but my grandma was there and everyone tried to be nice for me. I was also there at her last arrest a couple of years later. They grabbed her and took her away from me. I wanted to go with her but they made me stay with my father. We sat waiting and then they brought her out in handcuffs and took her to a patrol car and drove away. I was terrified and crying all the way home.

Jessamyn R., adult child of two incarcerated parents

In some cases, parental arrests provide relief and increase safety for children.

Though I frequently sat crying in some shadowed room while listening to my mom being beaten, I would never call the police nor ask anybody for help. This lifestyle lasted until just days after my eleventh birthday, when some neighbors called the police, who made him leave early in the morning and he would never live with us again.

Bruce B., adult child of two incarcerated parents

My dad's first prison terms were for armed robbery and happened before I was born. But by the time I was able to understand what was happening when my father got arrested, he was older and getting picked up just for being a crazy drunk. He was one of the only White guys in our area so the police (also White) were nice to him and sometimes they just took him to a detox center or released him. A few times I was glad to see him go and wished they held him longer.

Jessamyn R., adult child of two incarcerated parents

A study from the University of Illinois at Chicago reported that children in the child welfare system who had seen their parents arrested were more likely to have psychological trauma and posttraumatic stress disorder than other children in foster care.[4] A New York study reported that most children who have witnessed parental arrest saw their parents handcuffed and about half have also witnessed law enforcement officers draw a weapon during the arrest.[5]

In spite of these efforts, it is difficult to determine the significance of witnessing parental arrest. For example, what we know about parental arrest is derived from studies of incarcerated parents and extremely high risk children in foster care,[6] rather than from samples of child witnesses that include children whose arrested parents do not go on to be convicted or incarcerated.

Adjudication of Parents and Outcomes of Parental Arrest

There is no information available on these topics. We don't know the rate at which parents remain in detention during adjudication, the rate at which they are convicted or the types of dispositions they receive, although there is evidence that gender and family status affects sentencing.[7] The relative unimportance of this segment of the justice process for most children is reflected in our contributors' narratives, only one of which directly or indirectly addresses parental adjudication.

The courts labeled my mother a fugitive-from-justice because for a year and a half she successfully avoided being captured despite several close encounters ... She was being held in a county jail while awaiting trial and there was a strong possibility that she could be sent to state prison ... The courts were determined to make my mother pay for the time they'd spent searching for her as a fugitive.

Bianca B., adult child of an incarcerated mother

The great majority of children whose parents will serve sentences to incarceration face the more mundane, everyday reality of low-to-mid-level parental charges, parental detention throughout adjudication as the result of an inability to pay bail, and plea bargains that allow parents to plead "guilty" in exchange for a reduction in the their jail/prison time.

Parental Incarceration

The incarceration of parents causes several unique circumstances that do not occur in the lives of other children, even those facing multiple risks. However, throughout this section, it is important to remember that many children of incarcerated parents have never or only intermittently lived with those parents and that this reality significantly limits the importance of telling children about parental incarceration, parent–child contact during parental incarceration and shame/stigma associated with parental incarceration.

To Tell or Not to Tell

There is no reliable information about the proportion of prisoners' children who are told about their parents' incarceration. Based upon the large percentage of children who have never lived with and/or do not know the whereabouts of those parents, it might be expected that many children are not told about parental incarceration simply because their caregivers are not aware of it.

There are valid reasons for withholding information about parental criminal justice system involvement from children, who cannot realistically be expected to keep it confidential. These include avoiding the possible loss of parental employment, the family's eviction from their housing or the removal of children to foster care. The stigma surrounding crime and sanctions for criminal activity may also encourage families to lie to a child about a parent's arrest or incarceration.

Children of prisoners may be told their parent is "away" or "in school" or "working in another town."[8] Such deceptions often prove futile, however, as children usually discover the truth. Sister Elaine Roulet, founder of the Bedford Hills Correctional Facility Children's Center, often told the story of a 10-year-old girl she had escorted from the prison visiting room; the girl asked Sr. Roulet to please not tell her grandmother that her mother was in prison because "my grandma thinks this is a college."

Occasionally, prisoners themselves will make the decision to withhold information about their incarceration from their children. Studies have found that this is because parents are embarrassed, do not want their children to see them incarcerated, or are trying to spare their children what they think will be too difficult for them.[9]

While the ethical issues of lying to a child about parental incarceration might be debated, there are also developmental issues involved.[10] Such lies must always involve children's primary caregivers; when the dishonesty is discovered, it undermines the trust that is the foundation of the child–caregiver relationship. In addition, lying signals to children that the truth about their parents' circumstances is not to be discussed; this may create "forced silences" in which children feel they must suppress their natural reactions, comments and questions about their missing parents, adding to any traumatic effects of the separation.[11]

Several contributors to this book were lied to about their incarcerated parents' whereabouts; other families avoided the issue.

> My grandmother would often call [prison] "college" to protect me from the embarrassment but as I got older, my mom told me the truth.
>
> *David S., adult child of an incarcerated father*

> Despite the press coverage I did not know that my father was incarcerated until I was bullied by some classmates. My mother never spoke of it.
>
> *Pamela H., adult child of an incarcerated father*

Some adults appreciate their parent's deception.

> Daddy spent months in county jail and Mom became an expert at doling out excuses when we didn't hear from him. "Daddy went on a trip," or "Daddy's working a double shift," or "Daddy was tired but he loves you girls very much." Our mother wanted to protect us and she did. In fact, I am grateful for her deceit … this well-kept secret allowed me to have a normal adolescence.
>
> *Hollie O., adult child of an incarcerated father*

Several of our contributors say there was media coverage of their parent's predicament, and many vividly recall where they were and how they found out. Upon reflection, some adult children recognize how the moment of their parent's arrest or incarceration changed their lives.

> I found out he was in prison one night when my mother came to get me after a school function. She showed me the newspaper article; my father had been arrested for murder … [Later, when I thought of what I considered] my other life, the life where there was no possibility I would have a normal relationship with my father, [I realized this other life] began the day he was convicted.
>
> *Danielle C., adult child of an incarcerated father*

But some children of prisoners are grateful for being respected and allowed to know and speak the truth about their parents.

> My mom always told me to say what I felt [about her incarceration] and ask questions if I needed to. On the day she got out I had just turned six. She and I were standing in a

long cashier line at the market and I was so happy that she was back that I was bouncing up and down and laughing. One of the old ladies in the line asked me why I was so happy and I yelled, "Because my mom just got out of jail!" The ladies got shocked faces and I could tell that I had said something wrong so I turned to look at my mom. Her face was pink and she was biting her lip but she nodded to the ladies and to me, telling them that it was true and telling me that what I said was okay. I didn't understand until I got older but then I was so proud of her for accepting the embarrassment and letting me feel okay about expressing myself.

Jessamyn R., adult child of two incarcerated parents

Most authorities on parental incarceration recommend telling children that their parents are in jail or prison.[12]

Parent–Child Contact during Parental Incarceration

Excluding visitation, parent–child contact among prisoners' families historically was limited to written correspondence and telephone calls. More recently, modern technology in some jails and prisons has allowed parent–child contact by videoconference and Skype. Most jailed and imprisoned parents and their children communicate,[13] with parents who lived with their children prior to incarceration having more contact than parents who did not.

Letters

About 70 percent of parents in state prisons and 85 percent of parents in federal prisons correspond with their children, and this includes through letters, cards and pictures.[14] There is no similar information available about correspondence between jailed parents and their children.

Through the years, I would occasionally visit my father and mail letters to him. Every so often, I would get a card from him.

Carie S., adult child of an incarcerated father

Letters may be a powerful form of communication. One recent study found the frequency of letter-writing, rather than of personal visits or phone calls, predicted more contact between children and parents.[15] For older children, written correspondence allows detailed expression of writers' feelings and thoughts. Although letters are not suitable for infants, toddlers, very young children, and parents or children who cannot read, many parents and children can exchange drawings, photographs or even pictures cut from magazines in place of the written word. In addition, almost all correctional facilities provide paper, writing implements and postage to indigent prisoners.

However, only a third of our contributors mentioned corresponding with their parents in jail/prison and only one identified letters as a valuable support during parental incarceration.

Telephone Calls

Telephone communication works for children of all ages, except infants. It also works for parents and children who cannot read. About half of parents in state prisons and 85 percent of parents in federal prisons report having phone calls with their families.[16]

> My dad used to call almost every day while he was in jail. He always had a new joke to tell me and sometimes he would pass the phone to a friend who would give me some entertaining "advice." Because we were so close all my life and because he called so much, I didn't really miss visiting him.
>
> *Jessamyn R., adult child of two incarcerated parents*

> Whenever [my step-dad] got arrested, he would call constantly on the phone, talking for hours upon hours to anybody (this was before jails put time limits on phone calls). Even when there was nobody for [him] to talk with, we'd just leave the phone off the hook and he could listen to our day or talk to anyone who came by, until the phone would get turned off.
>
> *Bruce B., adult child of two incarcerated parents*

Until the 1980s, prisoners made collect phone calls using regular pay telephones operated by local service providers. Then the Federal Bureau of Prisons began to contract with correctional telephone service providers; state and local correctional agencies followed suit. The rates charged by the new providers were often many times those charged for the same calls made from phones in the community and included correctional agency commissions, limiting the ability of families to pay for telephone calls with prisoners.[17] These changes are reflected in the stories of our younger contributors, few of whom write about telephone calls with their incarcerated parents. However, more recently, legislation, correctional policies and payment mechanisms for telephone calling from correctional facilities have reduced its costs.

Parent–Child Visitation

More than 50 years of child welfare research has established the importance of visitation during parent–child separations.[18] While there is no similar body of research on the families of incarcerated parents and visitation, there is also no mandate to intervene in or monitor in-person contact between most prisoners and their children.

Although parent–child visits in correctional settings have been the focus of many studies and publications,[19, 20] most children do not visit their incarcerated parents. Less than half of imprisoned parents of both genders and only a third of jailed parents receive visits from their children.[21] There has been much speculation about why more prisoners do not get visits from their children. But perhaps the primary and most obvious reason – the fact that a large minority of the children have never lived with their parents and an equal proportion have lived with them only intermittently – has been mostly overlooked.

Another reason for lack of parent–child visitation is lack of support for visits and other parent–child contact by children's caregivers. Research shows the relationship between the caregiver and the incarcerated parent is significant and will impact whether a child visits a parent.[22] Jails and prisons require a visiting child under the age of 18 to be accompanied by an adult; children are also dependent upon adult caregivers to transport them to visit.[23] Some caregivers are willing and able to take children to visit their parents. For others, the task is more nuanced. A recent report speaks to the sometimes complex relationships between caregivers and incarcerated parents and argues that understanding the impact of incarceration on families and family systems requires, among other things, appreciation of how the parent was influencing family functioning prior to being incarcerated.[24] Conflicts in this arena often directly affect whether or not caregivers support parent–child visits.

Incarcerated parents and their co-parents often have the most conflicted of parent–caregiver relationships.[25] A contributor to this book recalls going to the prison to visit her father:

> His new lover and her child had come to visit at the same time my mom, brother, sister, and I had. He was only allowed to see five people, but there were six of us there to visit him. My dad had to choose between seeing us and seeing his new family. I stood on our side with a smirk on my face, because I know my dad was going to choose us. He had to, of course he will!, I said to myself. I had no doubt in him at all. But to my surprise, he didn't. Before we left, my mom said to him, "You don't have to worry about me coming here anymore." … That was the last day my mother stepped anywhere near that prison.
>
> *Larri C., adult child of an incarcerated father*

Other, long-recognized barriers to parent–child correctional visitation include the distance between the child's home and the parent's jail/prison, and the high cost of travel.[26] Most parents in state and federal prisons are housed at least 100 miles away from their primary residences.[27] The small percentage of prisoners who are female means that there are fewer prisons for women in each state, so women prisoners are housed an average of 160 miles from their children while men are housed an average of only 100 miles away. In addition to distance, it is costly to visit people in prison or jail. One study found that families spend at least 15 percent of their monthly income to stay in touch with incarcerated members.[28]

A contributor to this book recalls her girlhood experience of visiting her father. Her recollection demonstrates the difficulty families have traveling to the prison and the cost involved:

> Eventually I was able to visit him at Sing Sing … From our house in Brooklyn, getting to Sing Sing took a walk, a bus, two trains and then a longer walk up to the main gate. It was costly, so I went once a month, and always walked the last part to save the 50 cents it would cost to get there. The trip, about two to three hours each way, was arduous.
>
> *Shari O., adult child of an incarcerated father.*

The type of correctional facility where the parent is held, the facility's policies regarding visitation, and the kind of contact available may also affect whether or not a child visits.[29] Correctional facilities that require long waiting periods before a visitation can occur, conduct searches of families, and offer noisy, crowded visiting areas may deter families.[30] One of our contributors clearly felt unnerved by the prison's rules and regulations:

> Going inside a prison ... is not a pleasant experience ... every person who enters is a suspect, even a young child. If I wore a belt, I had to take it off. If I had on jewelry, I had to leave it outside the visiting room in an envelope until I left. I was not allowed to carry the card I had handmade for my father ... the visiting rules were dependent on what level of security he was in at the time. Some limited [contact] to a hug before and after the visit and you faced each other across a table. Some wouldn't allow any physical contact at all and made sure of it by separating you by glass.
>
> *Carie S., adult child of an incarcerated father*

Another contributor writes exclusively about visiting her father in prison. Her reflections confirm the disturbing effect of prison security on some children and families, the long distances people often travel to see their loved ones, and the emotional costs and rewards for maintaining the parent–child relationship through visits:

> After driving eight hours ... we must first be inspected for any contraband or paraphernalia ... finally, the line to the Visiting Room ... after hours of visiting and pretending ... the guard ... shouts out "five minutes."
>
> *Vannette T., adult child of an incarcerated father*

Among the contributors to this book, about two-thirds report no type of parent–child contact during parental incarceration.

Social Challenges and Stigma

Many of our contributors speak about the social challenges they felt as children, teens and young adult children of incarcerated parents. Social challenges are circumstances or factors that make it difficult for people to have a sense of belonging or to connect with and feel accepted by others. Many, if not most publications on families and incarceration have suggested that families of incarcerated parents face social challenges stemming from the fact that a loved one is in prison.[31] One of these social challenges is stigma.

No matter how others actually do respond, children and families of incarcerated people are often anxious about how they will be perceived or understood. One older, large-scale study found that while about 40 percent of the children studied were aware of their mother's incarceration, only 6 percent gave that information to others to explain maternal absence.[32] Children of prisoners often report that they know the assumptions others make about prisoners and their families and, as a result, are reluctant to tell people their parents are incarcerated.

> I only told a few close friends about her arrest. I was completely humiliated … My friends didn't really care … but still I felt so much shame and embarrassment.
>
> *Natalie C., adult child of an incarcerated mother*

> I never knew why [my father] was in jail. The family never spoke of it; they just avoided the subject if it ever came up.
>
> *David S., adult child of an incarcerated father*

> [My grandmother] always told me not to talk about my mom being in jail. She was worried about what people would say.
>
> *Jessamyn R., adult child of two incarcerated parents*

Their fears are not unfounded. Although many children receive sympathy upon the loss of a parent, children of incarcerated parents may face disapprobation. The San Francisco Children of Incarcerated Parents Partnership (SFCIP) suggests the problem is important for reasons beyond a child's initial discomfort, since children may internalize stigma and, as a result, develop low self-esteem.[33]

Especially troubling is a recent study that finds children may be stigmatized by teachers.[34] Researchers discovered some teachers feared their colleagues would prejudge a student whose parent was incarcerated; these teachers also thought their colleagues' expectations about the academic competency of students might be negatively influenced if the student had an incarcerated parent. These findings resonate with the experience of one of our contributors:

> For some reason, [my teacher] never liked me and he would punish me as often as he could, often without cause. I tried to stay out of his way but one day I saw him getting chewed out by a school administrator. This made him mad at me. Later, he scolded me in class and ordered me out into the hall, where he began to yell and push me around. I started to fight back. He was banging me up against the lockers when another teacher who heard the sounds of the beating stopped him … I had always liked and done well in school but that experience ended my positive relationship with education.
>
> *Michael C., adult child of an incarcerated father*

It is clear from his story that Michael sees the experience with his teacher in the context of the stigma he felt from his peers:

> One day [Petey and I] were arguing, and he said something about my father. I told him my father was working in the mountains, which is what my mother and grandfather had always said to explain his absences. Petey laughed at me and said, "Your dad isn't working in the mountains. He's in prison. Everybody knows that."
>
> *Michael C., adult child of an incarcerated father*

Michael is writing about life in a small town. The fact that "everybody" knows his father is in prison suggests his teachers know as well. Whatever the teacher's beliefs about him are, Michael experiences these beliefs in the context of his father's incarceration. Furthermore, writing decades after the event, Michael sees a relationship between the teacher's view of his student and Michael's disillusionment with school.

Of course, the majority of teachers are appropriately concerned about the well-being of all their students.

> I had one teacher in particular who was very kind to me. When our AP English class took a field trip, and I couldn't afford it, he paid for me to attend. He later sat me in the classroom seat where the first Latina Rhodes scholar had sat years before, to encourage me. He was an amazing teacher, an older gay man who knew what it was like to have a secret, and he helped me tremendously.
>
> *Natalie C., adult child of an incarcerated mother*

It's important to recognize that there is research that did not identify shame and stigma as a major problem for prisoners' children.[35] However, it should be noted that at least two of these studies were conducted among very-low-income families of color where the higher prevalence of parental incarceration may have reduced the level of social stigma experienced among the children. Indeed, some studies have found that caregiver concerns about the social implications of parental incarceration predict children's sense of stigma.[36]

When a Parent Is Released: Reentry and Reunification

What we know about prisoners' children and families suggests that more focus must be placed on supporting the parent–child relationship before, during and *after* parental incarceration. Because of the difficulty of reentry, it is an especially stressful time for the parent, so experts recommend that reunification start before the parent leaves prison or jail.[37] Furthermore, studies have shown family visitation increases the likelihood that prisoners will have a more successful reentry and lower levels of recidivism.[38]

In 2009, the most recent period for which data is available, persons incarcerated in state prisons served an average of 65 months.[39] Jailed persons serve much shorter sentences. This means that most prisoners – including most incarcerated parents – return to their communities. Many of these parents will reunify with their children in the sense of resuming the parent–child relationship. But we have no data on the proportion of formerly incarcerated parents who actually reside with their children after release. It can be expected to be small for several reasons:

- At least 15 percent of imprisoned parents have had their rights to at least one child terminated.[40]
- Pervasive multi-partnered fertility among parents involved in the criminal justice system[41] makes it clear that many former prisoners will be unable or unlikely to reside with all of their children at the same time – and especially those kids who have resided with their other birth parent their entire lives.
- Other factors also affect parent–child reunification. According to The Urban Institute, when they are released from prison or jail, formerly incarcerated parents often face

homelessness, unemployment, inadequate healthcare and financial debt (especially related to child support payments) that prevent parent–child co-residence.[42]

- The lack of effective rehabilitative services in the prisons (as reflected in high recidivism rates[43]), the stresses of reentry[44] and the lack of substantive supports for formerly incarcerated parents[45] increase their return to drug use and criminal behavior. For these and other reasons, incarcerated parents are rearrested or fail to meet the terms of conditional release at a rate that slightly exceeds that of prisoners who are not parents.[46]

The vulnerability of children of prisoners continues when their parents are released and reenter society. Our contributors' stories mirror those of the larger population of prisoners' children and include a range of parent–child reentry experiences.

Some Parents Don't Return after Incarceration

There is absolutely no published information about parents who do not reunify with their children because they die during incarceration or reentry. Among our contributors, one experienced the death of her father during his incarceration, and the parents of three contributors died shortly after release.

> My father was in jail most of [my early life]. They took me to visit him but I don't remember it. He got killed in jail when I was three. I don't remember that or anything about him except that he was a very big man and when he picked me up it felt like I was high up in the air.
>
> *Mary, adult child of two incarcerated parents*

> I wanted to go and meet [my father] but [my mother] said he had died right after he got out of prison in 1968.
>
> *Betty M., adult child of an incarcerated father*

> On my fifteenth birthday, I got in trouble with my brother and got sent to the California Youth Authority. One of the counselors was trying to find my mom and he found out that she had been murdered in 1998 while I was living in foster care. Later I found out she was strangled and raped and left behind a dumpster in El Monte … I never visited my parents in prison and never got a phone call from them. I have looked for my father in the prison system but there is no one by his name. He would be in his seventies now, so maybe he died there.
>
> *Abel H., adult child of two incarcerated parents*

Some Parents Return but Don't Reunify with Their Children

The parents of a few of our contributors were released from incarceration but did not re-enter their children's lives. This was sometimes the result of the parent's unavailability and sometimes the result of the child's.

In October 2001, two years after his release and at the age of 38, my dad, Mark Vernon Read, was found dead in his flat in England. He died from a heroin overdose. At the time, I was 19 years old and only in the third year of a 28-year sentence. Needless to say, I was devastated.

Jeremy R., adult child of an incarcerated father

As I got older and began to deal with the system more, my mother was slowly abstaining from being a jail bird. But it came too late for me. I was too deep into the system to turn back. The neglect and loneliness I felt in the beginning had made my heart a stone.

Manuel R.W., adult child of an incarcerated mother

Some Parents Return and Reunify Briefly with Their Children

For many reasons, formerly incarcerated parents may return briefly before leaving their children's lives once again. Most often this is due to re-involvement in drugs and/or criminal behavior.

[That first imprisonment] was not his last incarceration. There were others to follow.

Pamela H., adult child of an incarcerated father

I reunited with my father, disregarding court orders not to be with him again. Less than a year has passed and my father is now looking at 29 more felonies. I am currently incarcerated in a county jail and my fate is undetermined for now.

James C., adult child of two incarcerated parents

Some Parents Return and Reunify with Children in Nontraditional Ways

Although not at the rate suggested by many publications on incarcerated parents and their children, some former prisoners reunify with their kids. However, the idealized return of the prodigal father or mother to their children's home is rare and many parent–child reunifications occur in other places and other ways.

As for my father, by some quirk of fate, we ended up living near one another. Following his final prison term – which was still in the pre-background-check days – he was once again the fair-haired boy of the company he worked for. He retired at 77. He still read three newspapers a day, was still recognized as a former football hero; he was still handsome, and was still a con man. He lived into his eighties and my brother and I were with him in his hospital room when he drew his last breath. From his estate, we inherited 123 spotless neckties and a bowling trophy.

Pamela H., adult child of an incarcerated father

By the age of 17, I had been around the U.S. committing crimes and had been in juvenile halls, jails and prisons in California, New York and Wisconsin. My mom had entered my life again but we had a partner-in-crime relationship more than a mother-and-son relationship.

Marcus R., adult child of an incarcerated mother

Just a month ago, I learned that Cliff was here in the same prison. He reached out to me, sending his love. Though I was affected profoundly, I was also bitter, emotional and did not respond. Then he was moved into my housing unit and I now see him almost every day. He's prematurely old, ravaged by heavy drug abuse and his unchanged outlaw lifestyle. As I talk with him at yard, I am profoundly repulsed by most everything he still embraces and represents, and I simultaneously ache with childhood memories, both good and bad.

Bruce B., adult child of two incarcerated parents

[Since his release], my father and I struggle with how to fit into each other's lives. I don't consider his home my home. I feel too intimidated to invite myself for fear of rejection. Although he lives only 15 minutes away, I haven't seen him for years … I continue to try to give him the benefit of the doubt, knowing that he was institutionalized. Perhaps he may not know how to make conversation like others can. I suppose it's easy enough to talk for two hours during a prison visit, but when you have to make an effort to be involved in someone's life, that isn't as easy. The other part of me is not as forgiving. I still continue to be angry that he is absent in my life even now he has his freedom.

Carie S., adult child of an incarcerated father

Some Parents Return to Reunify and Live with Their Children Again

This may be the least common of parental reentry and parent–child reunification scenarios. For example, among our contributors, only the children of four jailed or imprisoned mothers and one imprisoned father reunified in this way.

Incarcerated mothers appear to reunify and reside with their children at a rate several times higher than that of incarcerated fathers.[47] There are some likely reasons for this. First, females are convicted of less-serious/violent offenses and serve shorter sentences to incarceration than males. Second, women prisoners more often lived with their children before incarceration. And, third, multi-partnered fertility is more likely to prevent fathers from living with all of their children than mothers.

It still hurts me to think that the court let our mom have custody of us again.

Nate L., adult child of an incarcerated mother

My mother had stopped getting arrested and incarcerated after serving her fourth sentence in three years. My father didn't stop until he got cancer. He was in a court-ordered treatment program when he found out and from there he went into other institutions like hospitals and nursing homes. But we were always together in our hearts.

Jessamyn R., adult child of two incarcerated parents

My mother had an alcohol problem … On occasions she was arrested for being drunk or driving under the tnfluence. Those nights that they kept her in jail, me and my brother stayed with my aunts. I don't remember what I thought about my mom being in jail. A lot of people we knew had been arrested. I never visited her in jail because she was never there very long, at the most only a few days. I think I was 11 the last time she went.

Mary, adult child of two incarcerated parents

That was my plan to "feed [my mother] from a long-handled spoon" since I developed this bit of emotional intelligence as a teenager. However, God, as he often does, had a different plan for me. The year that I received my undergraduate degree, while I was on summer vacation, and still basking in the glory of a major goal accomplished in my life, my birth mother was almost killed … When I saw her in the fatal condition, my heart was tender and I thought she'd die. As a mature Christian, God began to speak to me more about forgiving her and loving her unconditionally to reflect and replicate His relationship with me. So for the last eight years, I've gone from figuratively "feeding her out of a long-handled spoon" to literally feeding her as well as bathing, dressing, and grooming my mother in her paralyzed state. It has been a very challenging, growing and testing process.

Victoria G., adult child of an incarcerated mother

One Family's Story

Daniel B., one of our contributors, writes expressly about the reentry process, and his essay speaks to the myriad problems children and families face when a parent is released. His essay also provides a compelling story that illustrates what research finds: the challenge of reentry is a challenge for the entire family, and the effects of parental incarceration can sometimes be shown to exist from cradle to grave.

Research indicates that a parent's incarceration may be associated with child outcomes even if it occurs prior to the child's birth.[48] Currently a lawyer who specializes in reentry issues, Daniel understands his family's story in the context of reentry more generally. He has written:

My father was released from custody and put on parole in the fall of 1985. I was only a few months old at his homecoming, I have no recollection of his incarceration of the years after his release. Accordingly, our family's story is not so much one of incarceration as it is reentry. Our collective struggle to move beyond my father's felonious past has been, I believe, the most defining aspect of who we are as a family. As is often the case, the long and destructive reach of the collateral consequences of his criminal record impacted not just our access to resources and opportunities, but also how we viewed ourselves and our place in the community.

Althrough he was too young to remember his father's incarceration, Daniel's family struggles with the same challenges as do many families of formerly incarcerated people: under-employment, a criminal record, substance abuse and shame. And yet Daniel's family does succeed. Daniel attributes this to his parents' respect for each other and their commitment to parenting. He recognizes his father's good fortune in securing a job when he was released from prison and his parents' ability to work hard and provide for their children. As he has said, however, Daniel realizes his father's reentry journey is also the family's journey, and he underscores the long-term consequences of parental incarceration on an entire family.

An Unexpected Adult Outcome of Parental Incarceration

We made a surprising finding in compiling *Parental Incarceration: Personal Accounts and Developmental Impact*. About one in four contributors (23 percent) are advocates who work specifically with or on behalf of prisoners' children and their families.

> I got released in 2001, after 16 years in Pennsylvania and federal prisons. Right after I got out, I went to work for the Center as a child custody advocate for incarcerated fathers.
>
> *Michael C., adult child of an incarcerated father*

> I work and volunteer two days a week in a program for pregnant prisoners.
>
> *Jessamyn R., adult child of two incarcerated parents*

> Some might have expected me to end up in jails and prisons just like my mother and they were exactly right! But I am honored to say that I have never been arrested or incarcerated in my life, but gladly go to jail on a biweekly basis to inspire and empower others that might be mothers like mine.
>
> *Victoria G., adult child of an incarcerated mother*

> I am a civil rights attorney and practice exclusively on matters related to reentry – litigating employment and housing discrimination charges, lobbying for increased reentry-focused resources and reduced barriers to reentry, organizing individuals with criminal records and their families to speak out for restored opportunities for productive citizenship.
>
> *Daniel B., adult child of an incarcerated father*

This high level of involvement by individuals with first-hand understanding of parental arrest/incarceration/reentry is exciting in a field that is characterized by unrelenting complexity and few successful "solutions." It promises a future in which researchers, practitioners, policymakers and others working around the issues of parental incarceration will be able to expand the knowledge base of the field by drawing from both their professional and personal experience while modeling the ability to overcome the developmental challenges faced by children in justice-involved families.

Conclusions

Negotiating the logistics of parental criminal justice system involvement is always difficult. The relational aspects of these processes and issues like stigma add to the complexity of parents', children's and families' experiences. Yet there are some clear conclusions that can be drawn from the research about children of incarcerated parents and from their stories:

- Telling children about parental arrest/incarceration and encouraging them to express their feelings about these experiences will help their adjustment to these difficult circumstances.
- Parent–child contact during parental incarceration is determined to a large extent by the parent–child relationship prior to incarceration and the parent–caregiver relationship during incarceration.
- Parent–child correctional visitation is almost always beneficial for children and the parent–child relationship.
- Children of prisoners may experience the adverse consequences of social stigma, and this is most likely where their caregivers are concerned about the stigma of parental incarceration.
- Only a small proportion of children of incarcerated parents experience parent–child reunification in the traditional sense of residing with their parents again.
- Some children of incarcerated parents have a non-traditional parent–child reunification experience.
- Many prisoners' children never reunify – traditionally or otherwise – with their incarcerated parents.

In addition to the research on prisoners' children and the knowledge of practitioners who have conducted services for this population, the stories of adults who experienced parental incarceration as children are invaluable in helping us to understand the complex circumstances and outcomes of families involved in the criminal justice system. By following the research, attending to authoritative opinion and listening to the stories of those with first-hand experience, we can learn how to best help children and families survive and thrive under the difficult process that is parental arrest, incarceration and reentry.

Notes

1 Federal Bureau of Investigation. (2015). *Crime in the United States 2013: Persons Arrested*. FBI Uniform Crime Reports. Washington, D.C.: US Department of Justice. Available at: www.fbi.gov/about-us/cjis/ucr/crime-in-the-u.s/2013/crime-in-the-u.s.-2013/persons-arrested/persons-arrested.
2 Glaze LN, Marushak LM. (2008). *Parents in Prison and Their Minor Children*. NCJ 222984. Washington, D.C.: US Department of Justice, Bureau of Justice Statistics.
3 Blustain, R. (2013). Pushing Cops to Consider Kids when Arresting Parents. *City Limits*. New York: City Limits; Johnston D. (1995b). Jailed mothers. In Gable K, Johnston D. (Eds.). *Children of Incarcerated Parents*. New York: Lexington Books; NY State Division of Criminal Justice Services. (2013). *Children of Incarcerated Parents in New York State*. Albany, NY: Authors.
4 Phillips SD, Burns SJ, Wagner HR, Barth RP. (2004). Parental arrest and children involved with child welfare agencies. *American Journal of Orthopsychiatry*, 74(2): 174–186.
5 NY State Division of Criminal Justice Services. *Ibid*.
6 Dallaire DH, Wilson LC. (2010). The relation of exposure to parental criminal activity, arrest and sentencing to children's maladjustment. *Journal of Child and Family Studies*, 19(4): 404–418; Johnston D. (1995b). *Ibid;* Kinner SA, Alati R, Najman JM, Williams GM. (2007). Do parental arrest and imprisonment lead to child behavioral problems and substance abuse? *Journal of Child Psychology and Psychiatry*, 48(11): 1148–1156.

7 Doerner JK, Demuth S. (2012). Gender and sentencing in the federal courts. *Criminal Justice Policy Review*, 25(2): 242–269; Daly K. (1994). *Gender, Crime and Punishment.* New Haven, CT: Yale University Press; Daly K. (1989). Neither conflict nor labeling nor paternalism will suffice: Intersections of race, ethnicity, gender and family in criminal court decisions. *Crime and Delinquency*, 35(1): 136–168.

8 Adalist-Estrin, A. (n.d.). *Conversations: Questions Children Ask.* Children of Prisoners Library. Available at: http://nrccfi.camden.rutgers.edu/files/cipl103-conversations-questionschildrenask.pdf.

9 Hairston CF. (1990). Mothers in jail: Parent–child separation and jail visitation. *Affilia*, 6(2): 9–27; Walker C. (2003). *Parents behind Bars Talk about Their Children.* Pittsburgh, PA: Pittsburgh Child Guidance Foundation.

10 Ayers TS, Sandler IN, West SG, Roosa MW. (1996). Assessment of children's coping behaviors: Testing alternative models of children's coping. *Journal of Personality*, 64(4): 923–958; Compas BE. (1987). Coping with stress during childhood and adolescence. *Psychological Bulletin*, 101: 393–403.

11 Lister ED. (1982). Forced silence: A neglected dimension of trauma. *American Journal of Psychiatry*, 139(7): 872–876; Snyder-Joy ZK, Carlo TA. (1998). Parenting through prison walls. In Miller SL. (Ed.), *Crime Control and Women: Feminist Implications of Criminal Justice Policy* (130–150). Thousand Oaks, CA: SAGE Publications.

12 Adalist-Estrin A. *Ibid.*; Families & Criminal Justice. (2014). *Where's Daddy? Telling a Child about Parental Incarceration.* Los Angeles, CA: Authors; Prison MATCH. (1984). *Telling Your Child You're in Prison.* Berkeley, CA: Authors; Osborne Association. (1996). *How Can I Help? Working with Children of Incarcerated Parents.* New York: Authors.

13 Glaze, Marushak. *Ibid.*; Walker. *Ibid.*

14 Glaze, Marushak. *Ibid.*

15 Poehlmann J, Dallaire D, Loper AB, Shear L. (2010). Children's contact with their incarcerated parent: Research and findings. *American Psychologist*, 65(6): 575–598.

16 Glaze, Marushak. *Ibid.*

17 Hairston CF. (1998). The forgotten parent: Understanding the forces that influence incarcerated fathers' relationships with their children. *Child Welfare*, 77(5): 617–639; Also, please see a review of this issue by the Campaign to Promote Equitable Telephone Charges at www.etccampaign.com/progress.php.

18 See the review in Johnston D. (1995d). Parent–child visits in jails. *Children's Environments*, 12(1): 25–38.

19 For a comprehensive review of the early history of correctional parent–child visitation programs see Cannings K. (1990). *Bridging the Gap: Programs and Services to Facilitate Contact between Inmate Parents and Their Children.* Ottawa: Ministry of the Solicitor General of Canada.

20 Arditti JA. (2003). Locked doors and glass walls: Family visiting at a local jail. *Journal of Loss and Trauma*, 8: 115–138; Beckerman A. (1989). Incarcerated mothers and their children in foster care: The dilemma of visitation. *Children and Youth Services Review*, 11(2): 175–183; Bertram J, Lowenberg C, McCall C, Rosenkrantz L. (1982). *My Real Prison Is … Being Separated from My Child.* San Francisco: Prison MATCH; Block KJ, Potthast MJ. (1998). Girl Scouts beyond bars: Facilitating parent–child contact in correctional settings. *Child Welfare*, 77: 561–578; Bloom B, Steinhart D. (1993). *Why Punish the Children? A Reappraisal of the Children of Incarcerated Mothers.* New York: National Council on Crime and Delinquency; Boudin C. (2012). *Prison Visitation Policies: A Fifty State Survey.* ExpressO. Available at: http://works.bepress.com/chesa_boudin/1; Dixey R, Woodall J. (2012). The significance of "the visit" in an English Category B prison: Views from prisoners, prisoners' families and prison staff. *Community, Work and Family*, 15(1): 29–47; Hairston. (1990). *Ibid.*; Johnston D. (1993b). *CCIP Research Monograph No. 2: Parent–Child Contact Visitation in California County Jails.* Pasadena, CA: Center for Children of Incarcerated Parents; Johnston D. (1993c). *CCIP Research Monograph No. 7: Children's Reactions to Visitation in the Prison.* Pasadena, CA: Center for Children of Incarcerated Parents; LaVigne NG, Naser RL, Brooks LE, Castro JL. (2005). Examining the effect of incarceration and in-prison family contact on prisoners' family relationships. *Journal of Contemporary Criminal Justice*, 21: 314–355; Laughlin JS, Arrigo BA, Blevins KR, Coston CTM. (2008). Incarcerated mothers and child visitation: A law, social science, and policy perspective. *Criminal Justice Policy Review*, 19: 215–238; Massachusetts Department of Correction. (1987). *Joining Incarcerated Mothers with Their Children: The Lancaster Visiting Cottage Program.* Boston: Authors; Poehlmann J, Runion H, Burson C, Maleck S, Weymouth L, Pettit K, Huser M. (2015). Young children's behavioral and emotional reactions to plexiglass and video

visits with jailed parents. In Poehlmann-Tynan J. (Ed.), *Children's Contact with Incarcerated Parents: Implications for Policy and Intervention*. New York: Springer Briefs in Psychology; Weilerstein R. (1995). The Prison MATCH Program. In Gable K, Johnston D. (Eds.), *Children of Incarcerated Parents*. New York: Lexington Books.

21 Glaze, Marushak. *Ibid.*; Walker. *Ibid.*

22 Poehlmann et al. (2010). *Ibid.*

23 Lincroft Y. (2011). *When A Parent Is Incarcerated: A Primer for Social Workers*. Baltimore: The Annie E. Casey Foundation.

24 Turanovic JJ, Rodriguez N, Pratt TC. (2012). The collateral consequences of incarceration revisited: A qualitative analysis of the effects on caregivers of children of incarcerated parents. *American Society of Criminology*, 50(4): 913–959.

25 Carlin M. (2000). Asserting parental rights from prison. *Family and Corrections Network Report*, 22: 1–3.

26 Bloom B, Steinhart D. *Ibid.*; also see review in Poehlmann et al. (2010). *Ibid.*

27 Mumola, C. (2000). *Incarcerated Parents and Their Children*. NCJ 182335. Washington, D.C.: The Bureau of Justice Statistics.

28 Travis J, McBride EC, Solomon AL. (Revised 2005). *Families Left Behind: The Hidden Costs of Incarceration and Reentry*. Washington, D.C.: The Urban Institute Press.

29 Poehlmann et al. (2010). *Ibid.*

30 LaVigne N, Davies E, Brazzell D. (2008). *Broken Bonds: Understanding and Addressing the Needs of Children with Incarcerated Parents*. Washington, D.C.: The Urban Institute Justice Policy Center.

31 Arditti JA. (2005). Families and incarceration: An ecological approach. *Families in Society: Journal of Contemporary Social Services*, 86(2), 251–260; Bakker LJ, Morris BA, Janus LM. (1978). Hidden victims of crime. *Social Work*, 23: 143–148; Braman D, Wood J. (2003). From one generation to the next: How criminal sanctions are reshaping family life in urban America. In Travis J, Waul M. (Eds.), *Prisoners Once Removed* (157–188). Washington, D.C.: The Urban Institute Press; Hannon G, Martin D, Martin M. (1984). Incarceration in the family: Adjustment to change. *Family Therapy*, 11: 253–260; Nesmith A, Ruhland E. (2006). Children of incarcerated parents: Challenges and resiliency in their own words. *Children and Youth Services Review*, 30(10): 1119–1130; Zalba S. (1964). *Women Prisoners and Their Families*. Sacramento, CA: Department of Social Welfare and Department of Corrections.

32 Zalba. *Ibid.*

33 San Francisco Children of Incarcerated Parents Partnership. (2005). *Children of Incarcerated Parents Bill of Rights*. Available at: www.sfcipp.org/images/brochure.pdf.

34 Dallaire, DH, Ciccone A, Wilson LC. (2010). Teachers' experiences with and expectations of children with incarcerated parents. *Journal of Applied Developmental Psychology*, 131(4): 281–290.

35 Baunach PJ. (1979, November). *Mothering from Behind Prison Walls*. Paper presented at the annual meeting of the American Society of Criminology, Philadelphia; Johnston D. (1992). *The Children of Criminal Offenders Study: A Report to the California Assembly Office of Research*. Pasadena, CA: The Center for Children of Incarcerated Parents; Schneller DP. (1978). *The Prisoner's Family*. San Francisco, CA: R&E Research Associates.

36 Zalba. *Ibid.*

37 Jacobs A. (2001). Give 'em a fighting chance: Women offenders reenter society. *Criminal Justice*, 45(16); Travis J. (2005). *But They All Come Back: Facing the Challenges of Prisoner Reentry*. New York: The Urban Institute Press.

38 Barrick K, Lattimore PK, Visher CA. (2014). Rentering women: The impact of social ties on long-term recidivism. *The Prison Journal*, 94(3): 279–304; Cochran JC. (2013). Breaches in the wall: Imprisonment, social support and recidivism. *Journal of Research in Crime and Delinquency*, 51(2): 200–229; Hairston, CF. (1998). Family ties during imprisonment: Do they influence further criminal activity? *Federal Probation*, 48–52; Minnesota Department of Corrections. (2011). *Effects of Prison Visitation on Offender Recidivism*. St. Paul, MN: Authors.

39 Bonczar TP. (2011). *National Corrections Reporting Program: Sentence Length of State Prisoners, by Offense, Admission Type, Sex, and Race*. Washington, D.C.: Department of Justice, Bureau of Justice Statistics. Available at: www.bjs.gov/index.cfm?ty=pbdetail&iid=2056.

40 Applied Behavioral Health Policy. (2005). *An Epidemiological Study of the Prevalence and Needs of Children of Incarcerated Parents within the State of Arizona*. Phoenix, AZ: University of Arizona.

41 Carlson MJ, Furstenberg FF. (2005). *The Consequences of Multi-Partnered Fertility for Parental Involvement and Relationships.* Fragile Families Publication 2006–28-FF. Available at: http://crcw.princeton. edu/publications/publications.asp; Geller A. (2013). Paternal incarceration and father–child contact in fragile families. *Journal of Marriage and the Family,* 75(5): 1288–1303; Hairston CF. (1989). Men in prison: Family characteristics and family views. *Journal of Offender Counseling, Services and Rehabilitation,* 14(1): 23–30; Harknett K, Knab J. (2007). More kin, less support: Multi-partnered fertility and perceived support among mothers. *Journal of Marriage and the Family,* 69(1): 237–253.

42 Travis et al. *Ibid.*

43 Langan P, Levin D. (2002). Recidivism of prisoners released in 1994. *Federal Sentencing Reporter,* 15 (1): 58–65; Phelps MS. (2011). Rehabilitation in the punitive era: The gap between rhetoric and reality in U.S. prison programs. *Law and Society Review,* 45(1): 33–68.

44 Binswanger IA, Stern MF, Deyo RA, Heagerty PJ, Cheadle A, Elmore JG, Koepsell TD. (2007). Release from prison: A high risk of death for former inmates. *New England Journal of Medicine,* 356 (2): 157–165; Geller A, Curtis MA. (2011). A sort of homecoming: Incarceration and the housing security of urban men. *Social Science Review,* 40(4): 1196–1213; Turney K, Wildeman C, Schnittker J. (2012). As fathers and felons: Explaining the effects of current and recent incarceration on major depression. *Journal of Health and Social Behavior,* 53(4): 465–481.

45 Covington S, Bloom B. (2003). Gendered justice: Women in the criminal justice system. In Bloom B. (Ed.), *Gendered Justice: Addressing Female Offenders.* Durham, NC: Carolina Academic Press; Dill LJ, Mahaffey C, Mosley T, Treadwell H, Barkwell F, Barnhill S. (2015). I want a second chance: Experiences of African American fathers in reentry. *American Journal of Men's Health,* doi: 10.1177/ 1557988315569593; Spjeldnes S, Goodkind S. (2009). Gender differences and offender reentry: A review of the literature. *Journal of Offender Rehabilitation,* 48(4): 314–335; Travis. *Ibid.*

46 Glaze, Marushak. *Ibid.*

47 Johnston, D. (2002). What works: Children of prisoners. In Gadsden V. (Ed.), *Heading Home: Offender Reintegration in the Family – What Works.* Lanham, MD: American Correctional Association.

48 Roettger M, Swisher R. (2011). Associations of fathers' history of incarceration with sons' delinquency and arrest among Black, White and Hispanic males in the United States. *Criminology,* 49(4): 1109–1147. doi: 10.1111/j.1745–912.5.2011.00253x.

PERSONAL STORIES

My Name is Tony Shavers by Tony Shavers, III

When a son is given the name of his father, there is a unique permanent attachment between the two. In my case, the nature of the attachment is something I've struggled not to feel imprisoned by, but instead to find freedom in.

There was a time when I would walk around my neighborhood and people would ask me, "You're Tony's son?" "And I would say, "Yes," but without much enthusiasm. My dad is Tony Shavers, Jr., and I am Tony Shavers, III.

"When does he get out?" they'd next want to know. I would freeze, stare blankly at them, and walk away. Those types of comments created permanent wounds on my heart. I did not want to be questioned about my dad's incarceration. My dad has been incarcerated for more time than he has been actively present in my life. I've had my share of migraines and tears because of his absence. It hurts when people ask me when my dad is getting out of jail. And the fact that I can't lie and just say he's doing awesome also hurts.

My dad was pretty popular in my community, so everyone knows me as "Lil Tony." In a way, it makes me popular too, but it's not the kind of popularity that I want to have. Having the same name as my father made me fear that I would be the mirror image of him: I would become an absentee father or never learn from my mistakes.

I was deemed Tony Shavers, III on November 5, 1992. I was born one pound, four ounces. The doctors told my mom I was not going to live, and that if I did, I would not make it past the eighth grade. But I proved them wrong, continually exceeding expectations. But even as I thrived in my development, my name was a heavy burden. Having a name passed down, a third generation name is unique, and should hold value. I was never pleased with it, though. I used to write only "Tony Shavers" on all my homework assignments, poems and name cards, because having the roman numerals III annexed after Shavers made me feel as if I would never amount to anything. Maybe if my name was Anthony Darnell Shavers, the name my mom had originally planned for me, then I would not doubt myself so much. Maybe if I switched names I'd have a better approach to life and would become a new individual, not the person I feared becoming.

The name held me hostage. It made me feel as if I was going to walk the same path and encounter the same trials as my father. I was trapped between two different directions – do I make something out of myself, or do I follow the road of my dad?

I used to question my mom about my name, asking her why they had agreed on Tony Shavers, III.

"Well son," she'd say, "Your grandpa was named Tony Shavers, Sr., and he wanted all of his first sons to take his name. Your dad is the second and then you are the third. Make sense?"

"Yes, but when I have kids, do I have to name my son Tony Shavers too?"

"Well, I can't tell you what to name your kids, but your dad would like this name to be passed down for a long time."

"That's not fair. I don't want to name my son Tony Shavers, IV. I barely want to be named that. I don't want to follow in the same footsteps as my dad. Will I end up in jail like he is? Will I turn to drugs, too?"

"Tony, I understand you believe it's not fair to be named after your father. At the same time, don't let his actions make you think you're less of a person. If you don't want to go down the same road your dad is on, then you set a new meaning for Tony Shavers, III. Set a positive example for Tony Shavers, IV, so that he may take ownership and speak with purpose that he is named after a great father."

Maybe a name should not have so much power over your life. Maybe.

Because of my dad's imprisonment he has missed out on a lot of events in my life. An event that really hit home for me was my high school graduation from Oakland School for the Arts. Graduating high school is a stepping stone for people and having my family cheer me on would have meant the world to me. Unfortunately, as bad as I wanted my father to attend my graduation, I knew that it couldn't be so; I knew that he would be cheering me on from behind bars. While the rest of my family was in the crowd, I only wished that there was a way to have my dad released from jail just for the graduation. I wanted him to be able to say that he attended his first-born son's high school graduation. He never made it past the eighth grade. I made it, despite those doctors' predictions for me.

In 2008, my dad went to Richmond County Jail. I went to the computer, logged on the website and typed, "TONY SHAVERS." His sentence appeared along with the robbery charges. Seeing that made me realize that I have to excel and make my life worth living. Following in the same direction as my father was not an option. One generation of Tonys has to stand for something positive and it must start with me. I sat there at my computer, my hands stroking the keys and wondered if I should erase what I had typed and start over. Maybe it was a mistake! That was the first time my dad's incarceration felt real. No matter how bad I wanted his name to disappear, it was permanent.

I have the right not to be judged, blamed, or labeled because of my parents' incarceration.

I realize now that even more than having others judge me because of my father's incarceration, I judged myself harshly for being the direct descendant of a man who wanted me to be named after him, but could not teach me the fundamentals of what a man should be. In a way I am grateful today that I did not learn values and morals from someone who did not even know them himself. He does not know these things partly because his father died at an early age. He, too, did not have a father figure around to guide him.

But there is always room for learning how to be a man. I am a son who does not have a responsible father in his life, but am determined to be responsible. My dad is a human who makes mistakes but fails to learn from them. I know I will make my own mistakes in life, but I also know I am determined to grow from them. Ever since my dad has been incarcerated he has told me, "You don't want to end up like me. Serving time for crime." I don't, and something that I want to ask him is, "Why do you? Why are you always behind bars or a reflective mirror when I see you?"

The actions of your parents can paint the mural of what your life is going to be like, if you allow it. As a child of an incarcerated parent it is expected that you will be immersed in the lifestyle of prison, that there is no future or success in the years ahead of you. But just because I was named after my dad does not mean that I will end up in the same situation that he is. Even though we share the same name, our directions in life are very distinct. Today I know that.

My dad has spent a lot of years in prison physically; I've spent years in an emotional prison. In my sixteenth year, I found my release from this internal prison through a passion that would allow me to express myself, connect with others, and cope with detrimental experiences: I found writing. Writing became my creative outlet, allowing me to use the animosity, anguish, and the shame within me in a positive manner. Writing helped me claim myself, the man I want to be. I want to be able to speak truth about issues that most people are afraid to speak about: racism, sexism, abuse, and sexual orientation. Because I am walking down the course of success my writing path is headed towards greatness, away from Tony Shavers, Jr., and toward Tony Shavers, III. I am inspiring my audience with my poetry. I finally began writing my full name after reclaiming it when I wrote my poem "16 years." It was a pivotal year when I came to the awareness that the alliance with my dad would not happen and that the complications at my birth had made me more secure in who I am.

> 16 years I've been living on this planet called earth. Weighing one pound four ounces at birth. 16 years, a relationship between a father and his son did not get the chance to blossom but hid in the cracks covered by darkness. But with every step that I take, every breath I inhale, every person that I come in contact with lets me know Tony Shavers III is and always will be Destined 4 Greatness.

When we are judged because of our parents' incarceration – whether by others or by ourselves – our creativity is halted. It makes us feel that our aspirations and desires will never be reached. We need the support of community organizations, community activists, politicians, and others. We need them not to judge us because of the actions of our parents. We need them to believe in us, and we need to believe in ourselves. In many ways the incarceration of my father still hurts me, but I will not let his path erase the steps that I am taking toward a new life. I am now an 18-year-old young man who is claiming the destiny he was always set for. I am still a fatherless son, but a son who will exceed the expectations of doubters and live up to his name, Tony Shavers, III.

In the words of Ralph Waldo Emerson, "Do not go where the path may lead, go instead where there is no path and leave a trail."

★★★

The White Bridge by Carie Spicer

As a child I often dreamed about the magic of life and how I could live happily ever after in a carefree cartoon world. My favorite stories were the dramatic fairy tales where the princess was saved from danger and the villain was defeated. Unlike many of my peers, I always had empathy for the villain. I couldn't help but to wonder what happens to the children of the villain? Maybe I wondered that because the child of the villain was me.

I was about 5 years old when I was told my father was going to prison. My relationship with him was already very difficult since my parents had gone through what I know now to be a bitter divorce. I remember crying for him and waiting at the window to see if he would come for me. Now I was being told he could never come for me. I remember being confused that I would not be able to see him because of this thing called prison. What was prison anyway? Of course one of my relatives kindly explained it as being a place where "bad" people go. Was I going to go there too if I was bad? How bad did I have to be? This new situation was scary for me. I didn't want to go to this place called prison even though I loved my father.

I remember my family discussing my father's trial and the outcome. There were whispers in the family about how to protect me. What did this mean? Protect me? I didn't understand why I needed protection or what protection was exactly. I just didn't get the enormity of the situation. So finally, my mom, step-dad, and grandparents sat me down to discuss what was happening. My father had shot someone at a bar after a dispute regarding repayment of a loan. The man was dead. The man's family was publically angry at the situation and threatened revenge on my father's family. When this got back to my mom, she decided that the threat warranted my adoption by my step-dad and that my name should be changed to protect me. It would also be several years before I was allowed to visit my father in prison, but that was okay because he wasn't going anywhere. He was sentenced to 25-years-to-life with possible parole after 15 years.

When I was finally old enough to understand the concept of prison, I still had no way to relate it to anything in my daily life. I remember my aunt picking me up one Saturday morning with a prison reservation form in hand. We drove up to an old scary brick building and crumbling parking lot. It looked a lot like an old church from a scary movie. We walked up the stairs and into the building and from that point on my perspective on the world changed. I saw hundreds of men in a prison yard dressed in what looked to be medical uniforms. Then, I noticed that each man had a number sewn on the front of the shirt. Their identity was now just a number belonging to the state of Ohio.

Going inside a prison is something many people will never experience in their lifetime. It is not a pleasant experience, to say the least. Every person who enters is a suspect, even a young child. If I wore a belt, I had to take it off. If I had on jewelry, I had to leave it outside the visiting room in an envelope until I left. I was not allowed to carry the card I had handmade for my father. I was quickly scanned and stripped of my dignity before I could be cleared for entrance. The sound of the gate unlocking is still embedded in my mind. The cold steel doors that kept people in the walls felt like they were keeping me in a nightmare.

The visiting rules depended on what level of security he was in at the time. Some prisons limited you to a hug before and after the visit, and you faced each other across a table. Some wouldn't allow any physical contact at all and made sure of it by separating you with glass. There were vending machines and the sound of quarters being fed and microwaves burning popcorn. The chairs were hard and cold and there were no creature comforts. Just a loud room full of strangers' voices talking over each other. The visits quickly came and went, and when I left the gate behind me, my life went back to what was now normal.

Growing up I would hide the fact that I had a parent in prison. It was a lot easier to do since I had my adopted father's name, but it didn't change the fact that I was in pain from that part of my life. I was fearful at times that someone would find out who I really was and that they would come and hurt me or my family. I wanted to be well liked. I worried about what would happen if the kids at school found out that I had a parent who murdered someone. That would make me bad too, right? I wondered who already knew my secrets. Did my teachers know? Did that lady staring at me know? I felt some type of paranoia wondering and evaluating each person I came in contact with. I was unintentionally shy and alienated myself from others outside of my family. I can count on one hand how many times I actually spent the night with a friend through all my school years. I was afraid to make friends who might find out who I was and where I came from. To this day, I noticeably struggle making friends. I attribute that very much to not building that skill when I was younger.

Through the years, I would occasionally visit my father and mail letters to him. Every so often, I would get a card from him. It wasn't the same as having the time and attention you desire with your parent. The older I grew the more I needed someone who was present in my life. My visits became fewer, but I still managed to see him as my schedule would allow. Before you knew it, I was driving my own car to the prison to visit him. Things were pretty much the same for him, but in my world I was growing up. I had become a young adult and started college. I was determined to bury the secret of who I was and make myself a successful contributor to society so I couldn't be compared to the sins of my father.

I started my own family and saw my father less. I was in my twenties. The thought of him ever being out of prison was a long-forsaken dream. Then one day, I received a call from my aunt, asking me to write a letter to the parole board on my father's behalf. With mixed feelings, I did. In my letter to the board, I wanted that family of the victim to know that I was respectful of the fact that their loved one was lost tragically and unnecessarily and that from the bottom of my heart, I was sorry for that. I wanted the family and the board to know that I too wanted a chance to have a relationship with my father that I had never had. The only way that this could happen was if he was released. I so badly wanted him to have a chance at building the relationship with my kids he had missed having with me. It wasn't long afterwards that the hearing day came. I decided to go to the hearing to finally face the family of the victim, which I had never done before. For the past 22 years, I had only feared them for the sake of my life. I looked at each one of them. They seemed to be very normal people that had lost someone important to them. I wanted them to know that I was not an enemy. It was a matter of several minutes before the board approved the parole. In a matter of days, my father would be free.

So this is where the fairytale should have begun for me. Unfortunately, it hasn't been that simple. My father and I struggle with how to fit into each other's lives. I don't consider his home my home. I feel too intimidated to invite myself for fear of rejection. Although he lives only 15 minutes away, I haven't seen him for years. The last time we had any contact was by text message after a family member passed. I continue to try to give him the benefit of the doubt, knowing that he was institutionalized. Perhaps he may not know how to make conversation like others can. I suppose it's easy enough to talk for two hours during a prison visit, but when you have to make an effort to be involved in someone's life, that isn't as easy. The other part of me is not as forgiving. I still continue to be angry that he is absent from my life even now that he has his freedom.

All these years, I envisioned the white stone bridge that I drove over to visit my father in prison in Orient, Ohio. I believed that someday that white bridge would signify the crossing of this new life for us as father and daughter. In reality, that bridge has been more of a reminder of pain and promises that never transpired. I live my life now just as before. I bury the secrets of the past and swallow the pain of it all, always wondering and waiting to see if someday our relationship will flourish.

★★★

That Place by Ifetayo Harvey

The state of Florida convicted and sentenced my dad to 15 years in prison for cocaine trafficking. I was 4 years old when he was sent to prison. During his incarceration, I communicated with him through letters – no phone calls or visits because those things cost money. We made do with the letters and this is how I grew to know my father for the eight years that he was in prison. He never spoke directly about his incarceration, my mom did. She told me that my dad went away because he sold drugs. My dad told me that he loved and cared about me; yet, he was not there physically. This confused me.

When I was 14 years old, the government deported my father back to his birth country, Jamaica, where he lives today. I became reacquainted with my dad when I was 16 years old during my visit to Jamaica. We hung out for about a week. He introduced me to a lot of friends and family because he was so happy to see me. During my short visit, there were awkward silences and conversations. I drove a car for the first time there. At one point when we were in the car together, my dad opened up about his absence from my life; he apologized for missing all of the monumental moments that father and child are supposed to experience together. I knew then that I had already forgiven him. I found that forgiveness was the only way for me to move on, but that route is not for everyone.

Growing up, I always wondered if I would be happier with my dad around. When I wrote my dad, my mom always told me to ask him for money, but I hardly did; it felt weird asking my estranged father for money, even though I knew that I deserved it. In my family, we sweep emotional and mental toil under the rug, so I never felt comfortable opening up about the isolation that I felt in social situations. There were nights when I cried myself to sleep because I struggled with intrusive thoughts of my dad being beaten or raped in prison. I never asked him about what happened to him in prison because he referred to it as "that place."

Speaking about my father's incarceration meant facing my fears of invalidation. Entering college was a turning point in my life. I grew up in Charleston, South Carolina, so moving to Massachusetts marked my first time leaving family and friends. When I reflect on my time in college, I remember Smith [college] as the first place where I spoke openly about my father's incarceration. During my last day at Bridge, a pre-orientation program for students of color, I opened up about my relationship with my dad. Two years later, I published a story in the *Huffington Post*, "Children of Incarcerated Parents Bear the Weight of the War on Drugs" and I spoke at the opening plenary of the 2013 International Drug Policy Reform Conference. At that point in my life, I had learned that no relationship is picture perfect and that you don't have to give up when situations turn tough. My father's incarceration taught me how to alter the way I conduct my everyday relationships.

My dad's incarceration has inspired some of my passion for social change. I want to learn from other children of incarcerated parents in order to continue being an advocate for people like me. I want the War on Drugs to end because it is indeed a war on people. I yearn for amnesty for the thousands of people in prison for non-violent drug offenses. I hope that ordinary citizens will destroy the system that allows wealthy CEOs to profit from the subjugation of vulnerable people in and out of the prison system. I want to live in a world where violence is understood and not encouraged. I want to live in a world where police and prisons are not necessary. Through my father's absence, I learned to treat people with compassionate kindness while demanding the same respect from them. I learned to take a step back before I judge someone else's situation.

Maintaining friendships are important because when I enter times of anguish I want someone to be there for me. I hope that over the years us humans will teach our children to take the time to treat each other's past vices with compassion rather than judgment.

★★★

Visiting Day by Vannette Thomson

As we pull into the parking lot, I hear the crunching of gravel under the vehicle tires. I think to myself, "Each little pebble is like the broken hearts that come to this place, some shoot out from under the pressure and some remain here year after year." After driving eight hours, Mamaw parks her car in the first available space. I curiously watch the other visitors make their way toward the building. Although I walk casually with a smile on my young face, my heart is beating like a moth against a window trying to get closer to the light just on the other side of the glass.

We stand outside the barbed wire fence waiting patiently for everyone to make their way from their car to the first of numerous guard-manned gates we must travel through to get inside the prison. I glare at the guard in the tower looking down on us behind his mirrored sunglasses and pale grey uniform. In my child's mind, I believe him an enemy. All the people who work here are enemies because they keep my Daddy here. Not until I am older do I realize Daddy's choices put him here, not the people who work at the prison.

Once the button is pushed, the buzz sounds, and the gate is unlocked. We walk into the main entrance of the Holman State Prison, but before entering the visiting room, we must first be inspected for any contraband or paraphernalia. The female guard who pats us down steps forward to begin her responsibility of insuring we are "all clean." She has blonde hair teased into the shape of a perfectly round bouffant ball, bright coral-colored lipstick, and a crisp, starched guard uniform that is a bit too tight for her plump, soft, physique. Contrary to her dated look, she is always kind toward me while she inspects the insides of my shoes and pats down my entire body – even the insides of my legs. I often wonder what she actually discovers on visitors that make it necessary to subject children to this. Her soft voice and gentle smile help make the moment less awkward.

Next, each family takes turns at the vending machines filled with shrink-wrapped soybean burgers, chili-dogs, and sandwiches packed in triangular-shaped plastic containers. The vending machine line is usually long because items in them taste better than the meals the men are given. When it is our turn, Mamaw and I gather as much food as is reasonable, being careful to leave enough for the other visitors behind us.

Finally, the line into the visiting room. It won't be long now until I see my Daddy walk through the door on the opposite side of the room! I can hardly wait and I begin to squirm and fidget. I look through the glass into the vacant visiting area, and at all the tables and benches around for the families and friends to share with their loved one. I hate the depressing color I see everywhere. The walls and floors are painted the same grey as the guards' uniforms – an ugly, sad grey. The color of grey the sky turns before a bad thunderstorm. The kind of grey that tells you something ominous is about to come your way and you had best run for cover.

Once we are allowed into the room, we briskly walk to our favorite spot. It is a corner of the large room that allows us to sit close together so we can see and hear each other clearly over the next few hours. It affords us a little bit of privacy. There are only two doors in the visiting room, one for us and one for them. Their door opens to a concrete platform that allows them to enter and immediately walk down a small flight of stairs, about five steps.

I know the men are about to arrive because we can hear them getting closer. The slamming of the bars and the jingling of the guards' keys, along with their yells for the next section to open up so they can pass through to the next set of security walls, tells us they are nearing. With each step they take, my heart beat quickens and my breath shallows. I am both excited and saddened to see him today – excited that I will have this brief moment to be with him and saddened that it is both fleeting and never-ending at the same time.

I can see him through the glass; he has only one more stop to make until our reunion. He turns so the guard can unlock his handcuffs and they finally open the door. At last, my dad arrives! This thought always screams in my mind once they finally allow him into the area. As he proceeds to walk down the steps, my heart races with excitement! Once our arms are locked around one another in a loving hug, our burden is lifted. For a few brief moments we are sharing our lives together face-to-face, not through letters or quick collect phone calls. As I look up at him, I admire his beautiful hair that is always so neatly cut and combed, his light blue eyes, and strong tattooed arms. It is obvious to all who are looking … I adore my Daddy. Even clad in white prisoner garb with "Daniels, John" stenciled on the front and "Alabama State Penitentiary/Holman Unit" on the back, he is still my Daddy and I think he is wonderful. After our hello hug, we walk to "our" corner to sit and begin our time together. He always greets me with, "Hey there, baby girl!", and once seated, we hold hands and mostly I excitedly talk about my mom, friends, school, and life.

At this particular facility, we are allowed to spend a full day with our loved one. We visit from 9am to 2pm, only leaving one another's side for bathroom breaks. After a while, and for a small fee, the guards come in and take Polaroid photos of us. They are always very kind to us; I think they can see past the strained smiles to the real pain in our souls. I also like to believe they recognize the good in my Dad and have witnessed the commitment and adoration we have for one another through the years.

After hours of visiting and pretending we were not actually in a state prison visiting room filled with men who were convicted of murder, the guard quietly comes through the door and shouts out, "Five minutes." How does a little girl who adores her Dad tell him goodbye in 300 seconds? There are no words to adequately end a visit that crushes your heart and leaves your soul weeping like an open wound for weeks to come. Daddy never fails to comfort me, even though he is the one returning to a 5 by 5 foot cell for 23 hours a day.

He says, "Don't cry, baby girl. I will be alright. I am so proud of you."

I try to be strong; I did get better at it as I got older. Better at masking the hurt, not better at dealing with the pain. Dad would kiss me and say, "I love you, baby girl. Be careful going home and take care of Mamaw." Once the tearful good-byes were finished, he would give me his handkerchief with the small initials "JRD" in the bottom corner. I collected many of these cherished square pieces of cloth through the years. So, with the hanky clutched in my hand, I would wave and blow kisses through the glass, always waiting until they had put the handcuffs back on him before I would move from the window. As they lead him down the hall with both hands cuffed behind his back, he would twist his body so he could wave at his little girl once last time. Once I heard the finality clang of the last door close and the sound of their clinking keys become fainter and fainter, I knew the visit was actually over. Now it was only a memory until next time.

Before exiting the facility, the coral-lipstick-wearing female guard would usually have something for us that Dad had either made or had made by one of the other inmates. Sometimes it's a leather wallet or purse, or maybe a painting made special for us. My favorite is a gazebo made from matches. It has little steps that lead up into the gazebo that could be pulled out and used to hold small things like jewelry. I keep it for many years, often placing one of the Polaroid photos in the little hiding place.

Once in the cocoon of the warm car, I am free to feel what I had been holding back as I watched Dad return again to his cell. I crawl into the backseat and quietly cry while clinging to his hanky. It smells like cigarette smoke and Yardley's lavender soap. Once we drive off the gravel-filled parking lot, I long to leave behind some of the emotion I hold close inside while inside the grey, depressing prison. Like the multitude of pebbles in the parking lot, my heart is crushed once again, and my tears and my Dad will remain here forever … unchanging … until the end.

★★★

Dad in Prison by Shari Ostrow Scher

I grew up in the 1950s as a middle-class Jewish child in Brooklyn, New York. My parents were college graduates, my mother worked part time when money was needed, and my father sold school furniture. We had a small, attached, brick house, but I thought we were rich. Our home was surrounded by "the projects," lower-middle-class apartment buildings of multiple floors that housed policemen, fire fighters, postmen and their families. In all, I thought I was a very lucky kid.

I struggled with ultra-sensitivity and being overly empathetic. I was definitely a Daddy's girl, and would spend time on the weekends going with my dad to the library or riding bikes in a local park. We spent hours talking, watching the news on television, and arguing politics. My dad made me lunch each day, drove me to school, and really looked after our family by doing the cleaning and even some of the cooking. He was a great story teller, and he would tell me about his childhood, his time in the war, and his time with friends. He also read me bedtime stories. He was my hero in so many ways.

One day, when I was about 15 and a junior in high school, I arrived home after high school to find a large group of very, very angry people screaming in my living room. My father had embezzled millions of dollars from his own company. Later we found out that it was used to pay loan sharks and mafia members, so the money was never used by my family. That evening began a long, painful period for my family; the police became involved, my dad attempted suicide, he spent a year in a mental health facility, and he was incarcerated at Sing Sing prison in Ossining, New York. I was embarrassed by the whole ordeal and continually worried about him. A few horrific years followed and those years and experiences have left their mark on me. While my memory is a bit scattered on this, I believe all of this happened from the time I was 15 to 20 years old.

My dad made it clear that I was not to come to his sentencing. Prior to that, he was incarcerated at The Tombs in New York City, a place famous for its filth and rough living. He sent me a letter during that time and told me about the rats, the bad food, and the rotten conditions. I did not sleep much during the time he was there; I was fraught with worry.

Eventually I was able to visit him at Sing Sing. While my mother insisted that I not visit, I refused to listen and was the first in my family to go. I still remember my dad walking into the visiting area, looking around to see who had come, and smiling and saying he should have known it would be me. From our house in Brooklyn, getting to Sing Sing took a walk, a bus, two trains and then a longer walk up to the main gate. It was costly, so I went once a month, and always walked the last part to save the 50 cents it would cost to get there. The trip, about two to three hours each way, was arduous. I would go from our plain neighborhood in Brooklyn to beautiful, wealthy places like "Crotin on the Hudson" (as the train engineer would sing out), to the poverty-stricken Sing Sing stop in Ossining where I was usually the only person not of color who got off the train. Once, the conductor of the train sat down with me and told me to stop visiting, since no man was worth it. Obviously he thought I was visiting my boyfriend!

Once I completed the walk up the hill, I would sit in the waiting room until I was called. I would go through an x-ray, be frisked, and then asked questions about the purpose of my visit. I would walk into a room where the guards were seated high up with guns, and wait for my dad to come to the visiting room. In those days, Sing Sing was a place where you could touch the one you were visiting, so that helped. However, it was always scary for me. I felt so out of any comfort level I had ever known.

My monthly visits, at the beginning, were always a surprise for my dad. I would also bring along food for him that my mother had put together, and the prison staff would carefully go through the boxes. My father explained that prisoners of different cultures would gather in their own groups and share all food. Thus, he had a Jewish service on Friday nights. I always felt so proud that I helped him by bringing the little cans of tuna and salmon.

In my family, my dad's imprisonment was never to be discussed. We were told never to tell friends, teachers or neighbors. Of course that added to our sense of shame. In addition, our economic state collapsed. My mother had to find a full time job. She could not tell anyone she had a college degree, or she would be seen as over-educated. She began working in downtown New York; she made very little money and hated every minute of it. At night she would stare out of her bedroom window for hours and hours.

Different personalities have different reactions to hardship. My sister, four years older than me, became angry. She only visited my dad once and she resented having to contribute her salary to the household. She and my mother fought continuously. In fact, when my dad left for prison, he told me I was now in charge. He said if they were left to one another, they would kill each other. This just added to my belief that I really could take care of the family, even though I was just in my teens.

The pressure I felt, coupled with not being able to tell anyone the big family secret, made life very hard. Friends would ask what happened to me; they wanted to know where my dad was and why I always had to race home. They wondered why I was not joining in on any of the usual activities of college kids. I did not have words for them, and knew I was alone. One day after school a friend told me that I had to go with her for a soda. She said she would not leave until I told her what was going on. I broke down and shared the "family secret," and I've always remembered that this confession lifted a bit of burden for me. I was no long totally alone.

The economic hardships just kept coming. Though we narrowly avoided losing our house, we did lose our car. Pancakes were often what we had for dinner, for meat was too expensive. There were no extras, no eating out, no new clothes – just survival. I was not used to this, so it was a very big change. When I turned 16, about 50 friends surprised me with a party held at someone's father's clubhouse. My mom and sister made the food, my boyfriend (and now ex-husband) made the decorations, and everyone brought presents. I remember how extra-ordinary the night was. I am guessing that by then lots of people knew what was going on but they were too kind to tell me. The presents I received lasted for a few years.

Whether I reflect upon my high school or college years, I see how my life changed dramatically. I had been a student leader, involved in every fun activity at my high school; I was a very good student, so the plan was that I would go away to college. That was the first change – I immediately had to find a job, and became an afterschool and weekend nanny. In later years I became a speed reading teacher, worked at a medical book store, and worked at the college registrar's office. My dreams of going away to school were over. I decided I would go to college in the evenings or not at all. My mother became quite hysterical, but I refused to listen. Several days later I was called into my principal's office. He told me that my mother had come to talk with him and that I had to go to college. I was shocked, for looking back it must have taken everything in her to admit to what was going on in our family. Thanks to the same principal, I won a $250 President Kennedy scholarship from a fund that I had actually started. It paid tuition and books; I lived at home and attended Brooklyn College. I would go to school all day and worked each evening and weekends. When I was not working, I went to the college library every night or to my boyfriend's house to study, because my house was a place of pain and depression. I would also be responsible for rushing home at the end of the day and making dinner for my mother and sister and making sure they were okay. With all of that, I still did volunteer work and kept busy on campus. It was a very dark period in my life, but I could not share what I was going through with anyone.

Finally I went to see a college counselor. She listened, and then she became very quiet. She told me that she did not know what to say, but I should tell my mother to be proud of me. I went home and told my mother that I wanted to talk with her. I was ready to share my conversation with the counselor, but my mother became furious; she thought I was pregnant. At that painful moment I knew I really had to suffer all of this in silence. Later I won the Sophomore of the Year Award at Brooklyn College. For whatever reason, the person who sponsored the award, a wealthy businessman whose offices were in the Empire State Building, asked me if I would like to interview for a summer job. I fell in love with the idea of working in Manhattan and a way out of my feelings about home and Brooklyn. The gentleman asked me how much money I needed to earn for the summer, and I told him I could accept whatever he thought he could afford. Once I got the offer and shared it with my Mom, she pointed out that I would not make enough money for clothes and transportation to the city. For some reason, this just broke my heart. I really saw Manhattan as a new world, and I could not accept the offer. If I had been able to tell him about my father, I'm pretty sure he would have offered me more money.

My life was very different from my friends'. I belonged to a school club that had a father–daughter dinner. I had no dad to bring. In the 1950s most parents did not divorce and in my culture everyone had a father. I asked my uncle, but it was not like having my dad. In addition to all this, my father had hurt many people we knew. Relatives, neighbors, and family friends had all lost money because of his actions. I could barely live with the embarrassment and shame I felt. When it was time for me to marry, my mother wanted me to have a normal wedding. She saved up the little she had, and I contributed whatever money I could earn and that was not needed to pay the bills. The night of the wedding, two of the guests grabbed me and told me I had no business having a wedding given all the hurt my father had caused. I can remember feeling complete sadness. I did not want the wedding, I knew it was wrong to have any kind of celebration, but my mother needed to feel that she could give her daughter something normal. I felt so caught in the middle. To this day I remember that night with embarrassment and distaste. I only wish I could have said no to my mother.

As I reflect on this essay, it feels like I have written about sadness and depression. However, as is always true about any difficult experience, I learned a great deal from what my father did. I found out that I was strong. I learned that I could survive tough times. I developed an empathy for the underdog that always existed for me, but that grew stronger. I learned that people of religion are not always kind, but people who cared about others could reach out and take away pain. I learned that sometimes people need things they cannot ask for, and that being kind to everyone is time spent well. All of this learning inspired me to found the

Children of Incarcerated Parents Partnership (COIPP). I am the president of this non-profit, and the volunteers who work with me help children and caregivers who have family members in prison. We provide parenting classes for women in the local detention center, small group workshops on separation and loss for caregivers, and resource-filled bags for children. We created a lending/giving library at the detention center and offer scholarships to our local community college for caregivers. We provide child/caregiver "fun" activities and individual support for caregivers. We also educate our community about incarceration and families. The list of activities COIPP performs continues to grow as do the needs of the children.

While things in my family were very sad for a long time, when my father returned home, life went back to a new state of normal. My parents stayed together, though their relationship was never the same. I learned that I could still love my father, something I did until the day he died. He had weaknesses that led him down a bad path. However, in so many ways, he was a remarkable man, father and grandfather. Despite all the pain, I am honored that he was my dad. To this day, my children, my husband and I remember him as being about the best grandfather one can have. My oldest son asked him to visit his college classes. My youngest son invited him to his college graduation. Everyone loved my father, and he made new friends wherever he went! In fact, we all have incredibly fond memories of both my mother and my father and miss them very much. It took some time, but I ultimately realized that every journey brings new understanding and new friendships. This experience was definitely life changing, and not one I wish others to have. However, looking back, I would not change the way it influenced my life and made me who I am.

★★★

My Family by Jessamyn Ramirez

I think I had an okay childhood. I lived with my mom, dad, sister and maternal grandparents. At the time of my first memory, my grandma worked as a seamstress and my grandpa had his own mechanic's shop. My sister was in school. My mom and dad were not working then, they were both using drugs.

My mom and dad were both arrested in their teens and my dad served a couple of prison sentences by his early twenties. Then he went to jail a few times and then he stopped. My mom had a big case when I was two and she had three trials but was not convicted, so she didn't go to jail then. Actually, a lot of people in our family have been in jail or prison. On my dad's side, there is his father, his uncle, his brother, his cousin and his nephews. On my mom's side, there is her grandmother, her uncle and some cousins.

We had started out in the working-class neighborhood where my mom was raised but as my parents got more addicted and they got deeper into criminal things, we moved closer and closer to the bad places. At the end, before my mom's last incarceration, we lived in this neighborhood with cheap apartments, sketchy little stores and long blocks of deserted warehouses.

Life at our house could be pretty crazy and I used to go to my friends' houses to get away and have fun. My friends' families were very good to me. Nikki was my best friend and we played with Whopper. Their parents used drugs and went to jail, too. Nikki's apartment was little but it was clean and there was always food there because her mother sold drugs. But Whopper's parents were what my dad called "hope-to-die dope fiends" and at their house there was never any food except a pack of hot dogs in the refrigerator.

But it was different when my mom started getting arrested. I saw her arrested for the first time when I was four. The marshals came in the morning while it was still dark and got her. I was frightened but my grandma was there and everyone tried to be nice to me. I was also there at her last arrest a couple of years later. They grabbed her and took her away from me. I wanted to go with her but they made me stay with my father. We sat waiting and then they brought her out in handcuffs and took her to a patrol car and drove away. I was terrified and crying all the way home.

When my mom was incarcerated, I had to change schools. I had some bad experiences at that new school. Overall, school was not a positive experience for me. I hated it and didn't want to go.

I stayed with my grandparents. My grandmother hated that my mom was incarcerated. She always told me not to talk about my mom being in jail. She was worried about what people would say. But my mom always told me to say what I felt and ask questions if I needed to.

My mom called me twice a week and we could only talk for 10 minutes. But my grandma would also take me to see my mom in jail. My dad couldn't take me because he was on probation or he had warrants. It was so good to see her and to be able to hold her. I was fortunate to be able to do this because of the special visiting program they had at the jail.

Eventually she got out and I was really glad. On the day she got out I had just turned six. She and I were standing in a long cashier line at the market and I was so happy that she was back that I was bouncing up and down and laughing. One of the old ladies in the line asked me why I was so happy and I yelled, "Because my mom just got out of jail!" The ladies got shocked faces and I could tell that I had said something wrong so I turned to look at my mom. Her face was pink and she was biting her lip but she nodded to the ladies and to me, telling them that it was true and telling me that what I said was okay. I didn't understand until I got older but then I was so proud of her for accepting the embarrassment and letting me feel okay about expressing myself.

After my mom got out of jail things got better. She had been in a long time and stopped using heroin. She got a really good job and we had a place of our own. But my dad kept drinking.

My dad was a wonderful father. He was my primary caregiver when my mom worked all the time. He was the closest person in my life. But his drinking kept getting worse. After my mom got out, he was drinking all the time and in and out of jail for drinking and warrants.

My dad's first prison terms were for armed robbery and happened before I was born. But by the time I was able to understand what was happening when my father got arrested, he was older and getting picked up just for being a crazy drunk. He was one of the only White guys in our area so the police (also White) were nice to him and sometimes they just took him to a detox center or released him. A few times I was glad to see him go and wished they held him longer.

My dad used to call almost every day while he was in jail. He always had a new joke to tell me and sometimes he would pass the phone to a friend who would give me some entertaining "advice." Because we were so close all my life and because he called so much, I didn't really miss visiting him.

When he wasn't in jail, my dad was often living in recovery programs. Our relationship deteriorated and wasn't the greatest then. When I was a teenager, we fought all the time. It started getting better when I was in my twenties but then things took a turn for the worse. He was diagnosed with a terminal illness.

My mother had stopped getting arrested and incarcerated after serving her fourth sentence in three years. My father didn't stop until he got cancer. He was in a court-ordered treatment program when he found out and from there, he went into other institutions like hospitals and nursing homes. But we were always together in our hearts. I took care of him until the end, but in those two years we got very close and had the greatest bond.

Even though my parents used drugs and went to jail, my childhood was not that bad. My parents loved each other and stayed together, we always had a place to live, they didn't beat me or molest me, and nobody in our house was mentally ill or suicidal or homicidal. I got into meth when I was 15 and 16 but then I settled down. I went to nursing school and got married. I work and volunteer two days a week in a program for pregnant prisoners. When I think about the worst thing that ever happened to me, I think about when my dad died. I really miss him, but I still have my mom and my sister and my husband, and I am doing all right.

★★★

We Never Part by Bianca S. Bryant

On the morning of my college graduation, May of 2015, my heart was filled with excitement and a great sense of accomplishment. I was proud to know that when my name was called to walk across the commencement stage into the land of alumni, my mother would be watching with tears in her eyes. Having my mom at graduation meant more than hugs, flowers, and congratulations; her presence was redemption for both of us, and we were in the same space, smiling, laughing, crying, and rejoicing. I finally had my mom back, but it didn't happen overnight. I suffered for five long years during my mother's incarceration for a nonviolent financial crime.

Whenever I want to hurt myself, I flashback to April of 2007, the day the police found my mother and I in a small hotel room where we'd been evading the authorities for several months. The courts labeled my mother a fugitive-from-justice because for a year and a half she successfully avoided being captured despite several close encounters. One of my most poignant memories of a close call happened at my grandmother's house. We sat in her living room having a "normal" conversation about my mom's next move in the chase, and suddenly my aunt ran in to tell us that the police had just left my cousin's house after questioning her concerning our location. I was terrified. I had never jumped and run so fast in my life. We dashed to the car and sped to the most inconspicuous hotel we could find. I didn't sleep that night; it took at least four hours and one thousand soft pats on the back for my heart to stop pounding and my stomach to stop its incessant churning. From this moment on, I knew that the police were getting closer to finding my mom on their own, or with the help of an informant, and on a blurry day it all came to an end.

Boom! was the sound as two small town cops violently banged the cheap wooden door of our hotel room on that sleepy afternoon. I was somewhere between waking up and falling asleep again when I was forced to leap from the bed.

"It's the police! Open up! We know you're in there! Don't play with us!"

Damn it, I thought; fuck, they found us! I didn't know what to do; my mind was racing so fast. The room was getting smaller and the number of things I had to hide before they forced the door open grew by the minute. I was afraid for the cops to find the incriminating documents, the phone, and worst of all my laptop. Meanwhile, my mom was simultaneously rushing around looking for a place to hide and holding the door closed as the policemen pushed from the outside. Then it was over. They finally broke through, placed my mother in handcuffs, and I quickly kissed her goodbye before she was carted off to the police car. They made me stay inside the room for an interrogation, which was unlawful because I was a minor and I didn't have a parent or a lawyer present.

"What's your name little girl? Are you a runaway? What's your social security number? Don't lie to us or we'll lock you up too!"

I tried to keep my composure, but it seemed too much to handle. I sat in a chair and cried as the cops yelled random questions at me. When I tried to stand up one officer screamed, "Sit! Sit down, now!" I was embarrassed and insulted that he'd shouted at me as if I was a German Shepherd. My temperament is more like a poodle; moreover, it was unnecessary for him to yell. In the end, my grandmother came to rescue me and my mom was sent to a nearby jail and later extradited to the state from which her charges originated. Looking back on that day, I understand why I'm so fascinated with drama and action films; the final hotel incident was like a scene from a movie, and as a coping mechanism I chose to think of it all as fiction. I chose to believe that the ensuing chaos wasn't my real life.

By the time summer came, my grandmother, my nieces, my nephew and I had driven countless hours to see my mom. She was being held in a county jail while awaiting trial and there was a strong possibility that she could be sent to state prison. I cringed at the idea of my mother being in a more secured and remote location; more isolated, confined, and trapped. The courts were determined to make my mother pay for the time they'd spent searching for her as a fugitive, so after several months she was sent to a medium security women's prison.

Our first time visiting my mom in prison was more jarring and terrifying than a county jail. The intensity in the atmosphere of a medium security prison scared me. There were men with scowling faces in watchtowers holding assault rifles and the prison guards did not use names, but called each person receiving a visit "inmate." The whole time I couldn't believe that my mother was wearing khaki and that I was sitting in a room full of strangers trying to have a meaningful conversation with her. Even though our visiting time was limited, I was speechless. Thankfully for me, we only visited her twice as she served her time in state prison. As selfish as that sounds I was glad, because it hurt my entire body to see my mother look weak and helpless instead of strong-willed and tenacious as she remained in my dreams.

In lieu of physical visits, writing letters was the main line of communication between my mother and the free world. Writing letters was a difficult task for me to complete because it pained me to know that I couldn't hear my mom's voice or see her in person. I would begin to write a letter and leave one paragraph on a page for weeks at a time, and then I'd receive an angry letter from my mom with a long prayer attached in which she pleaded with Jesus to encourage me to write her and continue to believe in God. This always made me angry at her and guilty with myself. She didn't understand that I hated having shallow conversations with her in a letter that would be opened, read, and possibly discarded by a correctional officer before she could see it. I also understood her frustration with me. I would go months without responding to her letters and I knew that had to hurt, but I could never decide which was more important, my feelings or hers.

The psychological turmoil I experienced during my mother's incarceration can be summed into one term: mental bondage. I have always been a shy and reserved person, but with the fear of my mother being shouted at and mistreated in prison I became severely depressed. I withdrew from socializing at school and I refrained from speaking unless I had to defend myself.

I built so many walls in my mind to cope with the circumstances! Finally, in August of 2012, they began to break. It was the summer after my sophomore year in college when I received a call from an unfamiliar phone number.

"Hello?" "Baby, I'm out!"

I was in utter disbelief that my mom was calling to tell me she had been released from prison. It came as a total surprise, but something melted inside me; I could breathe deeper than before. After my mother's release it was exciting to be able to call her and talk at any time without the dreaded recording chiming in for a one minute warning. The empty, distant, and bottomless feeling that I carried for five years began to shift into the past and I could finally envision myself as a whole human being again, with my mom.

★★★

Fathers and Sons by Michael P. Carlin

My father was a career criminal and frequently incarcerated. After years of severe beatings by his father, my dad fought back and was put out on the streets of the city when he was 12. From that time forward, he lived by his wits and his fists and eventually became a fearsome and feared man who worked as an enforcer for others as well as an independent.

My mother was from a proper working-class Irish family. She was dating one of my paternal uncles when she met my dad. They ran off to get married and moved to Atlantic City. My father worked the docks and they had a tiny apartment. My dad had always been a drinker but he began to spend more time in the waterfront bars and one night when I was two months old, he came home drunk and staggered into my crib, knocking me to the floor. My mother left him after that and returned to the small town in Pennsylvania where she had grown up.

Her father did not want us. My grandfather hated my father and felt that my mother had made her own bed and should lie in it. My mother implored him and he relented but later he frequently let me know that he regretted the decision.

My grandfather, my extended family and almost everyone in our town were afraid of my father. At neighborhood parties and family gatherings, where all my cousins were tumbling in the mud and wrestling with each other, the big girls kept me safe and clean. I was treated like a little prince. Everyone was scared of what my dad might do if I was harmed.

When I was small, my favorite toys were a set of small cars that I used to create scenarios that included many chases and crashes. One day, my father came in while I was playing with a black and white police car and a green sedan. I was making the two cars chase each other around the kitchen floor when my father looked in through the doorway and asked which car was me. Instinctively, I knew that this was an important question and hesitated, then chose the police car. My father pulled back, disappointed. Over my head, he told my mother that she wasn't raising me to know which side I was on. I don't remember what else was said, but I never forgot the lessons in that experience.

My father continued to do the crimes that sometimes led to his incarceration. As I grew up, I would see him every few months, and then not see him for a few years. Then he'd get out and come to see me. As I got older, instead of visiting me at my grandfather's house, he'd take me on outings. During these times, my father often tested me to see how I would handle new experiences. He was a hard man who'd had a hard life and expected hard times in the future. He tested me because he wanted to make sure that I could handle things for myself in a life without him there for me.

Once, in Newark, he gave me a $10 bill and sent me into a downtown bar to get change. I had never been in an urban bar. The men and few women in the bar looked bad and they looked at me in a bad way. Not in the annoyed, "Godammit, here's that kid again" way they looked at you in the taverns of my hometown but more like you were a piece of meat. It felt really bad. When I brought my dad his change he told me that the bar was known to be dangerous, a hangout for predators. He'd wanted to expose me to this extreme situation to weather me, and he wanted to see how I would handle myself. I had the impression that he'd thought I did good.

In spite of my dad's efforts to protect me from a distance, I got hurt in many ways growing up. Around the fifth grade, I had a series of bad experiences that marked a turning point in my life.

One of these involved Petey, a kid that I did not get along with very well. One day we were arguing and he said something about my father. I told him my father was working in the mountains, which is what my mother and grandfather had always said to explain his absences. Petey laughed at me and said, "Your dad isn't working in the mountains. He's in prison. Everybody knows that."

I had been to visit my father in prison a couple of times when I was younger but the circumstances hadn't been explained to me. So this information seemed new and terrible. My dad had never wanted those visits or even correspondence when he was incarcerated, and said that his experiences in the criminal life and the joint had taught him that he should never give anyone anything they could use against him. That would be me and my mother. So he kept us completely apart from the rest of his life. My mom knew and understood, but at nine, this view hadn't been shared with me. After what Petey said, I began to realize how little I knew about my father and began to wonder how he felt about me or if he even wanted me.

A worse experience involved my fifth grade teacher, Mr. Lombardo. For some reason, he had never liked me and he would punish me as often as he could, often without cause. I tried to stay out of his way but one day I saw him getting chewed out by a school administrator. This made him mad at me. Later, he scolded me in class and ordered me out into the hall, where he began to yell and push me around. I started to fight back. He was banging me up against the lockers when another teacher who heard the sounds of the beating stopped him. Later, my mom went to the principal and raised hell, but the damage was done. I had always liked and done well in school but that experience ended my positive relationship with education.

I don't talk about my worst experiences. But soon after they happened, I was playing with my BB gun in a field when a local kid came up and started annoying me. He was a fat boy who didn't know when to shut up. I got angry and turned the gun against his belly, shooting him with a splinter that lodged in the fat under his skin. It was a great feeling. Later that day, the chief of police came to our house and took the gun away, but he couldn't take away that feeling.

My mother was a single parent; my grandfather – who steadfastly refused to accept me and often told me that I was no good, just like my father – had lost a leg when he worked in the mines and was disabled. My mom worked in the local factory; we had very little income and lived in an older neighborhood. I don't know if it was that I missed my dad or that I just had a sense that something was missing, but I grew up knowing things weren't right, that I wasn't right.

The void that a father's absence creates in a boy's life has to be filled in the ways that children fill their unmet needs, often by reaching out to people immediately available to them. Without a father, the most significant males in a boy's life are often his peers. For whatever reason – who my father was, my anger, my feeling of being different from the other kids – I never saw kids my own age as my peers. I felt like I belonged around the big boys.

Many of the older guys that were accessible to me were struggling with problems created by their own deprivations. My attachments to them were made out of desperation to be accepted by older male figures. By my early teens, I was cutting school, hanging around bars, delivering weed and drinking. My mother had completely lost control of me and I came and went as I pleased.

During this time my dad would show up and take me down to Atlantic City to go fishing. He would continue his usual routine of telling me things and testing me, advising me and anticipating challenges. As I got older, he began to share more information about his criminal life and his philosophy. I felt like this was making us closer. But then he would go away again.

By my mid-teens, I had been arrested several times and been to juvenile hall. I was stealing cars, doing small burglaries, assaulting people and getting assaulted. I ran from the local police in cars and on motorcycles. If you had asked me, I would have said I was enjoying myself.

When I was 17, I met and fell in love with a local girl and got her pregnant. My son was a miracle, this incredible little boy with a light shining out of him. I loved him and wanted to protect him and be around him always.

During the first years of his life, my relationship with my son deepened. I never went anywhere without him. We became so attached it was a struggle for me to get to work because he wouldn't let go of me. I hated to leave him. I knew how he felt, as such a little boy, having to be apart from his father. We were very close.

My father continued to come in and out of my life. I remember he showed up one time where I was living with my 18-month-old son and my girlfriend. She had gone inside the house and had left the baby in the front yard on a swing. My dad found him there alone and watched him for a long time before she returned. Later, speaking about my son's mother, he said, "That one's no good and you should get rid of her." He was right. My relationship with my son's mother wasn't good and we separated many times. When my son was five, we separated permanently.

After my boy was born, I'd made an effort to stay out of trouble and earn money legitimately. I had been employed as an auto painter, a day laborer and on an oil derrick. I did all kinds of jobs. But when his mother and I split up, I lost my life with my son and kind of lost the point of other things, too, like having a job. Then, a year later, my mother died. It felt like there was no longer anyone to be good for. Within a couple of years, I been arrested for a series of bank robberies and sentenced to long, consecutive terms in state and federal prison.

My father and I corresponded during this period. He was beginning to slow down. He wrote occasionally about a woman who worked in an alcohol rehab program and I thought he might be staying with her. He got out for the last time after I went to prison and we lost contact. He was in his mid-sixties.

During the first year of my incarceration, while I was going to trial on my many cases, I had contact with my son and his mother. It wasn't constant but there was still a connection. Visiting was impossible because she flatly refused to bring him into the prison. Then she told me she was moving to another part of the country. I knew I was losing my boy for certain. All I could do was ask his mother to stay in contact with me.

That would be hard from prison but even harder from the part of the prison where I was kept. In the first years after my arrest, I had escaped several times and attempted to escape several more. As a result, I ended up in the Hole (or disciplinary unit) first in Huntingdon, a maximum security prison in eastern Pennsylvania, and then at the new correctional institution at Greene, in the west. From the Hole, it was difficult to get support – like stamps and contact with the outside – from other prisoners and phone calls were extremely limited. I tried, but couldn't find my son.

My father and I were still corresponding at this point. He had spent several years in the Hole in another state prison but I had been locked down for more than five years, longer than he had and far beyond the legal limit for solitary confinement. This is one of the incidents in my life that deeply moved my father. As he got older, he would speak sadly and bitterly about all the time they kept me in the Hole and how it had been way too long.

When my son's mother took him and left Pennsylvania, I realized he was probably gone for good unless I did something. I asked around to see how the other fathers in the prison kept in touch with their kids and the consensus was that if the mother didn't stay in contact, you could just forget about any contact with your kid. You could also forget about getting any help from anyone else. I'd learn that, in the general sense, these men were right.

My incarceration denied my son those things that every child should have and experience from his father: protection, caregiving, bonding and emotional support. Because I was not there for him, I think he did what I had done – he simply put aside those needs and resigned himself to the notion that they would not be met until his dad returned. Being the son of an incarcerated father myself, I knew the feelings he experienced. I knew he was pushing his needs deeper and deeper from the surface while he acted out his hurt and pain in his everyday life.

At the same time, I had many questions about my son and how he was managing without a father. What had he been told about me and how would we eventually overcome any negative images or notions based upon what he had been told? Was he angry? Was he worried about me? How did he think I felt about him? Most importantly, I wondered who his father's incarceration made him in his own eyes. I knew that my dad's criminal lifestyle, crimes and imprisonment had contributed to what I had become and didn't want that for my son.

I wrote to more than 50 agencies for help in finding my son. Without family, I was indigent, so this was a long process. I would take used envelopes, readdress them, erase the postal cancellation marks on used stamps and stick them to envelopes with syrup from my Sunday breakfast. Only two agencies answered my letters; one was the Center for Children of Incarcerated Parents. The Center began to look for my son. Every week, I wrote him a letter in care of the Center, which they would keep for him until they found him. During the years that followed, I began working with the Center on several articles about incarcerated fathers. Finally, after five years, my son and I made contact.

It had been seven and a half years from the time of my last phone call with him until I spoke to my boy again and a total of ten years in which we did not see each other. The next time I saw him was at the U.S. Penitentiary at Leavenworth where I was serving my federal sentence for bank robbery. My son visited me and handed me his five-week-old daughter.

The fear I had felt in my heart of losing my boy had come true. In that moment, it had completed itself. The loss of seeing and enjoying my boy's childhood was plainly in front of me. It was gone now and all we could do was get to know one another again. He'd slipped away, no matter how hard I'd tried to maintain our connection.

While this was developing, the Center had located my dad in a nursing home and arranged telephone calls. Being connected helped all three of us. It may be hard to imagine, but this was a good time for me in the federal penitentiary, my dying father and my son in the Marines. My son and his grandfather spoke for the first time in 12 years.

My father died before we could see each other again. As a former state prisoner, he was not allowed to visit me in the state prison system but would have been able to visit in a federal facility once I was transferred. We didn't make it. Just like he was unable to be there for a lot of my life, I could not be there for his death. I was refused permission to attend his funeral but, through a friend, I was able to participate in planning his memorial service.

I got released in 2001, after 16 years in Pennsylvania and federal prisons. Right after I got out, I went to work for the Center as a child custody advocate for incarcerated fathers. I visited my son and granddaughter, who live in another state, and they came to visit me. At first, we were very careful with each other and my son was emotionally distant. But over the past ten years, our relationship has become more normal and we now disagree, have arguments and even ignore each other for periods of time like other fathers and adult sons. I never had a chance to do it this way with my own dad.

My father was a tough sonofabitch and a bad man by society's standards. I still get mad at him. I still wish I'd gotten more of him and from him. He shouldn't have been gone all the time, I needed him. But the time he spent with me was spent trying to protect me and that is one of the most important things a parent can do.

As far as parental incarceration goes, it was significant in my development, but not as significant as many other things in my life. Having been both the child of a prisoner and an incarcerated parent myself has helped me put the experience in perspective. It was not more important than my father's drinking, or his violent persona or his separation from my mother, although it was in part the consequence of these things. It was not more important than my grandfather's cruelty or our family's poverty and isolation. Nevertheless, it was a bad experience. My father's incarceration made our separations formal, immutable, and lasting. It set in stone the loneliness and pain that characterized our relationship.

I guess I'm trying to find a balance in my mind between what I needed as a child and what my father could give or what his experience with his own father allowed him to give. I'm trying to find the same balance with my son. Maybe that's what all fathers and sons, all parents and children, must try to do.

★★★

Reentry Story by Daniel Bowes

Standing before 100 men imprisoned at Polk Correctional Institution in Butner, North Carolina, I experienced one of those rare moments in life that elicit immediate and deep reflection. I was at Polk to discuss barriers to reentry and potential legal relief as part of a seminar the men – all between the ages of 19 and 25 – were participating in because each was within six months of release. I am a civil rights attorney and practice exclusively on matters related to reentry – litigating employment and housing discrimination charges, lobbying for increased reentry resources and reduced barriers to reentry, organizing individuals with criminal records and their families to speak out for restored opportunities for productive citizenship.

By the time I arrived at Polk, I had presented on the issue of reentry dozens of times – to employers and directly impacted individuals, on television and radio, in court rooms and statehouses and churches. I should have been comfortable and composed. And yet, as I opened my mouth to speak to those young men, I felt my face turn red, my hands begin to sweat and shake, and I could not recall a single word of a presentation I knew by heart. After a few false starts, I managed to introduce myself as an attorney. I stopped and steadied myself, and then confessed to the men in front of me the only concrete thought I could seize in those moments. With a voice that I hope sounded more steady than it felt, I said, "I am the son of a man who sat in one of those same seats 30 years ago – he was 21 years old, he had multiple felony convictions, and he was about to be released from Polk."

A few weeks after my birth in 1985, I was introduced to my father just after he had been transferred from Polk to Morrison Youth Institution. I have no memory of the occasion, but imagine that it was relatively jovial as prison visits go. The transfer was a welcome indication that my father was on course to be released early, having served ten months of concurrent three-year sentences for several felony convictions, including breaking and entering, and receiving stolen goods. Only once in my life has he talked openly and at length about his crimes. Just after I graduated from college, he and I were driving to a family reunion and, without prompting, he explained that he was looking forward to seeing an uncle who had once put his house up as collateral for my father's bail bond. Though I am a very curious person by nature, I have always been reluctant to delve into the details of my father's crimes.

But disarmed by his candor, I asked him about what he was like back then and the circumstances of his crimes. "I was a punk and did stupid things, especially when I was drunk … and I was drunk a lot," he told me. He then described the transgressions of a crew of unruly young men. Divided into two groups, they broke into stores after hours for cash, electronics, and alcohol – tallying who stole the most. Describing it 25 years later, he was clearly remorseful for his reckless behavior. Over the years, he has often described prison as a bleak but beneficial ordeal that shook him of his wildness.

In taking me to Morrison, my mother made a decision that fundamentally altered the course of our lives. She had only begun dating my father while he was awaiting trial on the charges for which he was eventually imprisoned. My mother was no stranger to the criminal justice system. She was just 17 years old when she met my father, but she had already had several run-ins with the law as had much of her family. My mother kept her own criminal history hidden from me until I was in law school but she often shared details of her family's legal problems. And so while not naïve to my father's circumstances, she had not imagined that my father would be imprisoned until he was led out of the courtroom in handcuffs. She discovered she was pregnant with me a few months into his incarceration, and told him by letter while he was at Polk. He told her to do what she thought was right and he would support her as best he could.

I am unsure how my father felt holding me in his arms that first time. In recent years, I've wondered whether he saw us as anchors to a past he wanted to move beyond or something real to build a new life around. The faded picture immortalizing the occasion shows him smiling broadly, one eye hidden under his shoulder-length hair, a goatee struggling to add years and toughness to his boyish face. One of his arms is around my mother whose eyes look dark and exhausted. I am resting in his other arm, asleep but dressed for the occasion in a red bowtie and red corduroy trousers. My father is a man of few words, especially when those words regard his time in prison. When I asked him about the picture recently, he said that he felt proud and excited to be a father but ashamed of the circumstances of that first meeting. "Nobody wants to see their son for the first time in prison."

My father was released from custody and put on parole in the fall of 1985. I was only a few months old at his homecoming, so I have no recollection of his incarceration or the years just after his release. From what I gather, it seems clear that my mom and dad's maturation as providers, watch keepers, teachers, and caretakers was slow-coming at first and much of it occurred in the year or so after his release from prison. This earliest period was very bumpy and not at all indicative of their eventual progress. In 1986, my mother was convicted for driving while intoxicated for an automobile incident that occurred in the same week my sister was born. As my grandmother tells it, this incident was reflective of the general recklessness of their choices during this time period. Shortly thereafter, my sister and I were removed from my parents' custody by the state of North Carolina. We were placed in foster care and then with relatives. After a little more than a year, my sister and I were reunited with one another and returned to my parents. During our time apart and afterwards, my parents completed several programs that tutored them in parenting and provided them with educational credentials and other life supports. This intervention, which I was not aware had occurred until much later in life, seems to have solidified my parents' determination to secure our family, their early recklessness supplanted by an ever strengthening commitment to respectability. Some of my earliest memories captured signs of this commitment. I remember spending one summer day in the back yard with my sister, mom, and dad – we were having one of those truly fun, intimate days that nurture a family and can draw them together even years later. At dusk, we were chasing lightning bugs, putting them in a jar for a couple of minutes as if to have a lantern. My mother had just announced that she was leaving to visit a friend. And I remember a muted but tense conversation ensuing between my parents. Years before, my father might have gone with her or asked her to pick up a six-pack on the way home. But on that day, he held the car keys from my mother and said, "Think about how hard we've worked to get where we are – don't put all that at risk with a DWI." Instead of leaving us, she sat in a lawn chair and watched us parade around our lanterns.

By the time I was capable of having impressions, my parents seemed to me to be largely normal parents – just a bit more *Roseanne* than *The Brady Bunch*. By the time I reached middle school, my mother and father had both become fairly skilled in setting expectations and boundaries. There were early bedtimes, shows that were off-limits, daily and weekly chores, rewards for good grades, and spankings.

Within two weeks of his release from prison, my father was offered a job as a welder at a metal fabrication company. The owner knew of his criminal history but decided to take a chance on a young man with potential. One of my first memories is of visiting him in the shop and watching him through a huge helmet. I watched sparks shower around him as he made glowing cuts in the metal, all made more beautiful contrasted to the dark blue tint of the protective shield. It was easy to imagine us a crew of astronauts making emergency repairs to our space shuttle. Like moon rocks, I usually got to bring back souvenirs from these visits. While other kids were playing with stuffed bears and action figures, my favorite toys were these pieces of iron and steel my father had cut and twisted into playthings for me. My favorites were a coin box race car, a desktop Ferris Wheel, and a humongous set of monkey bars.

By the time I was 10 years old, my parents' fortunes began to improve significantly. After obtaining her GED and then her associate's degree while working third shift at the Waffle House, my mom found an entry-level job doing data entry at a Fortune 500 company. Still with that employer today, she has done everything from payroll to human resources to shipping and receiving. After rising from welder to head welder to shop foreman, my father was eventually invited "into the office" to train as a draftsman. As I understand it, he learned the craft quickly, and within a few years had gained a good reputation for his design of steel stairs, rails, and ladders. The most obvious indication of our improved fortunes during this time was our move from a dilapidated trailer to a brick home. As ironic as it was fortunate, this move to better living in the city also meant transitioning from a largely White school of normal means to a predominantly African American school perpetually identified for intervention as one of the poorest in the state. Whatever knowledge of math and American history I failed to learn at Broadview Middle and Cummings High was substituted with more valuable lessons about race, impoverishment, and inequity.

Being the child of a formerly incarcerated parent, one would think I gained most of my notions of prison from my father. But his few words about that period of his life left me in the dark. And so, like most people, my early impressions of prison life were primarily formed from movies – *The Shawshank Redemption*, *Birdman of Alcatraz*, *Cool Hand Luke*, *Attica*, *Escape from Alcatraz*, and many others. These films portray prison as a cage fraught with dangers that humble or harden men. It seemed to do both to my dad. Throughout much of my child-hood I perceived him to be a sort of Byronic hero – flawed and coarse, but strong and principled, admirable if not relatable. It could feel like being raised by a Clint Eastwood lead.

I imagine most boys would be grateful to have a father they perceived to be strong and fearless. And I was at times, particularly when I felt small and afraid. Some of my most vivid and meaningful early memories are of my father's comforting touch. If I had run into trouble at school, he would tuck me in and rub my back, comforting me until I fell asleep. These moments were special and not uncommon. As was the time he dedicated to supporting all my extracurricular activities, most memorably as a fellow karate student and as cub master of my Cub Scout troop. Still, I often experienced feelings of isolation and defensiveness, largely because I could not see myself in him. He was steely and reserved. I was anxious and talkative. As a boy, he had worked on his family's farm, pulling tobacco and capturing snakes to sell to a science supply company. My first job was teaching tennis at a country club, explaining the intricacies of the semi-western grip to eight-year-olds at Super Saturday and then topping off their parents' glasses at Margarita Monday. He was the disciplinarian. I was the disciplined. He was an ex-convict. I aspired to be a lawyer. As a kid, I often viewed the gulf between us as a measure of how far I was from being a man.

The nature of this gulf shifted over time. In high school, I began to receive accolades for my scholarship, athletics, and volunteerism. These external indicators made the gulf less and less a measure of my shortcomings and more a measure of his. I became increasingly ashamed of my father's criminal history, and hid my parents away as best I could. In some respects, I came to envision myself a prisoner of circumstance – suffering for the mistakes of my parents. It didn't matter that I was surrounded by kids in similar and worse situations.

My parents' support for my personal success grew to be emphatic and gave rise to inter-mittent but strong feelings of superiority. From the time I was 12 or so, my mother would regularly say to me, "You're better than all of this – you're better than us and everything you see around you." Particularly aware that she wasn't saying the same thing to my sister seated beside me, I told her she was exaggerating. But a part of me – a significant part – heard her words and said, "I am better." As ashamed as I feel now about my arrogance and its impact on my perspective and my relationships, I cannot help but consider that it may have been crucial to my success. At some crucial junctures it set me adrift, untethered to the expecta-tions and traditions of my immediate surroundings. I felt free to entertain goals and pursue ambitions that would take me beyond the destitution I saw all around me.

I committed myself to attending Duke University and then law school as a freshman at Hugh M. Cummings High School. I never visited Duke as a high school student – my decision was based solely on its reputation as the best university in the state. What strikes me now is how little I consulted with anyone about these ambitions and how little my parents involved themselves in this decision. At an early age and throughout my life, I recognized and embraced my parents' deference to my judgement and decisions on my future.

I matriculated to Duke University in the fall of 2003. While Duke was supposed to be my passage to a wholly new life, there were holes in my plan from the beginning. On the first day of freshman orientation, I visited the just-completed addition to the Divinity School. My father had designed several rails and stairs as part of the addition, including a particularly ornate staircase that seemed to be its centerpiece. Even if I was not yet capable of truly appreciating the complete contours of my father's journey to "arrive" at Duke with me, I did feel a distinct sense of pride to be standing on his staircase. A decade before I had stood on monkey bars he had welded on our mobile home lot, and now, as a member of the Class of 2007, I stood on a staircase he had designed on Duke's campus. In that moment, perhaps for the first time in my life, I saw that I was in some meaningful sense standing on his shoulders. Unfortunately, the weight of this insight was quickly lost in the commotion of freshman year.

For all the great things Duke gave me during my four years there – generous financial aid, rigorous academic instruction, health insurance–it did not, and could not, provide me the sense of self, acceptance, and purpose I now realize I was pursuing. The transition was trying, academically and socially. I went from never having earned anything less than an "A" to dropping my first math class to avoid failing it. I thought my written words were all eloquence and insight, and then I got a "C–" on my first English paper. With the aid of plenty of free tutoring, I eventually learned how to really study and my grades rebounded in my sophomore year. It wasn't soon enough to prevent me from losing my academic scholarship. Fortunately, a need-based scholarship simply replaced the full amount of the merit scholarship.

Mirroring my academic struggles, my discomfort with money grew at Duke as I became more aware of the great disparity in family wealth between myself and most of my classmates. In middle school, I was mocked for wearing broken glasses I had soldered back together. In high school, I was ridiculed for wearing off-brand sneakers known as "bobos." While frustrating, these criticisms did not make me feel alienated because similar signs of impoverishment were everywhere. In my four years at Duke, not a single classmate ever directed a critical word about money at me. Yet, I became much more self-conscious of indications that I was not of this America – parking my Saturn with its hood held on by a bungee cord in a lot full of BMWs, Mercedes, Volvos, and SUVs; not rushing a fraternity to avoid fees and dues; rarely purchasing any meal not included in the school plan. As I became more sensitive to money, I generally avoided sharing details of my background.

One of the defining moments of my Duke experience came early in my second semester. In what began as a typical late-night dorm hallway conversation, a classmate and friend said to me, "Most poor people deserve to be poor; they're poor because they're not talented or hardworking enough. Look at you – you are here and they are not because you worked harder." It was disorienting, hearing him say out loud what I had essentially said to myself many times throughout my adolescence. But if this was the coronation I had pursued, I felt no sense of vindication or cause for celebration. Instead, I felt only embarrassment and self-loathing – not simply because his prejudiced words reflected some of my own sense of entitlement, but also because I felt completely unprepared to adequately respond to my classmate. While I had spent much of my youth convinced I deserved more, it didn't mean I was completely oblivious to the good character and talents of my classmates or of the barriers and trappings that prevented many of them from excelling. But on that night, I could not take any sort of stand. I only managed to change the subject.

I went to bed that night questioning my sense of self, as well as my motivations and life goals. Over the next few months, I confronted and then tried to abandon my condescension, insecurities, and immaturities. I worked to understand the assumptions and beliefs that fabricated and maintained my illusions of entitlement, prestige, and acceptability. I tried to allow my experiences, old and new, to better frame my perspective and set my ideals. Through this effort, I came to recognize the many important lessons to be learned from my parents' struggle and the impoverished community I was so eager to escape. I came to see that my parents' deep commitment to me and my success allowed me to prosper. I understand now that for much of my life I was shielded from the most serious consequences of scarcity by their sacrifices. Thankfully, I was provided a unique vantage point from which I was allowed to witness the struggles of others – close enough to draw from them truths that will forever shape my perspective, my decisions, and my pursuits – without having to suffer them myself. While much of the "heavy lifting" of this self-confrontation occurred in the months following that hallway conversation, this effort is ongoing, vacillating, and always challenging.

I spent my last years at Duke trying to open my eyes and then the eyes of my peers to the varying faces of social and economic injustice. In doing so, I found a supportive community of progressive leaders. I also became more resolute in my goal of becoming a lawyer. No longer simply a means to achieve prestige and respectability, I re-envisioned the law as an opportunity to reengage with the people and community I left behind. This vision was burnished after college by my experiences as an Autry Fellow at MDC, Inc., an anti-poverty think tank focusing on disconnected communities in the South. In 2008, I was awarded a full-tuition Root-Tilden-Kern Public Interest Scholarship to attend the New York University School of Law.

Upon graduation from NYU, I received an Equal Justice Works Fellowship to advocate on behalf of North Carolinians with criminal records as an attorney, lobbyist, and community organizer. As an advocate, I have come to more fully understand the ubiquitous and far-reaching nature of the "collateral consequences" of a criminal record. For many individuals, these collateral consequences are more destructive than their actual criminal sentences. Branded a felon and denied job after job, one of my clients once described the 20 years of his life since his release from prison as "still serving time." In helping individuals and families overcome these deprivations, I have come to recognize the faces of reentry as a father trying to get past "the box" in order to support his infant daughter; a young immigrant reminded of her abuse each time she was denied employment based on a bogus charge she got for calling for help but not speaking English as well as her abuser; a teenage mother appealing her exclusion from public housing; an elderly man not wanting to die still defined by his 30-year-old felony conviction. Through these individuals and many others, I have continued to gain a better understanding of my parents' circumstances, strength, and determination.

My parents were married February 12, 1986, just a few months before my little sister was born. Beating long odds to grow up and raise a family together, they've now grown apart and have been separated for the last year. Their marriage never seemed easy, but it was filled with laughter and loyalty, if not always love and affection. Today, they are better apart. I've only just come to realize how much our family served as a safe harbor for my parents. It's difficult to watch and support them trying to make their ways forward separately – still who they were, but without each other. In this volatile period, I find myself rehashing old deliberations of when moving on is being healthy and when it's being selfish.

As I stood before those young men at Polk, I was cognizant of all of this at once. Looking out into that crowd of youthful faces, I was besieged by feelings of pride, sadness, and shame. Alongside these emotions, though, was the prevailing sense of resiliency that still defines our family.

CONCLUSIONS

What We Can Learn From Adults Who Experienced Parental Incarceration as Children

Denise Johnston and Megan Sullivan

This book represents the first effort to explore parental incarceration from the perspective of adults who experienced it as children. It introduces two new and important categories of questions about children of incarcerated parents:

- How does the experience of parental incarceration differ in successive generations of prisoners' children?
- What are the effects of parental incarceration across the lifespan?

Differences among Generations of Prisoners' Children

It is important to recognize that the usefulness of the adult perspective on parental incarceration in childhood may be somewhat limited by changes in criminal law, sentencing, law enforcement and correctional policies. For example, contributors to *Parental Incarceration: Personal Accounts and Developmental Impact* experienced the incarceration of their parents between 1956 and 2000. During that period, the relatively small mid-twentieth century prison population grew dramatically as a result of increasing drug use in the 1960s and introduction of the War on Drugs in the 1970s, but exploded in the 1990s "prison boom" that followed the expansion of the War on Drugs during the 1980s.[1]

Parents of this book's oldest contributors were incarcerated before 1970, most often for some form of theft. The majority of (65 percent) of U.S. prisoners in that era were identified as White, with most the rest identified as Black (33 percent).[2] Hispanics and other ethnic groups were not identified during this period.

The parents of the next generation of contributors were incarcerated during the introduction of the War on Drugs in the 1970s. More parents from this era were convicted of drug offenses. During this period, the proportion of White prisoners declined to less than 58 percent while the proportion of Black prisoners increased to 41 percent; Hispanics, first counted in the mid-1970s, made up 8 percent of all U.S. prisoners.[3]

The youngest group of contributors had parents incarcerated during the expansion of the War on Drugs in the 1980s and 1990s. Almost all of these parents were drug-involved and a significant number were recipients of the longer prison terms imposed by mandatory minimum and other sentencing reforms of that era. By 1991, less than 40 percent of U.S. prisoners were White, more than 45 percent were Black and about 17 percent were Hispanic.[4]

These generational changes produced different experiences for children of prisoners, with increasing racial disproportion in incarceration producing changes in the neighbor-hoods and communities of children of color;[5] increasing utilization and length of incarceration for drug crimes exacerbating the effects of parental addiction and mental illness;[6] and increasing sentence lengths separating children and their incarcerated parents for longer periods of time.

By comparison, over the last decade, while the majority of incarcerated parents continue to be drug-involved, racial disproportion among state and federal prisoners has decreased. For example, from 1997 to 2007, the proportion of White parents in prison increased from 29 percent to 33 percent while the proportion of Black parents in prison decreased from 50 percent to 41 percent.[7] In addition, sentencing statutes have also changed in several states and in the federal sentencing guidelines,[8] so that many incarcerated parents are now or will be serving shorter terms.

The stories of our contributors demonstrate that – even aside from differences in individual children and families – parental incarceration is not a monolithic experience over generations. Changing economic and political forces change the meaning of crime and the way it is punished. The effects of the incarceration of parents on communities, families and children are always shaped to some extent by current laws, law enforcement and sentencing.

The Effects of Parental Incarceration

Adults who experienced parental incarceration as children can tell us a lot about the effects of that experience. They can tell us how and why it happened, how it made them feel at the time, how it manifested in their material lives, and how it affected their life course. They can also demonstrate to us, with their current lives, the range of outcomes that are possible among children who have had a parent go to jail or prison.

Effects of Parental Incarceration in Childhood

As is clear from the stories of contributors to *Parental Incarceration: Personal Accounts and Developmental Impact*, at least some never knew their incarcerated parent. While a large number of prisoners' children were not living with their parents prior to incarceration,[9] a significant minority never lived with those parents.[10] So it is quite likely that some children, while possibly affected by parental absence, experience no effects of the incarceration of their parents at all.

Another group of prisoners' children appear to be minimally affected when their parents are incarcerated. Again, this is often because they have not lived with that parent. In other cases, it may be because the removal of their parents from their lives was a neutral or even positive event. Our contributors' stories reflect all of these circumstances.

However, based not only on the research literature but also on the stories in this book, it can be assumed that the majority of prisoners' children experience some effects of parental incarceration. Identification of exactly what constitutes those effects has long confounded advocates and researchers concerned with children of incarcerated parents.[11]

In this regard, it is useful to examine one piece of the puzzle – the effects of parental incarceration on children's cognitive function. It has long been thought that parental incarceration has a direct, negative effect on children's cognitive skills, as reflected by academic performance.[12] Many of the studies that anchored this perception were based on reports by incarcerated parents about how their children performed in school; virtually none examined children's performance prior to parental arrest/incarceration. More recent and methodologically rigorous studies have found no impact of parental incarceration on academic performance.[13] However, current research reconciles these disparate findings. Turney,[14] using a large Fragile Families data set, found that children who are the least likely to have a parent in jail or prison experience the most negative effects of parental incarceration on behavior and cognitive function while for children who are most likely to have a parent incarcerated – those who experience multiple other vulnerabilities – parental incarceration is "mostly inconsequential." Turney's study suggests that children from middle-class families will be more affected by parental incarceration in ways that are detrimental to school performance. This is important information. It suggests that there are at least two broad groups of prisoners' children and that their outcomes are determined by the group they belong to.

One group – children of prisoners who have few developmental resources and experience many developmental insults, including poverty, dangerous neighborhoods, highly stressed families and impaired parents – demonstrates few immediate or long-term effects of parental incarceration. As a contributor to *Parental Incarceration: Personal Accounts and Developmental Impact* who falls into this group says, "There are worse things that can happen to a child." The adult outcomes of this group are relatively poor and reflect the effects of social and relational adversity on child development.

However, the other group – children who have experienced few developmental insults and been supported by adequate developmental resources, often middle-class kids of intact nuclear families – have more negative immediate outcomes of parental incarceration. Recall the words used by this group of contributors to describe that experience: "awful," "paralyzing" and "devastating." Yet the adult outcomes of this group, at least among our contributors, are good relative to other children of prisoners.

All of this demonstrates that, like race, class cannot be ignored in considering the lives of prisoners' children. Class not only determines the likelihood that children will have an incarcerated parent but also appears to determine the few outcomes that parental incarceration has been found to produce.

Effects of Parental Incarceration in Adulthood

There has been virtually no research on adults who experienced parental incarceration in childhood. A recent study of "life-course" effects of parental incarceration considered it as a major disruption in the lives of prisoners' children, examining young adults who experienced parental incarceration as adolescents and identifying a number of adverse outcomes – including criminal offending, depression, substance abuse and lower educational attainment/income – that are associated with parental incarceration that occurs during later childhood.[15]

Parental Incarceration: Personal Accounts and Developmental Impact represents the very first effort to explore the narrative content of the lives of a diverse group of adults of all ages who experienced the jailing or imprisonment of their parents in childhood.

There seems to be at least one consistent theme in the stories of our contributors and that is regret. Whether they lived almost continuously with their incarcerated parent, saw that parent intermittently or never knew him/her at all, every one of our contributors' stories is infused with a sense of loss. Enraged, angry, disappointed, saddened and/or grieving about their parents, all clearly feel the absence of a happy childhood and wish that their experience with their parents had gone another way.

Beyond the emotional realm, it is difficult to identify one area of life in which all contributors have shared or even had similar adult experiences. Just as they had a variety of childhood experiences, they have had different lives as adults. Most are parents, but a significant proportion are not. While some are professionals, some are or have been prisoners. Although many have struggled with addiction, others are completely abstinent, rigorously avoiding the behaviors that contributed to their parents' troubles.

This lack of shared characteristics may mean that our contributors do not represent the larger group of adults who had parents in jail or prison and that there is a core set of characteristics representing outcomes of parental incarceration among that larger group. It may also mean that parental incarceration *causes* no more outcomes among adults than it appears to do among children.

Why Children of Incarcerated Parents Are Important

So, does this mean that society doesn't have to consider the majority of prisoners' children separately from other low-income children or that, in terms of their outcomes, children of incarcerated parents are simply not that significant? Of course not. Children of prisoners are important for several reasons.

Children of Incarcerated Parents Represent a Significant Proportion of U.S. Minors

In the U.S., the number of minors who have experienced parental incarceration is about two times the number of youth in Boy Scouts and Girl Scouts;[16] six times the number of youth who play Little League Baseball;[17] 40 times the number of child victims of sex trafficking;[18] and 65 times the number of juvenile diabetics.[19] Yet the amount of information available about each of those groups of children and the amount of resources devoted to them are far, far greater than what is available for prisoners' children. Continuing to overlook the sons and daughters of incarcerated parents in this way is unconscionable.

The Effectiveness of Services Can Be Increased by Targeting Children of Incarcerated Parents

For many years, policymakers and service providers have struggled with how to identify who will most benefit from health and human services. Historically, services that target individual children and families have had relatively low impact for the level of effort and cost expended.[20]

However, more recently, social scientists have found that the risk of poor developmental outcomes (like delinquency and criminal behavior) increases with the number of developmental insults a child experiences[21] and that targeting "multi-risk" children can improve the effectiveness of services. But how can such children be picked out from the larger group of disadvantaged kids?

The research presented in this book, and the stories it contains, suggests that identifying, selecting and directing resources to children of justice-involved parents may be an answer. As proposed by the Center for Children of Incarcerated Parents in the early 1990s, the designation "children of incarcerated parents" might most helpfully be considered to be a flag flying over the head of kids that need attention and assistance.[22] Almost all the children under this flag will lack material and emotional resources and will have had multiple adverse experiences; the minority who have had more than adequate developmental resources will also be most at risk for the immediate adverse effects of parental incarceration. This evidence-based approach allows us all – parents, relatives, neighbors, educators, health workers, service providers – to identify those children who most need and will most benefit from services.

Some Children of Incarcerated Parents Will Present a Risk to Society

Many children of criminal offenders become criminal offenders themselves and some of those become prisoners.[23] However, the rate at which this happens is often overstated. For example, the very first federal grants for services specifically to children of prisoners were justified in Senate Report 106–404 (2001) with the following statement:

> Statistics show that children of prisoners are six times more likely than other children to be incarcerated at some point in their lives. The Department of Justice has ignored the fact that 70 percent of children of prisoners will become involved with the nation's prison system.

Although the magnitude of the risk stated is incorrect – there are no empirical studies supporting either of the "statistics" cited – the children's high likelihood of future crime, arrest or incarceration is a fact. This risk – whether it produces a fear *of* the children of incarcerated parents or a fear *for* them – is indisputably important.

Children of Incarcerated Parents Are Important as Children

Children represent the future of humanity. According to a UNICEF analysis of the social and economic returns of investing in children,

Investing in children is a key component of human development, helping to reduce inequity and the intergenerational transmission of poverty. It also has considerable economic benefits ... Moreover, the costs of financing are significantly less than the economic benefits of the investment, making the impetus for investing in children even stronger. If we are serious about improving the growth rate of nations, reducing poverty and achieving greater equity and social stability, investing in children will be a crucial way forward.[24]

When we read about the lives of children – for example, the childhood lives of the contributors to this book – we can clearly see a difference in adult outcomes by the amount invested in the child. Those in whom little was invested had the least desirable outcomes. Those whose lives included many relational and material investments did much better.

Most children of prisoners are born to parents who had little invested in them when *they* were children; to families that have not received the investments in their stability and well-being necessary to effectively support child development; and in communities where lack of investment has produced widespread unemployment, inadequate housing, poor services and high levels of crime and violence. One solution to improving the outcomes of the children of incarcerated parents is a greater investment in all children by all of us.

Children of Incarcerated Parents Are a Reflection of Our Society's Values

For many years and in many places, prisoners' children have been described as the "hidden victims" of their parents' crimes. Although a powerful tool for fundraising and raising public awareness, this facile characterization is partly untrue. As can be gathered from the stories in this book, children of prisoners are more likely to be strangers to their parents than their victims. However, these children have definitely been an unrecognized population.

One reason children of prisoners have remained hidden from public view may be the overwhelming social issues their recognition requires society to face. In addition to those noted above, these include racism, discrimination and the massive overutilization of incarceration to address behavioral health disparities and other income-related social problems.

Similarly, prisoners' kids also require us to face our failure, as a society, to protect children. We have known for centuries where our future generations of prisoners are coming from. We know the general economic and social circumstances that frame their lives. We know the neighborhoods and communities where they live. We know some of the problem behaviors they will have in childhood and the kinds of crimes they will commit. And we also know how to help. We know which supports for families and parents will improve children's development. We know which social programs and human services reduce the childhood precursors of delinquency and adult criminality. And we know at least some of the interventions that will prevent re-offending.

Yet, it has taken advocates and service providers more than 40 years of efforts to achieve public recognition of children of incarcerated parents and their circumstances. The supports, services and interventions that may help them are in place for only a few.

This suggests that the lives and outcomes of prisoners' children are a mirror that allows us to see society's willful refusal to do the right thing for our most vulnerable members.

They allow us to see how little we truly value children and how little we do to meet all children's needs.

The study of these children may help to end this age of arrogance in which it has been assumed that some children in a wealthy nation can be raised with as few developmental resources as possible in the face of many developmental insults without dire consequences for the children, their families, their communities and the larger society.

Children of Incarcerated Parents Teach Us about Human Development

Most contributors to this book had difficult and sometimes tragic childhoods. Yet, whether they are now professors, attorneys, Hollywood producers, prisoners, homemakers or advocates, they look toward the future with the intention of doing better. This resilience is quite familiar to practitioners who work with families involved in the criminal justice system and one of the many unexplored strengths of this population.

Many of our contributors are doing well. Even those who experienced the worst developmental insults in childhood responded appropriately, adapting to their circumstances and experiences in ways that allowed them to survive, rather than giving up. In this respect, their lives are powerful models of how development works to insure the survival of our species. If children's needs are met, they integrate those experiences and adapt by developing skills and behaviors that allow them to become healthy, productive adults. If children are raised in danger and deprivation, with many unmet needs, they will integrate their experiences and adapt, developing the skills and behaviors that insure they survive in those environments. Looking at adults who grew up with a parent in jail or prison from a developmental perspective, it is quite clear that improving the long-term outcomes of prisoners' children will require improvements in their living environments and life experiences before and after as well as during parental incarceration.

Notes

1 Drug Policy Alliance. (2014). *A Brief History of the Drug War*. Available at: www.drugpolicy.org/new-solutions-drug-policy/brief-history-drug-war.
2 Langan PA. (1991). *Race of Prisoners Admitted to Federal and State Institutions, 1926–86*. Washington, D.C.: Bureau of Justice Statistics.
3 *Ibid.*
4 *Ibid.*
5 Clear T. (2009). Imprisoning communities: How mass incarceration makes disadvantaged neighborhoods worse. *Law & Society Review*, 43(3): 716–718; Justice Policy Institute. (2010). *A Capitol Concern: The Disproportionate Impact of the Criminal Justice System on Low Income Communities*. Washington, D.C.: Authors; Von Hoffman E. (2015). How incarceration infects a community. *The Atlantic* (March 6). Available at: www.theatlantic.com/health/archive/2015/03/how-incarceration-infects-a-community/385967/; Wakefield S, Wildeman C. (2013). *Children of the Prison Boom: Mass Incarceration and the Future of American Inequality*. New York: Oxford University Press; Wildeman C, Haskins A, Muller C. (2013). Implications of mass imprisonment for inequality among American children. In McDowell DE, Harold CN, Battle J (Eds.), *The Punitive Turn: New Approaches to Race and Incarceration*. Charlottesville, VA: University of Virginia Press. pp. 117–191.
6 Cloud D. (2014). *On Life Support: Public Health in the Age of Mass Incarceration*. New York: Vera Institute; Murphy K, Barr C. (2015). *Overincarceration of People with Mental Illness*. Austin TX: Texas Public Policy Foundation.

7 Mumola C. (2000). *Incarcerated Parents and Their Children*. Washington, D.C.: Bureau of Justice Statistics; Glaze L, Marushak LM. (2008). *Parents in Prison and Their Minor Children*. Washington, D.C.: Bureau of Justice Statistics.

8 Perez E. (2014). U.S. moves toward shorter sentences for drug crime. *CNN Justice Reporter* (April 24). Available at: www.cnn.com/2014/04/10/us/sentencing-commission; Subramanian R, Delaney R. (2014). *States Reconsider Mandatory Sentences*. New York: Vera Institute.

9 Glaze, Marushak. *Ibid*.

10 Johnston D. (2002). What works: Children of prisoners. In Gadsden V. (Ed.), *Heading Home: Offender Reintegration in the Family – What Works*. Lanham, MD: American Correctional Association.

11 Blakely S. (1995). California program to focus on new mothers. *Corrections Today*, 57(7): 128–130; Dalley L. (2002). Policy implications relating to inmate mothers and their children: Will past be prologue? *The Prison Journal*, 82(2): 234–268; Johnston D. (2006). The wrong road: Efforts to identify the effects of parental incarceration. *Criminology and Public Policy*, 5(4): 702–713; Phillips SD, Erkanli A, Keeler GP, Costello EJ, Angold A. (2006), Disentangling the risks: Parental criminal justice involvement and children's exposure to family risks. *Criminology and Public Policy*, 5(4): 677–702; Kinner SA, Alati A, Najman JM, Williams GM. (2007), Do paternal arrest and imprisonment lead to child behavior problems and substance use? A longitudinal analysis. *Journal of Child Psychology and Psychiatry*, 48(11): 1148–1156; McNeely F. (2002). Children of incarcerated parents: Prisoners of the future? *Prosecutor*, 36(6): 12, 28–30; Murray JP, Janson C, Farrington DP. (2007), Crime in adult offspring of prisoners: A cross-national comparison of two longitudinal samples. *Criminal Justice and Behavior*, 34(1): 133–149; Reed EL, Reed DF. (1997). Children of incarcerated parents. *Social Justice*, 24(3): 152–169.

12 Friedman S, Esselstyn TC. (1965). The adjustment of children to parental absence due to imprisonment. *Federal Probation*, 29: 55–59; Fishman LT. (1990). *Women at the Wall: A Study of Prisoner's Wives Doing Time on the Outside*. New York: SUNY Press; Bloom B, Steinhart D. (1993). *Why Punish the Children?* San Francisco: National Council on Crime and Delinquency; Kampfner C. (1995). Posttraumatic stress reactions in children of incarcerated mothers. In Gabel K, Johnston D. (Eds.), *Children of Incarcerated Parents*. New York: Lexington Books; Dallaire D, Ciccone A, Wilson LC. (2010). Teachers' experiences with and expectations of children with incarcerated parents. *Journal of Applied Developmental Psychology*, 131(4): 281–290.

13 Murray J, Loeber R, Pardini D. (2012). Parental involvement in the criminal justice system and the development of youth theft, marijuana use, depression and poor academic performance. *Criminology*, 50: 255–302.

14 Turney K. (2014a). *The Unequal Consequences of Mass Incarceration for Children*. Presented at the Center for Demographic and Social Analysis, November 4, University of California Irvine.

15 Mears DP, Siennick SE. (2015) Young adult outcomes and the life-course penalties of parental incarceration. *Journal of Research in Crime and Delinquency*. doi: 10.1177/0022427815592452.

16 Girl Scouts of America. (2014). *Fact Sheet*. Available at www.girlscouts.org/who_we_are/facts; Boy Scouts of America. (2012). *Annual Report*. Available at http://scouting.org/About/AnnualReports.

17 Little League. (2014). Available at www.littleleague.org/Little_League_Online.htm.

18 EPCAT International. (2012). *Child Sex Trafficking; United States*. Available at: http://ecpat.net/sites/default/files/a4a_v2_am_usa_2.pdf.

19 Centers for Disease Control and Prevention. (2011). Children and diabetes. *National Diabetes Fact Sheet, 2011*. Available at: www.cdc.gov/diabetes/pubs/pdf/ndfs_2011.pdf.

20 Frieden, TR. (2010). A framework for public health action: The health impact pyramid. *American Journal of Public Health*, 100(4): 590–595; Sabates R, Dex S. (2015). The impact of multiple risk factors on young children's behavioral and cognitive development. *Children and Society*, 29(2): 95–108.

21 Horan JM, Widom CS. (2015). Cumulative childhood risk and adult functioning in abused and neglected children grown up. *Development and Psychopathology*, 27(3): 927–941; Kraemer HC, Lowe KK, Kupfer DJ. (2005). *To Your Health* New York: Oxford University Press; Loeber R, Farrington D. (2001). Young children who commit crime: Epidemiology, developmental origins, risk factors, early interventions and policy implications. *Development and Psychopathology*, 4: 737–762; Sabates, Dex. *Ibid*.

22 Johnston D. (1994). *Working with Children of Incarcerated Parents and Their Families: A Training Manual for Practitioners*. Richmond, VA: Virginia Department of Mental Health and Substance Abuse Services.

23 Otterstrom S. (1946). Juvenile delinquency and parental criminality. *ACTA Pediatrica Scandinavica*, 33(Suppl. 5): 1–326; Robins LN, West PA, Herjanic BL. (1975). Arrests and delinquency in two generations: A study of black urban families and their children. *Journal of Child Psychology and Psychiatry*, 16:125–140; McCord JM. (1979). Some child-bearing antecedents of criminal behavior in adult men. *Journal of Personality and Social Pyschology*, 9: 1477–1486; Robins LN. (1979). Sturdy predictors of adult outcomes: Replications from longitudinal studies. In Barratt JE, Rose RM, Klerman GL. (Eds.), *Stress and Mental Disorder*. New York: Raven Press; Blumstein A, Cohen J, Roth JA, Visher CA. (1986). *Criminal Careers and "Career Criminals"*. Washington, D.C.: National Academy Press; Task Force on the Female Offender. (1990). *The Female Offender: What Does the Future Hold?* Laurel, MD: American Correctional Association; Dallaire D. (2007), Incarcerated mothers and fathers: A comparison of risks for children and families. *Family Relations*, 56(5): 440–453.

24 Rees N, Chai J, Anthony D. (2012). *Right in Principle and in Practice: A Review of the Social and Economic Returns to Investing in Children*. Social and Economic Policy Working Paper. New York: UNICEF.

PERSONAL STORIES

The Most Important Thing by Sharika Lockhart Young

As a young girl growing up, it was really hard for me because my mother was raising me alone as a single parent. I met my father for the first time when I was 2 years old. He was in and out of my life for many years and we only spent one whole day together before his going to prison. My father wasn't just in prison, he was on death row. I found out about my dad going to prison when I was about 7 years old and getting dressed for school one day watching the news with my mom. As we were watching the news, they were speaking about a man named Thomas J. Miller who had just been shot by the police department. At that time my mom looked at me and told me that was my father. Of course as a young girl I started crying and didn't want to go to school because for some apparent reason I thought all of my friends knew that was my father on television.

From that point on I was rather down because I just could not figure out why he wasn't there to take care of me like my mother was. As a child you see and hear things but after a while it is past and you are back to normal. Years went by and I was now in junior high school. My mother received a call from a lady that introduced herself as my father's wife. The reason for her call was to see if my mother had a problem with allowing me to visit with my father. My mother has never been the type of woman to hold a grudge, so she did not have a problem with it. My mother did inform his wife the decision was mine and she would speak to me about it. One day after school my mother sat down with me and engaged in a conversation about me going to visit my father in prison.

My mother basically wanted to know how I felt about going to a prison and visiting the man that had been absent from my life for so long. Of course I was so happy because I would finally get the chance to meet my dad as a young lady. After the conversation with my mother she made the arrangements for his wife and me to meet before we went to the prison. As I met with his wife I felt comfortable in going with her to visit and she also shared information about my father that I did not know. Once she and I finished visiting with each other, she informed my mother she would call with details about going to visit with my dad.

As promised she called and all the arrangements had been made for us to visit. Soon the day came and his wife came to pick me up to drive and visit him in Huntsville, Texas. As a young girl it was the longest drive of my life because I was anxious to see my father. While we were driving we would talk about a lot of different things, especially how happy my father was going to be to see me. Once we arrived, I was so nervous because looking at the prison I felt they were not going to let me back out once I got in because of all the security. As we parked and got out of the car, we began to walk toward the gate to check in. I was looking around, heart beating fast, and nervous all at the same time. My father's wife noticed how afraid I was and reassured me everything was going to be fine. When they completed the check-in process, we were given permission to go in and visit. After we got inside the building where they visit, we were escorted to our seats and waited for the guard to bring my father out.

While I was waiting I was holding my hands together real tight because I was even more nervous because it had been a long time since I saw him last. Eventually the guard brought him out and he was smiling from ear to ear. After he approached the seat we were sitting in I noticed he had to be locked in a cage to visit with us. Surely, I wasn't going to ask why on the first visit so I just left that question in the back of my mind. As we visited he really wanted to know what had been going on in my life the past years. For two hours we sat and talked about so many things until I had forgotten we were in a prison until the guard told us we had ten minutes left to visit. When the visit was about to end I made a promise to him that I would continue to visit when I had time. After the visit we drove back to Houston and his wife dropped me off at home.

I can recall after our first visit I would go and see my father on a regular basis with his wife because I wanted to build up a relationship with him. The reason for me wanting to build up a relationship with him was because I didn't have him in my life as a young girl. I really wanted that father and daughter relationship because as a young girl there are things a male can teach you that a woman can't.

When I found out my dad was actually on death row, I was 17 years old. To get the news about your parent being in prison is devastating enough as a child, but to hear about them being on death row is heartbreaking. The reason it was so heartbreaking for me was because I really didn't know if he was going to live or be executed at any given moment. Not only was it devastating about my father, but also stressful because my dad's case was very public.

By my father being incarcerated it left me without the father figure that I needed to deal with a lot of the issues I had to experience. As a female I really missed the role of my father because I looked for love in men. I believe if I would have had the guidance from my father I wouldn't have experienced physical abuse. I wouldn't have thought that a man putting his hands on me and talking to me in a disrespectful way was normal. With the issues I have experienced in my life they not only made me stronger, but it gave me a hard heart with trust issues.

Since my mom was a single mother, she raised me to be a very independent woman. Being an independent woman affects me because it makes a man look at me as not needing him for guidance. My father being incarcerated also gave me a high level of compassion. I am very strong on community service and reaching out to those that feel like they can't make it. I believe in giving everyone a second chance because you never know why that person chose to do what they did in the first place.

I really enjoy telling other people about my story because there are so many other people that have experienced what I have, but don't know how to deal with it. Even though my dad is in prison we have a really strong relationship because I don't judge him on his past. I also find myself mentoring other young people that feel they should be mad at a parent that is incarcerated. I try to tell them everyone deserves a chance to tell their side of the story.

The most important thing I have learned from my father being in prison is trust. When I visit my dad he has always taught me that everyone deserves to be trusted until they show you otherwise. Now that I have a relationship with my father, we really have an open relationship and talk about everything. As of now, whenever I enter into a relationship, whether it be business or friendship, I use the same method my dad taught me about trust. In using this method, it has not failed me yet. My dad has been locked up for 27 years now and 20 of those years were spent on death row.

The one thing I would like to share with those who have incarcerated parents is never give up on them. Please allow them the time to share with you why they did what they did. Also understand the circumstances that they are dealing with, being incarcerated, are far worse than you could imagine. For me I wanted to experience it for myself so I became a correctional officer to be able to understand and relate to my dad. Please be their support system and never lose sight of what you really want, and that is to build and mend the broken relationship you all have.

REFERENCES

Adalist-Estrin A. (n.d.). *Conversations: Questions Children Ask*. Children of Prisoners Library. Available at: http://nrccfi.camden.rutgers.edu/files/cipl103-conversations-questionschildrenask.pdf.

American Academy of Pediatrics. (2014). *Adverse Childhood Experiences and the Lifelong Consequences of Trauma*. Elk Grove Village, IL: Authors.

Appleyard K, Berlin LJ, Dodge KA. (2011). Preventing early child maltreatment. *Prevention Science*, 12(2): 139–149.

Applied Behavioral Health Policy. (2005). *An Epidemiological Study of the Prevalence and Needs of Children of Incarcerated Parents*. Phoenix, AZ: University of Arizona.

Arditti JA. (2003). Locked doors and glass walls: Family visiting at a local jail. *Journal of Loss and Trauma*, 8: 115–138.

Arditti JA. (2005). Families and incarceration: An ecological approach. *Families in Society: Journal of Contemporary Social Services*, 86(2): 251–260.

Arditti JA, Few-Demo AL. (2006). Mothers' reentry into family life following incarceration. *Criminal Justice Policy Review*, 17: 103.

Aronovici C. (1913). Punishing the innocent. *Annals of the American Academy of Social and Political Science*, 46: 142–146.

Ayers TS, Sandler IN, West SG, Roosa MW. (1996). Assessment of children's coping behaviors: Testing alternative models of children's coping. *Journal of Personality*, 64(4): 923–958.

Bakker LJ, Morris BA, Janus LM. (1978). Hidden victims of crime. *Social Work*, 23: 143–148.

Banyard VL. (1997). The impact of childhood sexual abuse and family functioning on four dimensions of women's later parenting. *Child Abuse and Neglect*, 21(11): 1095–1107.

Barber JS. (2001). Intergenerational transmission of age at first birth among married and unmarried men and women. *Social Science Research*, 30(2): 219–247.

Barreras RE, Drucker EM, Rosenthal D. (2005). Concentration of substance use, criminal justice involvement and HIV/AIDS in families of drug offenders. *Journal of Urban Health*, 82(1): 162–170.

Barrick K, Lattimore PK, Visher CA. (2014). Reentering women: The impact of social ties on long-term recidivism. *The Prison Journal*, 94(3): 279–304.

Bauman PS, Dougherty FE. Drug-addicted mothers' parenting and their children's development. *International Journal of the Addictions*, 18: 291–302.

Baunach, PJ. (1979, November). Mothering from Behind Prison Walls. Paper presented at the annual meeting of the American Society of Criminology, Philadelphia.

Baunach PJ. (1984). *Mothers in Prison*. Newark, NJ: Rutgers University Press.

Beckerman A. (1989). Incarcerated mothers and their children in foster care: The dilemma of visitation. *Children and Youth Services Review*, 11(2): 175–183.

Belsky J, Jaffee SR, Sligo J, Woodward L, Silva PA. (2005). Intergenerational transmission of warm–sensitive–stimulating parenting. *Child Development*, 76(2): 384–396.

Bertram J, Lowenberg C, McCall C, Rosenkrantz, L. (1982). *My real prison is … being Separated from My Child*. San Francisco: Prison MATCH.

Binswanger IA, Stern MF, Deyo RA, Heagerty PJ, Cheadle A, Elmore JG, Koepsell TD. (2007). Release from prison: A high risk of death for former inmates. *New England Journal of Medicine*, 356(2): 157–165.

Blakely S. (1995). California program to focus on new mothers. *Corrections Today*, 57(7): 128–130.

Block KJ, Potthast MJ. (1998). Girl Scouts beyond bars: Facilitating parent–child contact in correctional settings. *Child Welfare*, 77: 561–578.

Bloom B, Steinhart D. (1993). *Why Punish the Children? A Reappraisal of Incarcerated Mothers in America*. San Francisco, CA: National Council on Crime and Delinquency.

Blumstein A, Cohen J, Roth JA, Visher CA. (1986). *Criminal Careers and "Career Criminals"*. Washington, D.C.: National Academy Press.

Blustain, R. (2013). Pushing cops to consider kids when arresting parents. *City Limits*. New York: City Limits.

Bonczar TP. (2011). *National Corrections Reporting Program: Sentence Length of State Prisoners, by Offense, Admission Type, Sex, and Race*. Washington, D.C.: Department of Justice, Bureau of Justice Statistics. Available at: www.bjs.gov/index.cfm?ty=pbdetail&iid=2056.

Borelli J, Goshin L, Joestl S, Clark J, Byrne MW. (2010) Attachment organization in a sample of incarcerated mothers: Distribution of classifications and predictive associations with clinical symptoms, perceptions of parenting competency and social support. *Attachment and Human Development*, 12(4): 355–374.

Boudin C. (2001). In prison again. *Salon.com*. Available at www.salon.com/2001/01/18/visiting.

Boudin C. (2012). Prison Visitation Policies: A Fifty State Survey. ExpressO. Available at: http://works.bepress.com/chesa_boudin/1.

Braman D, Wood J (2003). From one generation to the next: How criminal sanctions are reshaping family life in urban America. In Travis J, Waul M. (Eds.), *Prisoners Once Removed* (157–188). Washington, D.C.: The Urban Institute Press.

Bronte-Tinkew J, Horowitz A, Scott M. (2009). Fathering with multiple partners: Links to children's well-being in early childhood. *Journal of Marriage and the Family*, 71(3): 608–631.

Brooks-Dunn J, Duncan GJ. (1997). The effects of poverty on children. *The Future of Children*, 7(2): 55–71.

Browne A, Miller A, Maguin E. (1999). Prevalence and severity of lifetime physical and sexual victimization among incarcerated women. *International Journal of Law and Psychiatry*, 22: 301–322.

Bruner C, Tirmizi SN. (2004*). Corrections and Making Connections: The Impact of Incarceration on Neighborhoods*. Des Moines, IA: The Child and Family Policy Center.

Cannings, K. (1990). *Bridging the Gap: Programs and Services to Facilitate Contact Between Inmate Parents and Their Children*. Ottawa: Ministry of the Solicitor General of Canada.

Carey C. (2014). *No Second Chance: People with Criminal Records Denied Access to Public Housing*. New York: Human Rights Watch.

Carlin, M. (2000). Asserting parental rights from prison. *Family and Corrections Network Report*, 22: 1–3

Carlin M, Johnston D. (2000, September 13). Incarcerated Fathers and Their Children. Presented at the North American Conference on Fathers Behind Bars and on the Street. Durham, NC.

Carlson MJ, Furstenberg FF. (2005). *The Consequences of Multi-Partnered Fertility for Parental Involvement and Relationships. Fragile Families Publication 2006–2028-FF.* Available at: http://crcw.princeton.edu/publications/publications.asp.

Carlson MJ, Furstenberg FF. (2006). The prevalence and correlates of multipartnered fertility among urban U.S. parents. *Journal of Marriage and Family*, 68(3): 718–732.

Carlson BE, Shafer MS. (2010). Traumatic histories and stressful life events of incarcerated parents: Childhood and adult trauma histories. *The Prison Journal*, 90(4): 475–493.

Center for Children of Incarcerated Parents. (2010a). *How Many Are There? Estimated Counts of the Children of Incarcerated Parents in the United States.* Eagle Rock, CA: Authors.

Center for Children of Incarcerated Parents. (2010b). *Research Monograph No. 3 (Revised): Intergenerational Incarceration.* Eagle Rock, CA: Authors.

Center for Research on Child Well-Being. (2008). *Parental incarceration and child well-being in fragile families.* Fragile Families Research Brief 42 (April, 2008). Available at: www.fragilefamilies.princeton.edu/briefs/ResearchBrief42.pdf.

Chaffin M, Kelleher K, Hollenberg J. (1996). Onset of physical abuse and neglect: Psychiatric, substance abuse and social risk factors. *Child Abuse and Neglect*, 20(3): 191–203.

Children's Defense Fund. (2015). *Ending Child Poverty Now.* Washington, D.C.: Authors.

Chui WH. (2015). Voices of the incarcerated father: Struggling to live up to fatherhood. *Criminology and Criminal Justice*, advance publication online. doi: 10.1177/1748895815590201.

Clarke L, O'Brien M, Godwin H, Hemmings J, Day RD, Connolly J, Van Leeson T. (2005). Fathering behind bars in English prisons: Imprisoned fathers' identity and contact with their children. *Fathering: A Journal of Theory, Research, and Practice About Men as Fathers*, 3: 221–241.

Clear T. (2009). Imprisoning communities: How mass incarceration makes disadvantaged neighborhoods worse. *Law and Society Review*, 43(3): 716–718.

Cloud D. (2014). *On Life Support: Public Health in the Age of Mass Incarceration.* New York: Vera Institute.

Cochran JC. (2013). Breaches in the wall: Imprisonment, social support and recidivism. *Journal of Research in Crime and Delinquency*, 51(2): 200–229.

Compas BE. (1987). Coping with stress during childhood and adolescence. *Psychological Bulletin*, 101: 393–403.

Conway T, Hutson R. (2007). *Is Kinship Care Good for Kids? Center for Law and Social Policy.* Available at: www.clasp.org/publications/is_kinship_care_good.pdf.

Covington S, Bloom B. (2003). Gendered justice: Women in the criminal justice system. In Bloom B. (Ed.), *Gendered Justice: Addressing Female Offenders.* Durham, NC: Carolina Academic Press.

Craigie TA. (2010). *Child Support Transfers Under Family Complexity.* Fragile Families Working Paper WP10–15-FF. Available at: crcw.princeton.edu/workingpapers/WP10-15-FF.pdf

Craigie TA. (2011). Effect of paternal incarceration on early child behavior problems. *Journal of Ethnicity in Criminal Justice*, 9(3): 179–199.

Dallaire DH. (2007). Incarcerated mothers and fathers: A comparison of risks for children and families. *Family Relations*, 56(5): 440–453.

Dallaire D, Ciccone A, Wilson LC. (2010). Teachers' experiences with and expectations of children with incarcerated parents. *Journal of Applied Developmental Psychology*, 31: 281–291.

Dallaire D, Wilson L. (2010). The relation of exposure to parental criminal activity, arrest and sentencing to children's maladjustment. *Journal of Child and Family Studies*, 19: 404–418.

Dallaire D, Zeman JL, Thrash TM. (2015). Children's experiences of maternal incarceration – specific risks: Predictions to psychological maladaptation. *Journal of Clinical Child and Adolescent Psychology*, 44(1): 109–122.

Dalley L. (2002). Policy implications relating to inmate mothers and their children: Will past be prologue? *The Prison Journal*, 82(2): 234–268.

Daly K. (1989). Neither conflict nor labeling nor paternalism will suffice: Intersections of race, ethnicity, gender and family in criminal court decisions. *Crime and Delinquency*, 35(1): 136–168.

Daly K. (1994). *Gender, Crime and Punishment*. New Haven, CT: Yale University Press.

D'Andrade AC, Valdez M. (2012). Reunifying from behind bars. *Social Work in Public Health*, 27(6): 616–636.

Davis JB. (2006). Distribution of property crime and police arrest rates across Los Angeles neighborhoods. *Western Criminology Review*, 7(3): 7–26.

Davis JL, Petretic-Jackson PA, Ting L. (2001). Intimacy dysfunction and trauma symptomatology: Long-term correlates of different types of child abuse. *Journal of Traumatic Stress*, 14(1): 63–79.

DeHart DD. (2005). *Pathways to Prison: The Impact of Victimization in the Lives of Incarcerated Women*. Available at: www.ncjrs.gov/pdffiles1/nij/grants/208383.pdf.

Dill LJ, Mahaffey C, Mosley T, Treadwell H, Barkwell F, Barnhill S. (2015). I want a second chance: Experiences of African American fathers in reentry. *American Journal of Men's Health*, doi: 1557988315569593.

Dixey R, Woodall J. (2012). The significance of "the visit" in an English Category B prison: Views from prisoners, prisoners' families and prison staff. *Community, Work and Family*, 15(1): 29–47.

Doerner JK, Demuth S. (2012). Gender and sentencing in the federal courts. *Criminal Justice Policy Review*, 25(2): 242–269.

Dong M, Anda RF, Felitti VJ, Dube SR, Williamson DF, Thompson TJ, Loo CM, Giles WH. (2004). The interrelatedness of multiple forms of child abuse, neglect and household dysfunction. *Child Abuse and Neglect*, 28: 771–784.

Drug Policy Alliance. (2014). *A Brief History of the Drug War*. Available at: www.drugpolicy.org/new-solutions-drug-policy/brief-history-drug-war.

Dubose DG. (1983). Incarcerated Mothers and Their Children in Texas. (Unpublished manuscript held by the Center for Children of Incarcerated Parents).

DuCharme J, Koverola C, Battle P. (1997). Intimacy development: The influence of abuse and gender. *Journal of Interpersonal Violence*, 12(4): 590–599.

Dutton D, Hart S. (1992a). Evidence for long-term, specific effects of childhood abuse and neglect on criminal behavior in men. *International Journal of Offender Therapy and Comparative Criminology*, 36: 129–137.

Dutton DG, Hart SD. (1992b). Risk markers for family violence in a federally incarcerated population. *International Journal of Law and Psychiatry*, 15: 101–112.

Earley L, Cushway D. (2002). The parentified child. *Clinical Child Psychology and Psychiatry*, 7(2): 163–178.

Ee E, Kleber RJ, Jongmans MJ. (2015, May 11). Relational patterns between caregivers with PTSD and their nonexposed children: A review. *Trauma Violence Abuse*. doi: 10.1177/1524838015584355.

Ehrensaft M, Khashu A, Ross T, Wamsley M. (2003). *Patterns of Criminal Conviction and Incarceration among Mothers of Children in Foster Care in New York City*. New York: Vera Institute of Justice.

Ehrle J, Geen R, Clark R. (2001). Children cared for by relatives: Who are they and how are they faring? In *The New Federalism: A National Survey of America's Families*, B-28. Washington, D.C.: The Urban Institute.

Ehrle J, Geen R, Main R. (2003). Kinship foster care: custody, hardships, and services . *Snapshots of America's Families*, III. No. 14. Washington, D.C.: The Urban Institute.

Erickson KG, Crosnoe R, Dornbusch SM. (2000). A social process model of adolescent deviance: Combining social control and differential association perspectives. *Journal of Youth and Adolescence*, 29: 395–426.

Families and Criminal Justice. (2012). *Where's Daddy? Telling a Child about Paternal Incarceration*. Los Angeles: Authors.

Families and Criminal Justice. (2014). How Many Are There? Estimated Counts of the Children of Incarcerated Parents in the United States. Available at: http://familiesandcriminaljustice.org.

Farrington D. (2004). Conduct disorder, aggression, and delinquency. In Lerner R, Steinberg L. (Eds.) *Handbook of Adolescent Psychology*. New York: Wiley.

Federal Bureau of Investigation. (2015). Crime in the United States 2013: Persons Arrested. *FBI Uniform Crime Reports*. Washington, D.C.: US Department of Justice. Available at: www.fbi.gov/about-us/cjis/ucr/crime-in-the-u.s/2013/crime-in-the-u.s.-2013/persons-arrested/persons-arrested.

Felitti VJ, Anda RF, Nordenberg D, Williamson DF, Spitz AM, Edwards V, Koss M, Marks JS. (1998). Relationship of childhood abuse and household dysfunction to many of the leading causes of death in adults: The Adverse Childhood Experiences (ACE) Study. *American Journal of Preventive Medicine*, 14(4): 245–258.

Fenton F. (1959). *The Prisoner's Family*. Palo Alto, CA: Pacific Books.

Fishman LT. (1990). *Women at the Wall: A Study of Prisoners' Wives Doing Time on the Outside*. Albany, NY: State University of New York Press.

Frieden, TR. (2010). A framework for public health action: The health impact pyramid. *American Journal of Public Health*, 100(4): 590–595.

Friedman S, Esselstyn TC. (1965). The adjustment of children to parental absence due to imprisonment. *Federal Probation*, 29: 55–59.

Gabel S. (1992). Children of incarcerated and criminal parents: Adjustment, behavior and prognosis. *Bulletin American Academy of Psychiatry Law*, 20(1): 33–45.

Galster G. (2010). The Mechanism of Neighborhood Effects: Theory, Evidence and Policy Implications. Presented to the ERSC Seminar, St. Andrews University, Scotland, UK (February 4–5).

Geller A. (2013). Paternal incarceration and father–child contact in fragile families. *Journal of Marriage and the Family*, 75(5): 1288–1303.

Geller A, Curtis MA. (2011). A sort of homecoming: Incarceration and the housing security of urban men. *Social Science Review*, 40(4): 1196–1213.

Geller A, Franklin AW. (2014). Paternal incarceration and the housing security of urban mothers. *Journal of Marriage and Family*, 76: 411–427.

Geller A, Garfinkel I, Cooper CE, Mincy RB. (2009). Parental incarceration and child well-being. *Social Science Quarterly*, 90(5): 1186–1202.

Gemmill WN. (1915). Employment and compensation of prisoners. *Journal of the American Institute of Criminal Law and Criminology*, 6(4): 507–521.

Genty PM. (2003). Damage to family relationships as a collateral consequence of parental incarceration. *Fordham Urban Law Journal*, 30(6): 1671–1684.

Girshick LB. (1999). *No Safe Haven: The Stories of Women in Prison*. Boston, MA: Northeastern University Press.

Glasser, I. (1990). *Maintaining the Bond: The Niantic Parenting Programs*. Niantic, CT: Families in Crisis.

Glaze LD, Marushak LM. (2008). *Parents in Prison and Their Minor Children*. NCJ Publication 222984. Washington, D.C.: US Department of Justice, Bureau of Justice Statistics.

Greenberg SW, Rohe WM, Williams JR. (1982). Safety in urban neighborhoods: A comparison of physical characteristics and informal territorial control in high and low crime neighborhoods. *Population and Environment*, 5(3): 141–165.

Greene S, Haney C, Hurtado A. (2000). Cycles of pain: Risk factors in the lives of incarcerated mothers and their children. *The Prison Journal*, 80(1): 3–23.

Grella CE, Lovinger K, Warda US. (2013). Relationships between trauma exposure, familial characteristics and PTSD: A case-control study of women in prison and in the general population. *Women and Criminal Justice*, 23(1): 63–79.

Hairston CF. (1989). Men in prison: Family characteristics and family views. *Journal of Offender Counseling, Services and Rehabilitation*, 14(1): 23–30.

Hairston CF. (1990). Mothers in jail: Parent–child separation and jail visitation. *Affilia*, 6(2): 9–27

Hairston C. (1991). Family ties during imprisonment: Important to whom and for what? *Journal of Sociology and Social Welfare*, 18: 87.

Hairston CF. (1998). The forgotten parent: Understanding the forces that influence incarcerated fathers' relationships with their children. *Child Welfare*, 77(5): 617–639.

Hairston CF. (2007). *Focus on Children with Incarcerated Parents: An Overview of the Research Literature.* Baltimore: The Annie E. Casey Foundation.

Hanlon TE, Carswell SB, Rose M. (2007). Research on the caretaking of children of incarcerated parents. *Child and Youth Services Review*, 29: 348–362.

Hannon G, Martin D, Martin M. (1984). Incarceration in the family: Adjustment to change. *Family Therapy*, 11: 253–260.

Harknett K, Knab J. (2007). More kin, less support: Multi-partnered fertility and perceived support among mothers. *Journal of Marriage and the Family*, 69(1): 237–253.

Henriques, Z. (1982). *Imprisoned Mothers and Their Children*. Washington, D.C.: University Press of America.

Henry B, Avshalom C, Moffitt TE, Silva PA. (1996). Temperamental and familial predictors of violent and non-violent criminal convictions. *Developmental Psychology*, 32: 614–623.

Homma Y, Wang N, Saewyc E, Kishor N. (2012). The relationship between sexual abuse and risky sexual behavior in adolescent boys. *Journal of Adolescent Health*, 51(1): 18–24.

Horan JM, Widom CS. (2015). Cumulative childhood risk and adult functioning in abuse and neglected children grown up. *Development and Psychopathology*, 27(3): 927–941.

Howard K, Martin A, Berlin LJ, Brooks-Gunn J. (2011). Early mother–child separation, parenting and child well-being in Early Head Start families. *Attachment and Human Development*, 13(1): 5–26.

Hunter, SM. (1984). The relationship between women offenders and their children. *Dissertation Abstracts International*. University Microfilms No. 8424436.

Incarcerated Parents Work Group. (2014, March 18). Incarcerated Parents and Their Children in the Juvenile Dependency System: A Judicial Training. Presented to the Los Angeles County Superior Court, Juvenile Dependency Division, Monterey Park, CA.

Jacobs A. (2000). Give 'em a fighting chance: Women offenders reenter society.. *Criminal Justice*, 45(16).

James N. (2015). *Offender Reentry: Correctional Statistics, Reintegration into the Community, and Recidivism.* Congressional Research Service Report, 7–5700. Washington, D.C.: Congressional Research Service.

Johnson EI, Waldfogel J. (2004). Children of incarcerated parents: Multiple risks and children's living arrangements. In Patillo ME, Weiman DF, Western B. (Eds.), *Imprisoning of America: The Social Effects of Mass Incarceration*. New York: Russell Sage Foundation.

Johnson RJ, Ross MW, Taylor WC, Williams ML, Carvajal RI, Peters RJ. (2006). Prevalence of childhood sexual abuse among incarcerated males in a county jail. *Child Abuse and Neglect*, 30(1): 75–86.

Johnston D. (1992). *The Children of Criminal Offenders Study: A Report to the California Assembly Office of Research*. Pasadena, CA: Center for Children of Incarcerated Parents.

Johnston D. (1993a). *Caregivers of Prisoners' Children*. Pasadena, CA: Center for Children of Incarcerated Parents.

Johnston D. (1993b). *CCIP Research Monograph No. 2: Parent–child Contact Visitation in California County Jails*. Pasadena, CA: Center for Children of Incarcerated Parents.

Johnston D. (1993c). *CCIP Research Monograph No. 7: Children's Reactions to Visitation in the Prison*. Pasadena, CA: Center for Children of Incarcerated Parents.

Johnston D. (1994). *Working with Children of Incarcerated Parents and Their Families: A Training Manual for Practitioners*. Richmond, VA: Virginia Department of Mental Health and Substance Abuse Services.

Johnston D. (1995a). Child custody issues of women prisoners: A preliminary report from the CHICAS Project. *The Prison Journal*, 75(2): 222–239.

Johnston D. (1995b). Jailed mothers. In Gabel K, Johnston D. (Eds.), *Children of Incarcerated Parents*. New York: Lexington Books.

Johnston D. (1995c). The effects of parental incarceration. In Gabel K, Johnston D. (Eds.), *Children of Incarcerated Parents*. New York: Lexington Books.

Johnston D. (1995d). Parent–child visits in jails. *Children's Environments Quarterly*, 12(1): 25–38.

Johnston D. (1995e). Care and placement of prisoners' children. In Gable K, Johnston D. (Eds.), *Children of Incarcerated Parents*. New York: Lexington Books.

Johnston D. (1999). *The Therapeutic Intervention Project: Final Report*. Eagle Rock, CA: The Center for Children of Incarcerated Parents.

Johnston D. (2001). Incarceration of Women and Effects on Parenting. Presented to the Institute of Policy Research, Northwestern University Conference on the Effects of Incarceration on Children and Families.

Johnston D. (2002). What works: Children of prisoners. In Gadsden V. (Ed.), *Heading Home: Offender Reintegration in the Family – What Works*. Lanham, MD: American Correctional Association.

Johnston D. (2006). The wrong road: Efforts to identify the effects of parental incarceration. *Criminology and Public Policy*, 5(4): 702–713.

Johnston D. (2010a). A developmental approach to work with children of prisoners. *S&F Online*, 8(2). Available at: http://sfonline.barnard.edu/children/johnston_01.htm.

Johnston D. (2010b). *CCIP Research Monograph No. 2 (Revised): Intergenerational Incarceration*. Eagle Rock, CA: The Center for Children of Incarcerated Parents

Johnston D, Gabel K. (1995). Incarcerated parents. In Gable K, Johnston D. (Eds.), *Children of Incarcerated Parents*. New York: Lexington Books.

Jones DJ, Runyon DK, Lewis T, Litrowrick AJ, Black MM, Wiley T, English DE, Proctor LJ, Jones BL, Nagin DS. (2010). Trajectories of childhood abuse and early adolescent HIV/AIDS risk behaviors. *Journal of Clinical and Adolescent Psychology*, 39(5): 667–680.

Justice Policy Institute. (2010). *A Capitol Concern: The Disproportionate Impact of the Criminal Justice System on Low Income Communities*. Washington, D.C.: Authors.

Juul SH, Hendrix C, Robinson B, Stowe ZN, Newport DJ, Brennan PA, Johnson KC. (2015, May). Maternal early-life trauma and affective parenting style: The mediating role of HPA-axis function. *Archives of Women's Mental Health*. doi: 10.1007/s00737-00015-0528-x.

Kalter N, Lohnes KL, Chasin J, Cain AC, Dunning S, Rowan J. (2002–03). The adjustment of parentally bereaved children. *Journal of Death and Dying*, 46(1): 15–34.

Kampfner C. (1995). Posttraumatic stress reactions in children of incarcerated mothers. In Gable K, Johnston D. (Eds.), *Children of Incarcerated Parents*. New York: Lexington Books.

Katarzyna C, Siegel JA. (2010). Mothers in trouble: Coping with actual or pending separation from children due to incarceration. *The Prison Journal*, 90: 447.

Kershaw T, Murphy A, Lewis J, Divney A, Albritton T, Magriples U, Gordon D. (2014). Family and relationship influences on parenting behaviors of young parents. *Journal of Adolescent Health*, 54(2): 197–203.

Kinner SA, Alati A, Najman JM, Williams GM. (2007). Do paternal arrest and imprisonment lead to child behavior problems and substance use? A longitudinal analysis. *Journal of Child Psychology and Psychiatry*, 48(11): 1148–1156.

Kjellstrand J, Cearley J, Eddy JM, Foney D, Martinez CR. (2012). Characteristics of incarcerated fathers and mothers: Implications for preventive interventions targeting children and families. *Children and Youth Services Review*, 34(12): 2409–2415.

Kraemer HC, Lowe KK, Kupfer DJ. (2005). *To Your Health*. New York: Oxford University Press.

Kubiak SP, Kasiborski N, Karim N, Schmittel E. (2012). Does subsequent criminal justice involvement predict foster care and termination of parental rights for children born to incarcerated women? *Social Work in Public Health*, 27(1–2): 129–147.

Langan PA. (1991). *Race of Prisoners Admitted to State and Federal Institutions, 1926–86*. NCJ Publication 125618. Washington, D.C.: US Department of Justice, Bureau of Justice Statistics.

Langan P, Levin D. (2002). Recidivism of prisoners released in 1994. *Federal Sentencing Reporter*, 15(1): 58–65.

LaPointe V, Picker O, Harris BF. (1985). Enforced family separation: A descriptive analysis of some experiences of children of black imprisoned mothers. In Spencer A. (Ed.), *Beginnings: The Social and Affective Development of Black Children*. Hillsdale, NJ: Erlbaum.

Lappegard T, Thomson E. (2012). *Intergenerational Transmission of Childbearing across Partnerships*. Presented at the Meeting of the Population Association of America, San Francisco.

Laughlin JS, Arrigo BA, Blevins KR, Coston CTM. (2008). Incarcerated mothers and child visitation: A law, social science, and policy perspective. *Criminal Justice Policy Review*, 19: 215–238.

La Vigne DG, Davies E, Brazzell D. (2008). *Broken Bonds: Understanding and Addressing the Needs of Children with Incarcerated Parents*. New York: The Urban Institute.

LaVigne NG, Naser RL, Brooks LE, Castro JL. (2005). Examining the effect of incarceration and in-prison family contact on prisoners' family relationships. *Journal of Contemporary Criminal Justice*, 21: 314–355.

Lee RD, Fang X, Luo F. (2013). The impact of parental incarceration on the physical and mental health of young adults. *Pediatrics*, 131(4): e1188–1195.

Lewis C, Garfinkel I, Gao Q. (2007). Incarceration and unwed fathers in fragile families. *Journal of Sociology and Social Welfare*, 34(3): 77–94.

Lincroft Y. (2011). *When a Parent Is Incarcerated: A Primer for Social Workers*. Baltimore: The Annie E. Casey Foundation.

Lister ED. (1982). Forced silence: A neglected dimension of trauma. *American Journal of Psychiatry*, 139(7): 872–876.

Littner N. (1956). *Some Traumatic Effects of Separation and Placement*. New York: Child Welfare League of America.

Loeber R, Farrington D. (2001). Young children who commit crime: Epidemiology, developmental origins, risk factors, early interventions and policy implications. *Development and Psychopathology*, 4: 737–762.

Loper AB, Phillips V, Nichols EB, Dallaire DH. (2014). Characteristics and effects of the co-parenting alliance between incarcerated parents and child caregivers. *Journal of Child and Family Studies*, 23: 225–241.

Lynch JP. (2012). *Corrections in the United States*. Washington, D.C.: US Department of Justice, Bureau of Justice Statistics.

Lyons-Ruth K, Block D. (1996). The disturbed caregiving system: Relations among childhood trauma, maternal caregiving, infant affect and attachment. *Infant Mental Health Journal*, 17(3): 257–275.

Macfie J, Brumariu LE, Lyons-Ruth K. (2015). Parent–child role confusion: A critical review of an emerging concept. *Development Review*, 35: 34–57.

Mahoney C, MacKechnie S. (Eds.). (2001). *In a Different World. Parental Drug and Alcohol Use: A Consultation into Its Effects on Children and Families in Liverpool*. Liverpool: Liverpool Health Authority.

Massachusetts Department of Correction. (1987). *Joining Incarcerated Mothers with Their Children: The Lancaster Visiting Cottage Program*. Boston: Authors.

Mazza C. (2002). And then the world fell apart: The children of incarcerated fathers. *Families in Society*, 83(5): 521–529.

McCarthy BR. (1980). Inmate mothers: The problems of separation and reintegration. *Journal of Offenders Counseling, Services and Rehabilitation*, 4(3): 199–212.

McCord JM. (1979). Some child-bearing antecedents of criminal behavior in adult men. *Journal of Personality and Social Psychology*, 9: 1477–1486.

McGowan BG, Blumenthal KL. (1978). *Why Punish the Children?* Hackensack, NJ: National Council on Crime and Delinquency.

McNeely F. (2002). Children of incarcerated parents: Prisoners of the future? *Prosecutor*, 36(6): 12, 28–30.

Meade CS, Kershaw TS, Ickovics JR. (2008). The intergenerational cycle of teenage motherhood. *Health Psychology*, 27(4): 419–429.

Mears DP, Siennick SE. (2015) Young adult outcomes and the life-course penalties of parental incarceration. *Journal of Research in Crime and Delinquency.* doi: 10.1177/0022427815592452.

Merikangas KR, Stolar M, Stevens DE, Goulet J, Preisiq MA, Fenton B, Zhang H, O'Malley SS, Rounsaville BJ. (1998). Familial transmission of substance use disorders. *Archives of General Psychiatry,* 55(11): 973–979.

Messina N, Grella C. (2006). Childhood trauma and women's health outcomes in a California prison population. *American Journal of Public Health,* 96(10): 1842–1848.

Mincy R. (2002). *Who Should Marry Whom? Multiple Partner Fertility among New Parents.* Fragile Families Publication 2002–2003-FF. Available at: http://crcw.princeton.edu/publications/publications.asp.

Minnesota Department of Corrections. (2011). *Effects of Prison Visitation on Offender Recidivism.* St. Paul, MN: Authors.

Minton C, Pasley K. (1996). Father's parenting role identity and father involvement. *Journal of Family Issues,* 17(1): 26–45.

Moehler E, Brunner R, Wiebel A, Reck C, Resch F. (2006). Maternal depressive symptoms in the postnatal period are associated with long-term impairment of mother–child bonding. *Archives of Women's Mental Health,* 9(5): 273–278.

Morris P. (1965). *Prisoners and Their Families.* London: George Allen & Unwin.

Mueser KT, Gottlieb JD, Cather C, Glynn SM, Zarate R, Smith LF, Clark RE, Wolfe R. (2010). Antisocial personality disorder in people with co-occurring severe mental illness and substance use disorder. *Psychosis,* 4(1): 52–62.

Mumola C. (2000). *Incarcerated Parents and Their Children.* NCJ Publication 182335. Washington, D.C.: Bureau of Justice Statistics.

Murphy K, Barr C. (2015). *Overincarceration of People with Mental Illness.* Austin, TX: Texas Public Policy Foundation.

Murray J, Farrington D. (2007). The effects of parental imprisonment on children. *Crime and Justice: A Review of Research,* 37: 133–206.

Murray J, Farrington DP, Sekol I. (2012). Children's antisocial behavior, mental health, drug use and educational performance after parental incarceration. *Psychological Bulletin,* 138(2): 175–210.

Murray JP, Janson C, Farrington DP. (2007). Crime in adult offspring of prisoners: A cross-national comparison of two longitudinal samples. *Criminal Justice and Behavior,* 34(1): 133–149.

Murray J, Loeber R, Pardini D. (2012). Parental involvement in the criminal justice system and the development of youth theft, marijuana use, depression and poor academic performance. *Criminology,* 50: 255–302.

National Center for PTSD. (2015). *Relationships and PTSD.* Washington, D.C.: US Department of Veterans Affairs. Available at: www.ptsd.va.gov/public/family/ptsd-and-relationships.asp.

Nesmith A, Ruhland E. (2006). Children of incarcerated parents: Challenges and resiliency in their own words. *Children and Youth Services Review,* 30(10): 1119–1130.

Nettle D, Coall DA, Dickins TE. (2011). Early life conditions and age at first pregnancy in British women. *Proceedings of the Royal Society of Biological Sciences,* 278(1712): 1721–1727.

New Jersey Department of Corrections. (2007). *What about Me? When a Parent Goes to Prison: A Guide to Discussing Your Incarceration with Your Children.* Trenton, NJ: Authors.

Newton RR, Litrownik AJ, Landsverk JA. (2000). Children and youth in foster care: Disentangling the relationship between problem behaviors and number of placements. *Child Abuse and Neglect,* 24(10): 1363–1374.

New York Initiative for Children of Incarcerated Parents. (2012). *Fact Sheet: Parental Incarceration's Impact on Children's Health.* New York: Authors.

New York State Division of Criminal Justice Services. (2013). *Children of Incarcerated Parents in New York State: A Data Analysis.* Albany, NY: Authors.

Nolan C. (2003). *Children of Arrested Parents.* Sacramento, CA: California Research Bureau.

Nurse AM. (2002). *Fatherhood Arrested: Parenting from within the Juvenile Justice System*. Nashville, TN: Vanderbilt University Press.

Olson SL, Lopez-Duran N, Lunkenheimer ES, Chang H, Sameroff AJ. (2011). Individual differences in the development of early peer aggression. *Development and Psychopathology*, 23: 253–266.

Osborne Association. (1996). *How Can I Help? Working with Children of Incarcerated Parents*. New York: Authors.

Otterstrom S. (1946). Juvenile delinquency and parental criminality. *ACTA Pediatrica Scandinavica*, 33 (Suppl. 5): 1–326.

Pearson, J. (2004). Building debt while doing time. *Family Court Review*, 43(1): 5–12.

Pearson J, Griswold EA. (2005). Lessons from four projects addressing incarceration and child support. *Corrections Today*, 67(4): 92–102.

Perez E. (2014). U.S. moves toward shorter sentences for drug crime. *CNN Justice Reporter* (April 24). Available at: www.cnn.com/2014/04/10/us/sentencing-commission.

Phelps MS. (2011). Rehabilitation in the punitive era: The gap between rhetoric and reality in U.S. prison programs. *Law and Society Review*, 45(1): 33–68.

Phillips SD, Burns SJ, Wagner HR, Barth RP. (2004). Parental arrest and children involved with child welfare agencies. *American Journal of Orthopsychiatry*, 74(2): 174–186.

Phillips S, Burns BJ, Wagner HR, Kramer TL, Robbins JM. (2002). Parental incarceration among youth receiving mental health services. *Journal of Child and Family Studies*, 11(4): 385–399.

Phillips S, Erklani A, Keeler GP, Costello EJ, Angold A. (2006). Disentangling the risks: Parent criminal justice involvement and children's exposure to family risks. *Criminology and Public Policy*, 5(4): 688–702.

Poehlmann J. (2005). Representations of attachment relationships in children of incarcerated mothers. *Child Development*, 76: 679–696.

Poehlmann J, Dallaire D, Loper AB, Shear LD. (2010). Children's contact with their incarcerated parents: Research findings and recommendations. *American Psychologist*, 65(6): 575–598.

Poehlmann J, Runion H, Burson C, Maleck S, Weymouth L, Pettit K, Huser M. (2015). Young children's behavioral and emotional reactions to plexiglass and video visits with jailed parents. In Poehlmann-Tynan J. (Ed.), *Children's Contact with Incarcerated Parents: Implications for Policy and Intervention*. New York: SpringerBriefs in Psychology.

Pogarsky J, Thornberry TP, Lizotte AJ. (2006). Developmental outcomes for children of young mothers. *Journal of Marriage and the Family*, 68: 332–344.

Prison MATCH. (1984). *Telling Your Child You're in Prison*. Berkeley, CA: Authors.

Prison Visitation Project. (1993). *Needs Assessment of Children Whose Parents Are Incarcerated*. Richmond, VA: VA Department of Mental Health, Mental Retardation and Substance Abuse Services.

Pynoos RS, Steinberg AM, Piacentini JC. (2009). A developmental psychopathology model of childhood traumatic stress. *Biological Psychiatry*, 46: 1542–1554.

Raine A. (1997). *The Psychopathology of Crime*. Houston: Gulf Professional Publishing.

Reavis JA, Looman J, Franco KA, Rojas B. (2013). Adverse childhood experiences and adult criminality: How long must we live before we possess our own lives? *The Permanente Journal*, 17(2): 44–48.

Reed EL, Reed DF. (1997). Children of incarcerated parents. *Social Justice*, 24(3): 152–169.

Rees N, Chai J, Anthony D. (2012). *Right in Principle and in Practice: A Review of the Social and Economic Returns to Investing in Children*. Social and Economic Policy Working Paper. New York: UNICEF.

Roberts R, O'Connor T, Dunn J, Golding J. (2004). The effects of childhood sexual abuse on later family life: Mental health, parenting and adjustment of offspring. *Child Abuse and Neglect*, 28: 525–545.

Robertson J, Robertson J. (1971). *Young Children in Brief Separation*. London: Tavistock Institute.

Robins LN. (1979). Sturdy predictors of adult outcomes: Replications from longitudinal studies. In Barratt JE, Rose RM, Klerman GL. (Eds.), *Stress and Mental Disorder*. New York: Raven Press.

Robins LN, West PA, Herjanic BL. (1975). Arrests and delinquency in two generations: A study of black urban families and their children. *Journal of Child Psychology and Psychiatry*, 16: 125–140.

Roche DN, Runtz MG, Hunter MA. (1999). Adult attachment: A mediator between sexual abuse and later psychological adjustment. *Journal of Interpersonal Violence*, 14(2): 184–207.

Roettger M, Swisher R. (2011). Associations of fathers' history of incarceration with sons' delinquency and arrest among Black, White and Hispanic males in the United States. *Criminology*, 49(4): 1109–1147. doi: 10.1111/j.1745-174912.5.2011.00253x.

Rojas JI, Hallford G, Tivis LJ. (2012). Latino/as in substance abuse treatment: Family history of addiction and depression. *Journal of Ethnicity in Substance Abuse*, 11(1): 75–85.

Rose DR, Clear T. (1998). Incarceration, social capital and crime: Implications for social disorganization theory. *Criminology*, 36: 441–479.

Rutter M. (1971). Parent–child separation: Effects on the children. *Journal of Child Psychology and Psychiatry*, 12(4): 233–260.

Sabates R, Dex S. (2015). The impact of multiple risk factors on young children's behavioral and cognitive development. *Children and Society*, 29(2): 95–108.

Sampson R, Lauritsen J. (1994).Violent victimization and offending: Individual, situational, and community-level risk factors. In Reiss AJ, Roth JA. (Eds.) *Understanding and Preventing Violence*. 3: 451–481. Washington, D.C.: National Academy Press.

Sandstrom H, Huerta S. (2013). *The Negative Effects of Instability on Child Development: A Research Synthesis. Low-Income Working Families Discussion Papers No. 3*. New York: The Urban Institute.

San Francisco Children of Incarcerated Parents Partnership. (2005). *Children of Incarcerated Parents Bill of Rights*. Available at: www.sfcipp.org/imges/brochure.ped.

Schirmer S, Nellis A, Mauer M. (2009). *Incarcerated Parents and Their Children: Trends 1991–2007*. Washington, D.C.: The Sentencing Project. Available at: www.sentencingproject.org/doc/publica tions/publications/inc_incarceratedparents.pdf.

Schneller D. (1978). *The Prisoner's Family*. San Francisco: R&E Research Associates.

Schwartz-Soicher O, Geller A, Garfinkel I. (2011). The effect of paternal incarceration on material hardship. *Social Service Review*, 85(3): 447–473.

Seider RP, Kadela KR. (2013). Prisoner reentry: What works, what does not and what is promising. *Crime and Delinquency*, 49(3): 360–388.

Sesame Street (2013). Little Children, Big Challenges: Incarceration. Available at: www.sesamestreet. org/cms_services/services?action=download&uid=24467219-1a98-4240-9fc3-cc738714e819.

Shaw CR, McKay HD. (1942). *Juvenile Delinquency and Urban Areas*. Chicago: University of Chicago Press.

Shlafer R, Gerrity E, Ruhland E, Wheeler M. (2013). *Children with incarcerated parents: Considering children's outcomes in the context of complex family circumstances*. University of Minnesota, Children's Mental Health eReview. Available at: www.extension.umn.edu/family/cyfc/our-programs/ereview/docs/June2013ereview.pdf.

Shlafer RJ, Poehlmann J. (2010). Attachment and caregiving relationships in families affected by parental incarceration. *Attachment and Human Development*, 12: 395–415.

Sinkewicz M, Garfinkel I. (2009). Unwed fathers' ability to pay child support: New estimates accounting for multiple-partner fertility. *Demography*, 46(2): 247–263.

Smith G. (2000). The Adoption and Safe Families Act of 1997: Effects on incarcerated mothers and their children. *Women, Girls and Criminal Justice*, 1(1).

Snyder-Joy ZK, Carlo TA. (1998). Parenting through prison walls. In Miller SL. (Ed.), *Crime Control and Women: Feminist Implications of Criminal Justice Policy* (130–150). Thousand Oaks, CA: SAGE Publications.

Spjeldnes S, Goodkind S. (2009). Gender differences and offender reentry: A review of the literature. *Journal of Offender Rehabilitation*, 48(4): 314–335.

Sroufe LA, Egeland B, Carlson EA, Collins WA. (2005). *Development of the Person: The Minnesota Study of Risk and Adaptation from Birth to Adulthood*. New York: Guilford Press.

Stanton A. (1980). *When Mothers Go to Jail*. New York: Lexington Books.

State of Washington, Department of Corrections. (2015). *Policy: Visits for Prison Offenders*. Available at: www.doc.wa.gov/policies/files/450300.pdf.

Subramanian R, Delaney R. (2014). *States Reconsider Mandatory Sentences*. New York: Vera Institute.

Suchman NE, Luthar SS. (2000). Maternal addiction, child maladjustment and sociodemographic risks: Implications for parenting behaviors. *Addiction*, 95(9): 1417–1428.

Swan A. (1981). *Families of Black Prisoners: Survival and Progress*. Boston: G.K. Hall.

Tasca M, Rodriguez N, Zatz MA. (2011). Family and residential instability in the context of maternal and paternal incarceration. *Criminal Justice and Behavior*, 38(3): 231–247.

Task Force on the Female Offender. (1990). *The Female Offender: What Does the Future Hold?* Laurel, MD: American Correctional Association.

The Sentencing Project. (2014) The Sentencing Project News – Incarceration. Available at: www.sentencingproject.org/template/page.cfm?id=107.

Travis J. (2005). *But They All Come Back: Facing the Challenges of Prisoner Reentry*. New York: The Urban Institute Press.

Travis J, McBride EC, Solomon AL. (Revised 2005). *Families Left Behind: The Hidden Costs of Incarceration and Reentry*. Washington, D.C.: The Urban Institute Press.

Trentacosta CJ, Shaw DS. (2009). Emotional self-regulation, peer rejection and antisocial behavior: Developmental associations from early childhood to early adolescence. *Journal of Applied Developmental Psychology*, 30(3): 356–365.

Trice A, Brewster J. (2004). The effects of maternal incarceration on adolescent children. *Journal of Police and Criminal Psychology*, 19: 27–35.

Tripp B. (2003). Incarcerated African American fathers: Exploring changes in family relationships. In Harris O, Miller R. (Eds.), *Impacts of Incarceration on the African American Family*. New Brunswick, NJ: Transaction Publishers.

Turanovic JJ, Rodriguez N, Pratt TC. (2012). The collateral consequences of incarceration revisited: A qualitative analysis of the effects on caregivers of children of incarcerated parents. *Criminology*, 50(4): 913–959.

Turney K. (2014a). *The Unequal Consequences of Mass Incarceration for Children*. Presented at the Center for Demographic and Social Analysis, November 4, University of California Irvine.

Turney K. (2014b). Liminal men: Incarceration and Family Instability. Fragile Families Working Paper WP 13–12-FF. Available at: http://crcw.princeton.edu/workingpapers/WP13-12-FF-2.pdf.

Turney K. (2014c). The intergenerational consequences of mass incarceration: Implications for children's contact with grandparents. *Social Forces*, 93(1): 299–327.

Turney K, Wildeman C, Schnittker J. (2012). As fathers and felons: Explaining the effects of current and recent incarceration on major depression. *Journal of Health and Social Behavior*, 53(4): 465–481.

Von Hoffman E. (2015). How incarceration infects a community. *The Atlantic* (March 6). Available at: www.theatlantic.com/health/archive/2015/03/how-incarceration-infects-a-community/385967.

Wakefield S, Wildeman C. (2013). *Children of the Prison Boom: Mass Incarceration and the Future of American Inequality*. New York: Oxford University Press.

Walker C. (2003). *Parents behind Bars Talk about Their Children: A Survey of Allegheny County Jail Inmates*. Pittsburgh, PA: Pittsburgh Child Guidance Foundation.

Warland C. (2014). *Healthy Relationships, Employment and Reentry*. Washington, D.C.: National Resource Center for Healthy Marriage and Families. Available at: https://library.healthymarriageandfamilies.org/cwig/ws/library/docs/MARRIAGE/Blob/88902.pdf?w=NATIVE%28%27TITLE+ph+is+%27%27healthy+relationships+employment+and+reentry%27%27%27%29&upp=0&rpp=25&order=native%28%27year%2FDescend%27%29&r=1&m=1.

Weeks R, Widom CS. (1998). Self-reports of early childhood victimization among incarcerated adult male felons. *Journal of Interpersonal Violence*, 13(3): 346–361.

Weilerstein R. (1995). The Prison MATCH Program. In Gable K, Johnston D. (Eds.). *Children of Incarcerated Parents*. New York: Lexington Books.

Western B, McLanahan S. (2001). Fathers behind bars: The impact of incarceration on family formation. *Contemporary Perspectives in Family Research*, 2: 309–324.

Weyand LD. (1920). Study of wage payment to prisoners as a penal method. *Journal of Criminal Law and Criminology*, 11(2): 222–271.

Wildeman C. (2010). Paternal incarceration and children's physically aggressive behaviors. *Social Forces*, 89(1): 285–309.

Wildeman C. (2014). Paternal incarceration, child homelessness and the invisible consequences of mass incarceration. *Annals of the American Academy of Social and Political Science*, 651(1): 74–96.

Wildeman C, Haskins A, Muller C. (2013). Implications of mass imprisonment for inequality among American children. In McDowell DE, Harold CN, Battle J. (Eds.), *The Punitive Turn: New Approaches to Race and Incarceration*(117–191). Charlottesville, VA: University of Virginia Press..

Wildeman C, Schnittker J, Turney K. (2012). Despair by association: Mental health of mothers with children by recently incarcerated fathers. *American Sociological Review*, 77(2): 216–243.

Wilson RE, Brown TH, Schuster B. (2009). Preventing neighborhood crime: Geography matters. *NIJ Journal*, No. 263. Available at: http://nij.gov/journals/263/Pages/neighborhood-crime.aspx.

Winokur M, Holtan A, Batchelder K. (2014). Kinship care for the safety, permanency, and well-being of children removed from the home for maltreatment: A systematic review. *Campbell Systematic Reviews*, 2.

Wolff N, Shi J, Siegel JA. (2009). Patterns of victimization among male and female inmates: Evidence of an enduring legacy. *Violence and Victimization*, 24(4): 469–484.

Wyman PA, Cowen EL, Work WC, Parker GR. (1991). Developmental and family milieu correlates of resilience in urban children who have experienced life stress. *American Journal of Community Psychiatry*, 19(3): 405–426.

Zalba, S. (1964). *Women Prisoners and Their Families*. Sacramento, CA: Department of Social Welfare and Department of Corrections.

Zilanawala A, Pilkauskas N. (2012). Material hardship and child socioemotional behaviors. *Children and Youth Services Review*, 34(4):814–825.

INDEX

Note: Page numbers followed by *s* indicate contributors' stories.

addiction *see* substance abuse/addiction
adults who experienced parental incarceration as
    children xi, xviii, xxxii–xxxiii, 152–153;
    advocacy work and 25*s*, 82*s*, 118, 128*s*, 129*s*,
    134*s*, 137*s*, 143*s*, 144*s*; criminal justice system
    involvement and 23*s*, 23–24*s*, 28*s*, 48*s*, 49*s*,
    56*s*, 60*s*, 61–62*s*, 63–64*s*, 82–83*s*, 83–87*s*, 92–
    94*s*, 95*s*, 95–97*s*, 97–100*s*, 139–144*s*
Adverse Childhood Experiences (ACEs) 4; effects
    on parenting 4–5; among children of
    incarcerated parents 39–42; among incarcerated
    parents 38; outcomes of 40
attachment among incarcerated mothers and their
    children 6, 9

behavioral problems among minor children of
    incarcerated parents ix–x, xviii, 69, 70, 74

care of children of incarcerated parents xxii–xxiii,
    1–2, 67–69; influence of care on
    developmental outcomes 1–2
caregivers of prisoners' children 7–8, 70;
    caregiver–child relationships 2, 9–10, 21–22*s*,
    47–48*s*; 51*s*, 107, 119; caregiver–parent
    relationships xvii, 110, 111; caregiver support
    for parent–child visitation xvii, 29–30*s*, 110;
    kin caregivers 37, 70–71, 83*s*, 101*s*; and stigma
    of parental incarceration 113; unrelated
    caregivers 47, 57*s*, 59–60*s*, 7, 101*s*
child abuse 34; among children of incarcerated
    parents 23*s*, 28*s*, 40, 48*s*, 51*s*, 53–56*s*, 57–59*s*,

60–61*s*, 63–64*s*; among incarcerated parents 38,
    53*s*, 61*s*, 82*s*, 94*s*, 96*s*, 139*s*
children of incarcerated parents: demographic
    characteristics xii–xiii; developmental outcomes
    xiii, xviii, xxvi, 4, 9, 42–43, 156
correctional policies and practices 37, 39; effects
    on children of prisoners 29–31*s*
criminal justice system involvement: among
    children of incarcerated parents 23*s*, 23–24*s*,
    28*s*, 48*s*, 49*s*, 56*s*, 60*s*, 61–62*s*, 63–64*s*,
    82–83*s*, 83–88*s*, 91–94*s*, 95*s*, 97–100*s*,
    139–144*s*; among family members of
    incarcerated parents 37, 48*s*, 62*s*, 83–88*s*,
    94–95*s*, 95–97*s*, 135*s*; and loss of child
    custody 49*s*

delinquency 66, 82*s*, 154, 155; among children of
    incarcerated parents xix, 21*s*, 23*s*, 55–56*s*, 59*s*,
    83*s*, 85*s*, 95*s*, 141*s*, among incarcerated parents
    62*s*, 85*s*, 96*s*, 98*s*, 141*s*
developmental outcomes xiii, xxii, 2, 4, 13;
    among dependent children of incarcerated
    parents xviii, xxvi–xxvii, 9, 42–43, 65, 117,
    156; among adult children of incarcerated
    parents xviii, xx, xxvi, 152–153, 155–156;
    and gender of incarcerated parent xiii–xiv,
    xxxiii, 8
domestic violence: among incarcerated parents
    xiv, 2, 5, 27–28*s*, 32*s*, 40–41, 48*s*, 53–56*s*,
    58–59*s*, 61*s*, 62–63*s*, 84*s*, 98*s*; among adult
    children of incarcerated parents 26–27*s*, 61*s*

economic strain in households of prisoners' children xxiii, 20s, 26s, 32–33s, 34, 36, 65–67, 73, 81s, 88s, 110, 133–134s, 141–142s

education and parental incarceration ix–x, xxiv–xxv, xxxiii; children's academic performance 82s; children's school experience xxiv, 75–76, 92–93s, 133–134s, 136s, 140–141s, 146–149s; stigmatization by teachers 112; truancy 76; school failure 76

effects of parental incarceration xiii, 21s, 143–144s, 151–153; in childhood 151–152; in adulthood 152–153

employment and work experience of incarcerated parents xiii, xxvi, 38–39, 84s, 142s

families of children of incarcerated parents 35–37, 65–67, 75, 110; ability to protect children 34–43; criminal justice system involvement of relatives 36–37, 135s

foster care and children of incarcerated parents xxxii–xxxiii, 5, 21s, 28–29s, 47s, 50s, 52s, 54s, 56s, 57–58s, 70, 72–73, 94–95s, 96s, 145s

forced silences 107, 133s, 136s

gender of incarcerated parents, effects of xiii–xiv, xxxiii, 8, 9

generational differences among children of prisoners 150–151

grandparents of prisoners' children 21–22s, 31s, 60s, 70, 74–75, 83s, 89s, 97s, 126s, 135–136s, 143s

guidance provided to children of incarcerated parents 66, 74–77, 160s

homelessness: among children of incarcerated parents xiv, xxx, 20s, 48s, 71, 94s, 100–101s

housing and parental incarceration 68–69; housing insecurity xxiii, 68

incarcerated fathers xiv, 20–21s, 21–23s, 25–27s, 29–31s, 31–33s; relationships with children 6–8, 25–26s, 97–98s, 128–129s, 133–135s, 139–144s, 144–149s, 159–161s

incarcerated mothers xiii–xiv; relationships with children 5–6, 23–25s, 47–48s, 53–60s, 83s, 88–91s–97s, 100–103s, 135–138s

incarcerated parents xii, xv, xvi, xvii, xxv, 13, 15, 73, 105, 110, 113–114, 151; parenting by xxxii, 2–9, 36–39, 84–85s; population size ix; social and economic characteristics 38–39, 65

intergenerational crime and incarceration xviii, xix, xxxiii, 21s, 28–29s, 48s, 60–64s, 83–88s, 97s, 123–125s, 139–144s, 154

life experiences of children of incarcerated parents xiv–xvii, 1–5, 39–42, 74, 76–77, 104–117

living arrangements of children of incarcerated parents: before parental incarceration 7, 9, 69; changes of placement during parental incarceration 8, 69, 74; during parental incarceration 69–73; following parental incarceration 73

mass incarceration i, 155

mental illness: among adult children of incarcerated parents 49s; among family members of incarcerated parents 27–29s, 62s, 95s; among incarcerated parents xiii, xiv, 2, 4, 41, 53–56s, 57–60s, 65, 132s, 151; effects on parenting 4

Minnesota Study of Risk and Adaptation from Birth to Adulthood 1, 10, 11–13

mothers of prisoners' children: ever-incarcerated mothers of prisoners' children see incarcerated mothers; never-incarcerated mothers of prisoners' children xiv, xix, 3, 7–8, 10, 20s, 25s, 31–32s, 36, 48–49s, 60s, 62s, 68, 81–82s, 124s, 131–135s, 139–142s, 145–147s, 159s

multi-partnered fertility 2, 10, 20s, 21s, 25s, 30–31s, 36, 113, 159–160; disadvantages for children 2–3; prevalence among incarcerated parents 2

neighborhoods and communities of prisoners' children xix, 26s, 34–35, 39, 43, 89s, 135s, 141s, 152

parental arrest 88s, 100s, 104–105; children's understanding of xv, 51s, 105; witnessed by children xiv, 23s, 32s, 136s–138s

parental identity among prisoners 39, 126s

parental incarceration 106–113; children's understanding of xv–xvi; and class xxiii; and loss of child custody 49s; and stigma x, xxiv, 32–33s, 71, 91s, 106, 107, 111–113, 123–125s, 127s, 134s, 136s

parental reentry: xvii, xxvi, 113–118, 144–149s; challenges to success 114

parent–child communication during parental incarceration 31s, 85s, 102–103s, 107–111; 128s, 136–139s

parent–child correctional visitation ix, xvi–xvii, 29s, 95s, 109–111, 126–128s, 129–133s, 138s, 142s, 159–160s; effects of correctional policies and practices 29–31s, 39, 100–111, 129–131s, 138s; obstacles to 110–111, 142s

parent–child relationships among children of incarcerated parents 1–9, 48s, 88–91s, 126–128s, parent–child attachment 6;

identification with parent 123–125*s*,
140*s*, 143*s*; parentification 8, 28–29*s*,
54–55*s*, 81–82*s*, 89–91*s*, 101–103*s*,
133*s*

parent–child reunification after parental
incarceration xvii, 25*s*, 28*s*, 54–55*s*, 57*s*,
62–63*s*, 82*s*, 87–88*s*, 96*s*, 101*s*, 114–118, 136*s*,
139*s*

parentification/family role reversal 8,
28–29*s*, 54–55*s*, 81–82*s*, 89–91*s*,
101–103*s*, 133*s*

peer relationships among children of incarcerated
parents 1, 10–13, 15, 23–24*s*, 91–94*s*,
126–127*s*, 133*s*, 140*s*, 141*s*

poverty and parental incarceration xxiii, 34–35,
65–67

public policy and children of incarcerated parents
x, 43, 118, 153–156

relationships in the lives of prisoners' children
1–16

romantic and reproductive relationships: among
adult children of incarcerated parents 26–27*s*,
63*s*, 81*s*, 141–142*s*, 160*s*; among incarcerated
parents xiv, 13–15

sibling relationships and parental incarceration
10–11, 20*s*; sibling separations 10–11, 15,
28–29*s*, 41, 52*s*, 95*s*, 96*s*

stigma and parental incarceration x, xxiv, 32–33*s*,
71, 91*s*, 106, 107, 111–113, 123–125*s*, 127*s*,
134*s*, 136*s*

substance abuse/dependence: among children of
incarcerated parents 20, 48–49*s*, 60*s*, 61*s*,
63–64*s*, 85–86*s*, 88–90*s*, 153; among
incarcerated parents xv, xxv, 4–5, 22*s*, 24*s*,
31–33*s*, 41, 49–52*s*, 57*s*, 63*s*, 94–95*s*, 96*s*,
101–103*s*, 135–136*s*, 143–144*s*, 145*s*; among
family members of incarcerated parents 37,
48–49*s*; 88–89*s*, 91–94*s*; effects on parenting 89*s*

telling children about parental incarceration xv,
21*s*, 25–26*s*, 81*s*, 88*s*, 106–108, 119, 126*s*,
128*s*, 140*s*

termination of parental rights among incarcerated
parents xvii, 64*s*, 73, 113

trauma in childhood: among children of
incarcerated parents xiv, xv, xxiv, xxv, 3–4,
23*s*, 24*s*, 26–28*s*, 32–33*s*, 42, 48–49*s*, 51–59*s*,
60*s*, 62–63*s*, 84–85*s*, 89*s*, 95*s*, 105, 107, 132*s*,
135–138*s*, 140–141*s*; among incarcerated
parents 3–4, 27–28*s*, 38, 39, 53–54, 57–60*s*,
63*s*, 84–85*s*, 95*s*, 139*s*, 140–141*s*; effects on
parent–child relationships 3–4

violence in the lives of prisoners' children xviii,
xxxiii, 34, 40–42, 47–48*s*, 57–59*s*, 62–63*s*,
84–87*s*, 92*s*, 139*s*, 142*s*